The Global Infrastructure of the Special Operations Executive

During the Second World War, the British government established the Special Operations Executive (SOE) for the purpose of coordinating 'all action, by way of subversion and sabotage, against the enemy overseas'. Although the overseas operations of this branch of the British Secret Services are relatively well known, few studies have explored the 'backroom sections' of this organisation. This book draws together the infrastructure developed to support an agent's 'journey' from recruitment to despatch to the field.

At the start of the Second World War there were few existing facilities established within the UK to support clandestine operations. As the conflict progressed, in parallel to learning the operational procedures of their trade, SOE also had to rapidly expand their support infrastructure around the world. The organisation could effectively support their agents only by establishing facilities dedicated to training, research and development, supply, transportation, communication, and command and control. By predominately focusing on the organisation's 'agent facing' infrastructure, this book provides a backdrop to the brave men and women who conducted operations abroad. In addition, it gives an overview of the facilities in which SOE's backroom staff lived and worked.

The book will be of interest to students and scholars of archaeology, history and war studies.

Derwin Gregory is the Programme Leader for Archaeology and Heritage at Bishop Grosseteste University in Lincoln, UK. Derwin specialises in militarised landscapes, modern conflict archaeology and material culture.

Routledge Studies in Second World War History

The Second World War remains today the most seismic political event of the past hundred years, an unimaginable upheaval that impacted upon every country on earth and is fully ingrained in the consciousness of the world's citizens. Traditional narratives of the conflict are entrenched to such a degree that new research takes on an ever important role in helping us make sense of World War II. Aiming to bring to light the results of new archival research and exploring notions of memory, propaganda, genocide, empire and culture, Routledge Studies in Second World War History sheds new light on the events and legacy of global war.

Recent titles in this series

The Novel *Das Boot*, Political Responsibility, and Germany's Nazi Past
Dean J. Guarnaschelli

World War II Historical Reenactment in Poland
The Practice of Authenticity
Kamila Baraniecka-Olszewska

Tourism and Memory
Visitor Experiences of the Nazi and GDR Past
Doreen Pastor

Shoah and Torah
David Patterson

The Global Infrastructure of the Special Operations Executive
Derwin Gregory

For more information about this series, please visit: https://www.routledge.com/Routledge-Studies-in-Second-World-War-History/book-series/WWII

The Global Infrastructure of the Special Operations Executive

Derwin Gregory

LONDON AND NEW YORK

First published 2022
by Routledge
2 Park Square, Milton Park, Abingdon, Oxon OX14 4RN

and by Routledge
605 Third Avenue, New York, NY 10158

Routledge is an imprint of the Taylor & Francis Group, an informa business

© 2022 Derwin Gregory

The right of Derwin Gregory to be identified as author of this work
has been asserted by them in accordance with sections 77 and 78 of
the Copyright, Designs and Patents Act 1988.

All rights reserved. No part of this book may be reprinted or
reproduced or utilised in any form or by any electronic, mechanical,
or other means, now known or hereafter invented, including
photocopying and recording, or in any information storage or
retrieval system, without permission in writing from the publishers.

Trademark notice: Product or corporate names may be trademarks
or registered trademarks, and are used only for identification and
explanation without intent to infringe.

British Library Cataloguing-in-Publication Data
A catalogue record for this book is available from the British Library

Library of Congress Cataloging-in-Publication Data
Names: Gregory, Derwin, author.
Title: The global infrastructure of the Special Operations
Executive /Derwin Gregory.
Description: Abingdon, Oxon; New York, NY: Routledge, 2022. |
Series: Routledge studies in Second World War history |
Includes bibliographical references and index.
Identifiers: LCCN 2021032963 | ISBN 9781138749900 (hardback) |
ISBN 9781032168074 (paperback) | ISBN 9781315180106 (ebook)
Subjects: LCSH: World War, 1939–1945—Secret service—Great
Britain. | Great Britain. Special Operations Executive—History. |
Intelligence service—Great Britain—History—20th century.
Classification: LCC D810.S7 G74 2022 | DDC 940.54/8641—dc23
LC record available at https://lccn.loc.gov/2021032963

ISBN: 978-1-138-74990-0 (hbk)
ISBN: 978-1-032-16807-4 (pbk)
ISBN: 978-1-315-18010-6 (ebk)

DOI: 10.4324/9781315180106

Typeset in Bembo
by codeMantra

To my parents Jane and Edward

Contents

	List of maps	ix
	Place names	xi
	Acknowledgements	xiii
1	Introduction	1
2	Training	31
3	Research and development	60
4	Supply	71
5	Transportation	90
6	Communications	108
7	Conclusion	124
	Index	133

Maps

Map 1	Global map showing the location of SOE's sites	xiv
Map 2	Map of the Americas showing SOE's sites	xv
Map 3	Map of the UK showing SOE's sites	xvi
Map 4	Map of the Mediterranean showing SOE's sites	xvii
Map 5	Map of Africa showing SOE's sites	xviii
Map 6	Map of India and Southeast Asia showing SOE's sites	xix

Place names

Throughout this book, the place names used are as they appear in the contemporary documentation.

Acknowledgements

I am indebted to the staff of The National Archives, the Imperial War Museum, the RAF Museum and the Norwegian Resistance Museum for their help in carrying out the research for this book. Penny and Nigel Oakey allowed me to survey Station 53b, which is located on their land. I would also like to thank the residents of Frogmore Hall, for allowing me to look around their estate, and Des Turner, for showing me around Frogmore and Aston.

The postgraduate work from which this book was developed was carried out at the University of East Anglia. Particular thanks must go to the Centre of East Anglian Studies at UEA, which funded this project. I am also sincerely grateful to my PhD supervisor Professor Robert Liddiard. Without his constant support, encouragement and enthusiasm, this project would have run far less smoothly. I would also like to thank Professor Tom Williamson, whose advice on early drafts was invaluable, Professor Tom Licence, Professor Carole Rawcliffe and Professor Katy Cubitt. My thanks go too to my former colleagues at English Heritage, particularly Wayne Cocroft, whose support and enthusiasm for contemporary military archaeology encouraged me to undertake postgraduate work. Finally, I am indebted to the Chartered Institute for Archaeologists, who were instrumental in my working with English Heritage's Archaeological Survey and Investigation Team. I learnt so much from my short time with this remarkable team.

On a personal note, I am especially grateful to Steve Nunn, discussions with whom have helped shaped my research. I would also like to thank Jo Porter for all the love and support she has provided. Finally, I would like to thank my family for their love and encouragement. Without my parents – Jane and Edward – I would not be where I am today and, in recognition of this, this book is dedicated to them.

Map 1 Global map showing the location of SOE's sites.

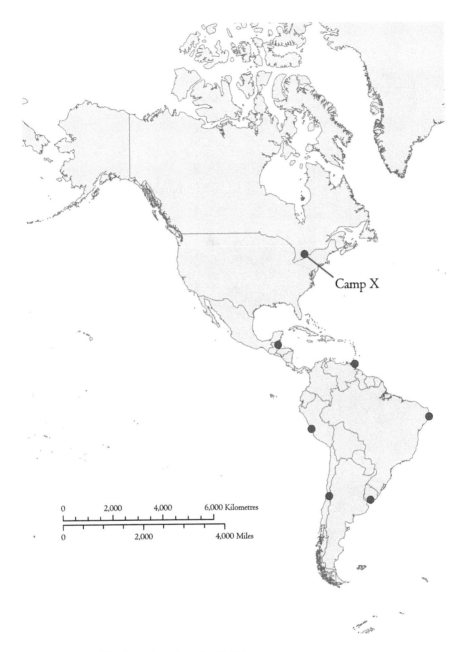

Map 2 Map of the Americas showing SOE's sites.

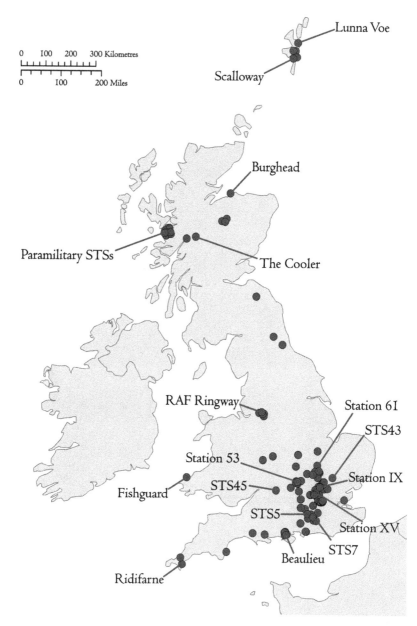

Map 3 Map of the UK showing SOE's sites.

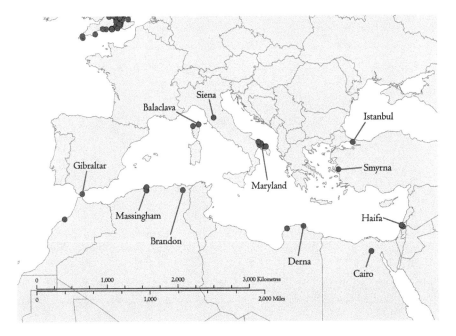

Map 4 Map of the Mediterranean showing SOE's sites.

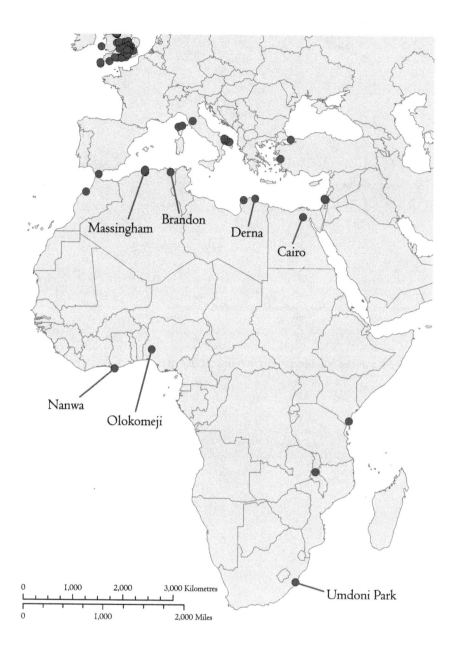

Map 5 Map of Africa showing SOE's sites.

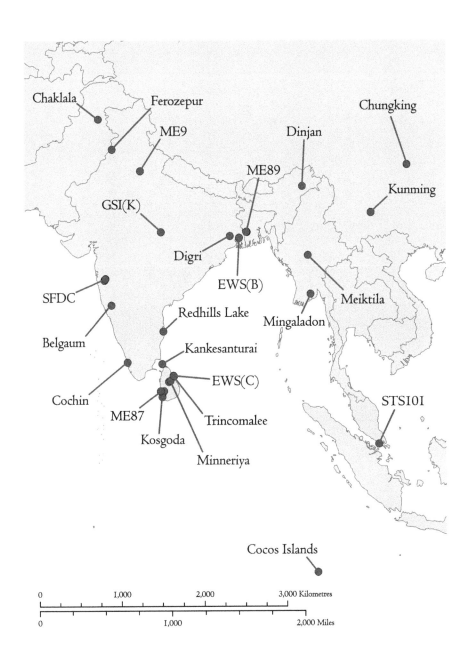

Map 6 Map of India and Southeast Asia showing SOE's sites.

1 Introduction

In 1940 the British Government established the Special Operations Executive (SOE) to 'co-ordinate all action, by way of subversion and sabotage, against the enemy overseas'.[1] From the time of its creation, SOE has been one of the most controversial of Britain's secret services,[2] historians regularly debating its military impact and political effect.[3] The focus of this book, however, is SOE's agent-facing global 'infrastructure'.[4] Although this is not the first work on the 'backroom sections' of this organisation, this study has brought together into a single book a discussion of the world-wide facilities that supported agents' 'journeys', from recruitment to despatch to the field. It is the aim of this book to provide the context in which the backroom staff operated.[5]

SOE was one of several branches of Britain's secret services during the Second World War. Its sister organisations included the Secret Intelligence Service (SIS, also known as MI6), the Secret Service (MI5), the Government Code and Cypher School (GCCS) and the Political Warfare Executive (PWE). Although each organisation had a different function, they often came into conflict owing to overlapping interests. SOE was formed by the British Government to operate in a manner similar to the Sinn Fein movement in Ireland and Chinese guerrillas fighting the Japanese. Inspiration was also taken from the Spanish Irregulars who fought alongside Wellington.[6] In order to function, SOE was provided funding through the 'Secret Vote' of Parliament[7] and by April 1942 their expenditure was approximately £2,500,000 per annum.[8] Although operational for only six years, SOE grew to employ a maximum of 10,000 men and 3,200 women. Of these, one in four men and one in eight women were of officer status.[9] Under their control were tens of thousands of resistance fighters operating on a global scale.[10]

Contextualising the study of SOE's agent-facing infrastructure

Since the end of the Second World War, the gradual release of classified documents into the public domain has transformed the study of the SOE.[11] The first attempt at writing a history of SOE occurred prior to its disbandment: as

DOI: 10.4324/9781315180106-1

2 Introduction

the war came to an end, a series of 'in-house' histories was commissioned,[12] the purpose of which was to ensure that SOE's hard-learnt lessons were not forgotten. They also provided a historical record of the organisation's achievements.[13] The task of combining these accounts together into an 'official' history was allocated to William Mackenzie.[14] To aid him in his work, Mackenzie was granted complete access to SOE's surviving archive[15] and was given the authority to request any document that he could not locate within SOE's files from other governmental departments.[16] On the completion of his monograph, it remained classified until finally being published in 2000.[17]

The public appetite for tales of clandestine operations meant it was inevitable that agents' 'accounts' rapidly appeared in press after the war. Even before Germany had surrendered, the War Office had cleared the first of these for publication. George Millar's *Marquis*, written shortly after he returned from operations in France, eventually ran to 70,000 copies.[18] Such memoirs are, however, not always entirely truthful: minor inaccuracies were sometimes incorporated as a result of misinformation or as a way to build suspense.[19] Many of the early accounts of SOE were characterised by courageous stories that both appealed to the public's desire to read about adventures and helped book sales.[20] Post-war British culture was inundated with tales of daring that have done much to shape public perception of SOE.[21]

The post-war period coincided with increased public scrutiny of SOE's activities in France. During the mid-1950s, reporters found that articles on controversies relating to the organisation sold newspapers, and features and exposés, therefore, began to appear regularly in the popular press. As a result of controversies appearing in the press, Whitehall commissioned Michael Foot to write the official history of SOE in France. Despite having access to the organisation's archive, his attempts to undertake interviews with key figures were severely restricted; nevertheless, the monograph, published in 1966, was the first publicly available scholarly study of SOE.[22]

During the period in which SOE was making newspaper headlines, there was a gradual deterioration of relations between East and West. This was a time when the Comintern was threatening a global workers' revolution and British troops were being regularly deployed to conduct operations against communist forces.[23] Techniques and procedures that had been perfected by SOE were now threatening British global interests.[24]

By 1950, Basil Liddell Hart, a leading figure on military strategy, was condemning British support for the European Resistance during the war. It was his belief that it had a 'wider amoral effect on the younger generation as a whole to defy authority and break the rules of civic morality'.[25] It was inevitable that an organisation that had supported, equipped and trained radicals would become the focus of criticism when the new threat became Soviet revolutionaries. Within this new geopolitical environment, intelligence became an increasingly important commodity, and the promotion of SOE as an irresponsible and amateurish organisation enabled other branches of the secret services to justify their own existence in a post-war world.[26] Indeed, in 1969 Richard Deacon stated that 'in achievements, in professionalism, and in organisation it [SOE] never matched up to SIS; in many respects it was downright inefficient, wasteful, and even damaging to the war effort'.[27] At the time, a number of historians believed SOE to have been in a constant state of disorder, overworked at headquarters, inefficient in the use of wireless and amateurish.[28] Writing ten years later, David Stafford[29] advocated a far less critical assessment. Although he accepted elements of the 'bumbling amateurishness of the British public school tradition, the muddling through, the inefficiency, the eccentricity ... [this was a] strategic disguise for what was in reality the clandestine arm of a determined attempt to further British interest in Europe'.[30] Stafford felt SOE functioned efficiently within the paralysing limits imposed by the Foreign Office and the SIS, and had accomplished their role as effectively as any other branch of the British war effort.[31]

The second official history of SOE was commissioned in 1980 and Charles Cruickshank published *SOE in the Far East* three years later. In 1986 it was followed by Cruickshank's official history of SOE's work in Scandinavia.[32] Deliberations by Foot during the early 1980s over whether SOE was any good were eventually answered 'with an emphatic Yes'.[33]

Since 1993 SOE's files have gradually been released into the public domain, leading to a proliferation in the quantity and quality of popular and academic studies of the organisation. The archives, however, are unlikely to provide all the answers, as those files capable of offering a comprehensive assessment of SOE's strategic value have been destroyed.[34] By 2005 Neville Wylie thought that 'the amateurishness for which SOE was routinely maligned had probably as much to do with any innate or institutionalized incompetence as with the legendary informality of the organization and the self-proclaimed "revolutionary" nature of the warfare it espoused',[35] while Mark Seaman was of the opinion that, although 'short-lived and frequently (and inappropriately) labelled "amateur" by its detractors, SOE nevertheless acquired a prominent position in most theatres of operations and exerted British influence on a truly global scale'.[36]

Unsurprisingly, the vast majority of work on SOE hitherto has focused on the 'glamorous' exploits of the organisation's agents abroad,[37] and research into SOE's Country Sections is so firmly entrenched in the mentality of SOE scholars that there is a danger that topics that do not fit into operational boundaries will be overlooked. It is, however, only with a comprehensive overview of an organisation in its entirety that a balanced assessment can be made: greater attention has to be given to the non-geographical sections.[38] Although lacking the prestige of acts of sabotage, SOE's global support infrastructure was vital to the operation of the organisation. These sites facilitated the organisation's training, research and development, supply and transportation networks, communications, and command and control, prepared the men and women for their operations and supported them in carrying their tasks out. An analysis of SOE's global network of bases will thus provide context to the work of SOE's agents abroad.

4   *Introduction*

One of the greatest challenges faced by scholars of the secret services is the fact that

> unless a secret service remains secret, it cannot do its work. As it has to remain secret, it ought not to keep any sort of records in the field. Even at its home base, security risks are not needlessly multiplied by putting more than necessary on paper ... the traces left for him [the historian] to study are likely to be few.[39]

In the case of SOE, this is compounded by the chaotic nature of the organisation's surviving archive.[40] The origins of this confusion can be partly attributed to the haphazard nature of the organisation's formation. When SIS's Section D, Military Intelligence (Research) (MI(R)) and Department EH were combined to form SOE, the new organisation failed to establish a central registry.[41] Each section and sub-section was responsible for organising its own filing system. In 1945, further confusion was introduced when SOE imposed a top-down approach to departmental filing based on thematic topics. By the time SOE was disbanded in 1946, the reorganisation had only just scratched the surface. For a brief period thereafter, a small body of staff was retained to complete this undertaking. When financial support was finally withdrawn, only 25 per cent of the archive had been reorganised. SOE's surviving archive, therefore, comprises of two overlapping, yet incomplete, filing systems.[42]

Within the secret services, there also exists a tendency to avoid keeping many records that were made. Only documents deemed operationally essential are favoured for preservation. As the Second World War drew to a close, reports began to circulate of bonfires of documents originating from within SOE's outstations. During these burnings, significant quantities of files produced by the organisation's UK Special Training Schools (STSs) were also incinerated. There are also reports of a large fire at SOE's Baker Street headquarters in February 1946.[43] By the middle of 1946, plans were in hand to transfer SOE's remaining files into the care of the SIS. In preparation for this move, it was necessary to reduce the size of the archive. Between August 1946 and May 1947, the contents of 119 filing cabinets were destroyed. Of this material, approximately half related to the organisation's administration, stores, training and communications.[44] Further episodes of destruction subsequently occurred, so that by the 1950s over 87 per cent of SOE's original archive had been lost.[45] Despite the organisation's archive remaining classified, by the 1980s many aspects of SOE's operational history had become public knowledge following the publication of a number of books and memoirs. It was not until 21 October 1993 that the first of SOE's files was released to The National Archives,[46] and this process of releasing documents is still ongoing.

Owing to the nature of the secret services, their archives are often incomplete, restricted or chaotic in nature. In these situations, an organisation's infrastructure offers an independent source of information, providing a physical representation of the actions of the organisation.

The historical background to SOE

On 27 September 1938 the British Cabinet decided to organise a Department of Propaganda to Enemy Countries. To run this new organisation, Whitehall approached Sir Campbell Stuart.[47] Previously, Stuart had been responsible for controlling the British propaganda effort during the final years of the First World War.[48] With the signing of the Munich Agreement three days later, the British Government postponed the organisation's formation. It was not until 23 December 1938, when Stuart was appointed chair of the propaganda sub-committee of the Committee of Imperial Defence, that the issue was once more raised.[49]

On 3 April 1939 Stuart moved his operations into Electra House, Victoria Embankment,[50] which, at the time, also housed the Imperial Communications Advisory Board. It was from this new accommodation that Stuart's Department EH gained its name.[51] In Room 207 of this building the department had access to a Reuter's tape machine, wireless equipment, maps and other relevant resources. In addition, Department EH was provided with the services of a stenographer. Prior to mobilisation on 1 September 1939, the department existed on a purely informal basis, with no Treasury grant.[52]

When Department EH mobilised at 10:00 on 1 September 1939, Stuart, his personal staff, the chief printing officer and the Military Wing were based at Electra House, while Stuart's deputy, along with the Planning, Editorial and Intelligence sections, was based at Woburn Abbey Riding School.[53] Following the outbreak of hostilities, 60 members of staff relocated to offices in the Riding School at Woburn Abbey.[54]

To prepare the Riding School for the arrival of Department EH's staff, a number of alterations were made. Partitions were inserted into the building to make cubicles, while sleeping accommodation was arranged on the second floor of the stable block.[55] At the beginning of the war, the organisation had to share the grounds with various other governmental departments.[56] As these moved out, Department EH took over the estate.

Department EH also acquired the use of the Old Rectory in Eversholt, plus Paris House, Foxfield and Maryland, all close to Woburn Abbey.[57] These properties were used to accommodate visitors and as places 'where discussions with them can be held. Certain senior members of the staff not only live there, but do a considerable part of their work there'.[58] On the formation of the PWE in 1941, Department EH's facilities passed from SOE to the new executive.

At the start of the Second World War, part of Department EH's role was being replicated by a section within SIS.[59] In 1938, SIS had established Section D to research subversive methods of warfare and to investigate 'every possibility of attacking potential enemies by means other than the operations of military force'.[60] By 5 June 1939 Section D had already begun experimenting with clandestine propaganda and was examining ways to undertake raids on enemy installations. Operational plans were developed for the seizure of oil wells in

6   Introduction

Romania and the disruption of the enemy's vital communications following the outbreak of war.[61] By the end of June 1939 SIS staff operating in British embassies, under the cover of the Passport Control Offices, were informed that there existed a 'centrally controlled organisation which is already equipped with arms and explosives, and prepared for action at ten days' notice'.[62]

Section D's first headquarters was established at 2 Caxton Street, London. This grand Victorian red-brick hotel was conveniently located 100 m south of SIS's HQ in Broadway Buildings.[63] One of the first facilities established by this section outside London was at SIS's base at Bletchley Park. By mid-1939 Section D had constructed a small magazine for explosives and incendiaries in the grounds of this property. These facilities enabled the section to conduct experiments with primitive sabotage weapons.[64] As it became apparent that war was likely, Section D began expanding. Following the requisition of The Frythe Residential and Private Hotel, Welwyn, on 26 August 1939, the section quickly acquired this site for their wireless research department.[65]

When war was declared on 1 September 1939, the rapidly expanding GCCS forced out Section D's five officers at Bletchley Park. Two months later, Section D relocated its research activities to Aston House, Stevenage, a facility that was to expand to include the manufacturing and storage of equipment. To aid the work of Aston House, machine and carpenters' shops were constructed in the grounds. In addition, Section D erected a miniature filling factory to prepare and pack explosive charges. It was not long before the storerooms at Aston House were holding several tons of high explosives and incendiaries. Section D also used the grounds for the *ad hoc* training of saboteurs.[66]

It was not until June 1940, however, that Section D established a specialist industrial sabotage school.[67] Known as Station XVII and located at Brickendonbury, Hertfordshire, this facility was run by Commander Peers, Royal Navy. The instructional staff included Major Hill, Mr Philby, Mr Burgess and Professor Paterson, whose aim was to train European exiles to act as instructors and recruiters. On returning to mainland Europe, these agents would be able to raise resistance networks and commit specific acts of sabotage.[68] Following the formation of SOE, The Frythe, Aston House and Brickendonbury would become important centres for the new organisation.

Preceding the creation of Section D by two years was the formation of a similar department set up within the War Office. Established in 1936, the War Office's General Staff (Research) (GS(R)) was comprised only of a major from the Army Education Corps and his typist.[69] In 1938 Major Jo Holland, Royal Engineers, took over the running of GS(R). Deciding to concentrate his meagre resources on researching unorthodox methods of warfare, Holland focused his efforts on studying Boer tactics, Lawrence of Arabia, the Russian and Spanish Civil Wars and the British experience in Ireland. In the spring of 1939, the War Office split its operations and intelligence into two new departments. During this reorganisation, GS(R) was renamed Military Intelligence (Research) (MI(R)).[70]

By the winter of 1939, Section D and MI(R) were discussing the future division of labour between the two competing organisations. Eventually, they reached a settlement whereby MI(R) would focus on activities that could be undertaken by troops in uniform, while Section D would devise operations that could not be officially linked to the British Government.[71] This distinction was not always clear to operational commanders. In January 1940 the Czechoslovakian Chief of Staff, Colonel Hutnik, requested MI(R) supply his agent in Belgrade with explosives intended to sink German barges stuck in ice on the Danube.[72] MI(R) was concerned that this 'business is really D's pigeon, and not an M.I.R. matter, but as the Chief of Staff came to me officially about it, we must take it up and pass it on'.[73]

Unlike Section D, which mainly established facilities associated with research and development, MI(R)'s infrastructure was aimed towards training agents. By May 1940 MI(R) had established a Special Training Centre (STC) at Lochailort, Scotland, to provide instruction to Polish wireless operators.[74] The unit also developed a training facility at Arisaig House, Inverness-shire. Under the command of Major Munn, the role of this base was to train students in demolitions, weapon training, combined operations, forward reconnaissance and clandestine intelligence work. Following an inspection of the local area by Major Davis and Major Wilson, Inverie House, Rhubana Lodge and Meoble Lodge were requisitioned to serve as satellites to Arisaig House.[75]

As early as 25 May 1940, the Chiefs of Staff had foreseen the collapse of France. In this event, the creation of widespread revolt within German-occupied territories was to become a major British strategic objective. It was inevitable that the overlapping roles of Department EH, Section D and MI(R) led to infighting over who should be responsible for clandestine warfare in this scenario. The task of facilitating a settlement between these organisations was given to Lord Hankey, the first formal secretary of the cabinet. At a meeting held on 13 June 1940, Hankey persuaded Holland and Major Grand, head of Section D, that raiding and subversion had to be coordinated by a single ministry.[76] On 1 July Lord Halifax,[77] Lord Hankey, Lord Lloyd,[78] Dr Hugh Dalton,[79] Sir Alexander Cadigan,[80] Gladwyn Jebb,[81] Sir Stewart Menzies,[82] and Sir Desmond Morton[83] agreed that subversive warfare needed to be controlled by a single body with 'dictatorial' powers.[84] The following day, Dalton wrote:

> We have got to organize movements in enemy-occupied territory comparable to the Seinn Fein movement in Ireland, to the Chinese Guerrillas now operating against Japan, to the Spanish Irregulars who played a notable part in Wellington's campaign or – one might as well admit it – to the organizations which the Nazis themselves have developed so remarkably in almost every country in the world. This 'democratic international' must use many different methods, including industrial and military sabotage, labour agitation and strikes, continuous propaganda, terrorist acts against traitors and German leaders, boycotts and riots.[85]

8   *Introduction*

On 10 July the lord president of the council, Neville Chamberlain, presented SOE's founding charter to the War Cabinet. Six days later, Prime Minister Winston Churchill invited Dalton to take charge of the new body.[86] The charter was approved on 22 July and Section D, MI(R) and Department EH were subsequently amalgamated into SOE.[87] In the month following SOE's formation, Dalton tasked Sir Frank Nelson with the daily running of the organisation.[88]

Following SOE's formation, the new executive was organised into three branches: SO1, responsible for propaganda; SO2, for active operations; and SO3, for planning and administration.[89] Despite the creation of SOE, interdepartmental rivalries over who should control propaganda continued. Internally, both SO1 and SO2 maintained the right to undertake 'covert' propaganda. Concerns were also raised as to whether it was feasible to separate covert from overt propaganda, the latter being the responsibility of the Ministry of Information (MoI).[90] Eventually, a decision was taken to form a new independent executive under tripartite ministerial leadership. Operational control of the PWE was entrusted to Robert Bruce Lockhart, while the ministers in charge were Sir Anthony Eden, Foreign Office; Dalton, Ministry of Economic Warfare (MEW); and Brendon Bracken, MoI.[91] On 12 September 1941 Winston Churchill announced to parliament that PWE had been established, formally splitting SOE in two.[92]

In the history of SOE a number of individuals deserve special mention. One of the most important figures in the history of the organisation was Churchill. On various occasions, it was only through the prime minister's influence that SOE survived attacks by her sister organisations. Fascinated by the 'cloak-and-dagger' world of the secret services, Churchill was no stranger to clandestine activities. Early on in his career he had not only been shot at by Cuban guerrillas but also managed to escape from a Boer prisoner-of-war camp. As home secretary he had also been involved in the creation of Britain's intelligence community.[93]

While at the Admiralty during the early stages of the Second World War, Churchill became aware of a plan by Section D to seize Swedish ore fields. As the prime minister, Neville Chamberlain, and the cabinet were dragging their feet in authorising the operation, Churchill lost patience. Summoning Major Grand to the Admiralty, he demanded an explanation for the delay. On hearing Grand's version of events, Churchill cornered Chamberlain and persuaded him to lift the veto against the mission. Following this bureaucratic procrastination, SOE was established as an independent executive within two months of Churchill becoming prime minister in May 1940. His lifelong interest in unorthodox warfare ensured that the resistance organisations were supported throughout the war.[94]

Churchill's conduit to the secret services was Desmond Morton. As an SIS officer, he had fed Churchill intelligence throughout the 1930s.[95] Morton's close connection with SIS meant that he was often eager to draw Churchill's attention to SOE's failures.[96] Despite Morton's personal bias, the prime minister tasked him with ensuring the fragile peace between SOE and SIS survived.[97]

The head of SIS throughout the Second World War was Sir Stewart Menzies, also known as 'C'. Sir Hugh Sinclair, who died on 4 November 1939, had previously held this position. Two days prior to his death, Sinclair had written a letter pressing the case for his deputy Menzies to be his successor. As there were a number of suitable candidates in the running for the position, it took until 28 November for the prime minister, the armed forces and the foreign secretary to come to agree unanimously on Menzies. Despite knowing little about intelligence gathering, Menzies was a shrewd bureaucrat. While head of SIS he managed to forge a strong alliance with the Foreign Office, which agreed that SOE would only ever be a wartime organisation.[98]

Menzies' opposite number in SOE, known as 'CD', changed three times over the course of the Second World War. On his appointment as minister in charge of SOE, Dalton's first task was to find someone to take operational control of the new executive. Dalton had originally intended to give the position to Brigadier General Sir Edward Spears, but he was passed over in favour of Sir Frank Nelson, a 56-year-old former Indian merchant and seven-year Conservative backbencher. This choice gained C's approval.[99]

In February 1942 Dalton was replaced by Lord Selborne as minister of economic warfare. Almost immediately, Selborne deemed Nelson unfit to continue as CD. His deputy, Sir Charles Hambro, replaced him in April 1942. Before joining SOE, Hambro's varied career had including working as a merchant banker and acting as the director of the Bank of England. Following his appointment, Hambro and Selborne arranged to meet on a daily basis. By keeping abreast of SOE's activities, the minister could support the organisation politically.[100]

This close relationship did not last long and eventually the pair fell out. The key area of contention was Hambro's desire to maintain SOE's independence. He was also keen on keeping Selborne at arm's length from the organisation's operational procedures. Following a ministerial meeting in which Selborne was humiliated by Hambro's withholding important information, Selborne decided to find a new CD. In September 1943 Major Colin Gubbins was appointed as Hambro's replacement.[101] Joining MI(R) in 1939, Gubbins had not only been involved in the Norwegian Campaign but was also the central figure in establishing Britain's resistance network, the Auxiliary Units.[102] He was ideally suited, therefore, to run SOE. As a regular soldier, Gubbins also agreed with Selborne that, in a conflict zone, SOE should be subservient to the battlefield commander.[103] Gubbins was to remain CD for the remainder of the war.

The role of SOE

SOE was established as a 'democratic international' responsible for the coordination of 'all action, by way of subversion and sabotage, against the enemy

10 Introduction

overseas'.[104] Throughout the Second World War, the organisation was involved in a wide range of clandestine operational activities, including sabotage, assassination, intelligence gathering and setting up resistance networks.

One of SOE's most famous acts of sabotage was undertaken during Operation GUNNERSIDE. On 16 February 1943 Lieutenant Joachim Ronneberg, Captain Knut Haukelid and Privates Fenriks Fredrik Kayser, Kasper Idland, Hans Storhaug and Birger Stromsheim, from the Norwegian Independent 'Linge' Company, parachuted onto the frozen Bjarnesfjord, Norway. Their task was to attack the Norsk Hydro Plant, Telemark.[105] Lying in a remote valley 150 miles (241.4 km) west of Oslo, this factory was the world's largest producer of heavy water, which was an essential element in controlling nuclear reactions. When the Germans ordered that the plant should increase its output to 10,000 lbs (4,536 kg) per annum, it became a strategic concern to the British.[106]

Previous attempts in November 1942 by Combined Operations to insert troops into Norway to destroy the factory failed. In the aftermath of this disaster, the task was given to SOE.[107] Following the unsuccessful operation, the Germans strengthened the defences in the area. The sabotage team decided that the only way to access the factory was via the sheer cliff face on top of which the plant had been constructed. Entering the compound on the night of 28 February, the demolition parties managed to set their charges within the electrolysis chamber without raising the alarm.[108] Operation GUNNERSIDE clearly demonstrated the value of clandestine warfare.

One of the most audacious plots devised by SOE was Operation FOXLEY. In the summer of 1941 Section X, the German Country Section, was given authorisation to assess the feasibility of assassinating Hitler. By the autumn of 1944 sufficient intelligence had been gathered for the section to contemplate undertaking a serious attempt on Hitler's life. Plans included infiltrating snipers into the vicinity of the Berghof, RAF bombing raids and targeted biological weapons. Debates over the strategic value of assassinating Hitler blocked attempts being made on his life. These continued until Hitler's suicide on 30 April 1945.[109]

SOE's agents were required to pass on all intelligence collected in the field to SIS. In certain regions, the resistance were the only allied forces operating and were SIS's sole source of information.[110] One of the most successful collaborations between SOE, SIS and the European Resistance was Operation MOST III. In the spring of 1944, a V2 rocket fired from a test range near Blizna, Poland, fell into the bank of the River Bug. When the Polish Home Army discovered the rocket, they quickly hid it from the Germans. After being disassembled and smuggled into Warsaw, scientists managed to extract the fuel and send samples back to London. Determined to see the rocket, SIS, in collaboration with SOE and Polish intelligence, arranged for it to be airlifted to the UK in July 1944.[111]

None of the operations conducted and planned by SOE could have occurred without the support of the backroom staff and the organisation's

Introduction   11

infrastructure. Without an appreciation of SOE's agent-facing infrastructure, which included training regimes, research and development facilities, transportation network, communications, and command and control, it is not possible to assess the operational activities of the organisation abroad. To understand the important role that SOE's infrastructure played in supporting agents, the operational life of two agents, Albert Robichaud and Max Manus, is outlined here.

Albert Robichaud

Born on 18 February 1916 in Cabano, Canada, Albert Robichaud was the son of a Canadian father and an American mother.[112] He received an excellent education and had become a schoolmaster by the age of 23, teaching French Literature and Latin. In 1941 he joined the US Army, where he was regarded as 'quiet, unassuming and rather colourless and does not appear to have any qualities of leadership'.[113] Shortly afterwards, Robichaud was recruited by the Office of Strategic Services (OSS) and trained to work as a 'Jedburgh'.[114] He was then seconded to SOE's Section RF, Free French, but no suitable role could be identified. Despite this setback, the organisation's F, French, Section were willing to employ him if he passed his medical.[115] On completion of these tests, Captain Benn became responsible for arranging Robichaud's training.[116]

On 16 January 1944 Robichaud arrived at STS50 with group 27FF-COB102 for paramilitary instruction. During his time there he was regarded as a 'cheerful and intelligent character who has worked well during the week he has been here. Has gone away with a sound knowledge of all subjects ... [However, he was] afraid of getting wet'.[117] By 23 January 1944 Robichaud had moved to Dunham House in preparation for his parachute training at RAF Ringway, STS51. There First Air Nursing Yeomanry (FANY) Heim, Lieutenant Fraser and Captain Rees joined him for six days of ground-based instruction, provided by Miss Daniels.[118] Despite being regarded as a 'rather youthful immature student who spent much of his time in the company with the F.A.N.Y's.', he successfully completed his two jumps and graduated from RAF Ringway.[119]

Robichaud then joined group 27FFC for 'finishing' training at Beaulieu. Here he gave the impression of being

> below the average in intelligence and rather more practical than academic. He is slow, rather scatterbrained and lacking in shrewdness and cunning ... [and] He has no powers of leadership and should be employed, if at all, in a very minor capacity under strict supervision.[120]

As a result of the reports made by his instructors, SOE decided Robichaud would be suitable as a 'guinea pig'.[121]

On the night of 21 March 1944 Robichaud, codenamed ROBIN, travelling by boat, successfully infiltrated into the north coast of Brittany.[122]

12 *Introduction*

On entering France, his orders were to test the newly established CHERUB Circuit by using it to leave France.[123] After moving between two safe houses that night, ROBIN left for Paris the following day. As his train to Bordeaux did not leave until the evening, he managed to fit in some sightseeing. Arriving later than expected at his destination, ROBIN had to locate the address of his contact, M. Renard, by himself. When he finally reached the safe house, he was informed that his contact, Benito, had left, after waiting two weeks for his arrival. When Benito returned the following morning, he was concerned that ROBIN was a Gestapo agent. His fears were dispelled after ROBIN used the correct passwords.[124] ROBIN was now ready to begin his journey on the CHERUB Line.

The first part of the line involved ROBIN catching the midnight train to Bayonne that Sunday.[125] On arrival, ROBIN and Benito continued towards St Jean de Luz by foot. Just outside Biarritz the pair boarded another train for the remainder of the journey to St Jean de Luz. Over the next couple of days ROBIN and Benito were moved between various safe houses while they prepared to cross the Spanish border.[126] Eventually crossing into Spain in the early hours one morning, ROBIN and Benito continued their journey cross country to avoid sentries. After travelling between safe houses and receiving lifts from local contacts, they eventually reached San Sebastian. Staying there for four days while arrangements were made, the pair finally bordered a train for Bilbao. They arrived at their destination, the end of the CHERUB Line, at 11:00 on 29 March 1944.[127]

Subsequent to the successful completion of his first mission, SOE ordered ROBIN to test the CELINI Line, which ran from Bilbao to Lisbon, Portugal.[128] His guide for this journey presented himself at a bus stop on 5 April, but they could not leave until new papers and clothing had been acquired.[129] On 11 April, following an altercation with a ticket inspector, they managed to catch the 19:00 train to Leon. They left Leon and, travelling by train, bus and foot, they eventually reached Barcencia, where they were met by George Montal, the head of the local network, who arranged for them to catch the train to Lisbon the following evening. Following their arrival in Lisbon the British embassy arranged ROBIN's transportation back to the UK. At 23:00 on 18 April 1944 ROBIN boarded a plane destined for Britain under the cover name of Joseph Albery Roberts.[130] On safely landing in the UK, Robichaud was immediately subjected to a series of interrogations.[131] The intelligence gathering from these debriefings was used by SOE in planning future operations.

After being fully debriefed, SOE enrolled Robichaud onto further training sessions.[132] Joining party 27.OB at STS39, Wall Hall, he was instructed in microphotography, where he exhibited a sound knowledge of copying documents, using different cameras and films and working under field conditions.[133] Robichaud was also sent on a three-day reception committee course at STS40, Howbury Hall.[134] His instructors at this school felt that he worked

Introduction 13

'well and has a very good all round knowledge. He should not have any difficulty in organising and controlling this type of operation'.[135]

Based on his training reports, SOE decided to send Robichaud to France via Spain to be in charge of the JESCHKE Circuit's carrier pigeon service.[136] For his new assignment, Robichaud was issued 100 ft (30.48 m) of microfilm, two Leica cable releases, one reel of cellophane, one pair of scissors, a No. 1 lens and 250,000 francs.[137] In order to disguise the equipment, Station XV, The Thatched Barn, was ordered to manufacture a custom-made seed box in which all the items could be concealed.[138] When all the preparations were complete, Robichauld had to wait until SOE was ready to send him to the field. On 26 June 1944 he boarded plane UG25 for Gibraltar under the cover name of Second Lieutenant Stephen Maitland.[139] His orders were to 'proceed to FRANCE to act as one of JUANITO's lieutenants, to operate under his orders a mail pigeon service from FRANCE to U.K.'.[140]

The day after arriving in Gibraltar, ROBIN travelled by car to Barcelona, where he was delayed for two weeks, as members of the line into France had been arrested. On 11 July ROBIN, accompanied by two guides and fellow agents, left Barcelona by car. After covering 155 miles (249.4 km) they had to abandon their vehicle and continue on foot, as it was no longer safe to travel by road. During this hike, one of the agents fell behind and was lost. The group, pressing on, finally stopped for a break at 23:00 on 13 July.[141]

Over the next few days the group had to keep to high ground and the mountain routes to avoid sentry posts. When they finally descended they were met by a new guide, disguised as a fisherman.[142] After walking along the road for some time, they were eventually approached by a car driven by members of the Maquis, who gave them a lift to a nearby hotel. From there they continued their journey to Tarbes by bus and car. On reaching their destination they met another contact, Edouard, who agreed to accompany them to Paris.[143]

Before leaving, Edouard noticed errors in the papers SOE had supplied to ROBIN. Their departure was, therefore, delayed as the circuit's forgers had to produce new documents. When they finally reached Toulouse by bus, the group had to wait 8.5 hours because a bomb had destroyed the train line to Nîmes. As it was estimated that the repairs would take two days, Edouard persuaded the driver of a mail van to take the group to Avignon. On this part of their journey they were accompanied by a Gendarme, whose presence ensured that they were not searched at checkpoints.[144]

Leaving Avignon, they reached Lyon, where they were forced to wait until they could board a train heading north. As they approached the demarcation line the train was stopped at a Gestapo checkpoint. Successfully completing these checks, they eventually reached Gare de Lyon, Paris. Proceeding to Gare d'Austerlitz, they caught the Metro to Montparnasse, before heading to No. 4 Rue Bertrand. Over the next 13 days, ROBIN moved between three further safe houses.[145]

14   *Introduction*

One of ROBIN's roles was to identify suitable landing grounds and drop zones for a new circuit JUANITO was establishing. The locations of these sites would be communicated back to the UK using a radio SOE had parachuted into France for use by the circuit. Despite locating a number of suitable sites, ROBIN went into hiding as the Allied troops advanced.[146] During this period in hiding he managed to assist a number of downed airmen through the circuit's escape routes.[147] On 5 September 1944 the Allied forces liberated ROBIN and sent him back to the UK.[148] For his actions Robichaud was mentioned in dispatches, as he

> not only made the [escape] line safe for evaders, but he broke all records for speed by being back in this country in less than a fortnight of his departure. The journey across the Pyrenees and Estrella Mountains into Portugal entailed great hardship, and it is a magnificent tribute to his great powers of endurance and determination that Lieut. Robichaud was able to accomplish his mission with such outstanding success in so short a space of time.
>
> Lieutenant Robichaud was sent on a second mission to France in June 1944 and although the intervention of D–Day curtailed his activities, Lt. Robichaud again showed the same spirit of determination by reporting to his organiser in Paris after travelling through enemy-held areas.[149]

Max Manus, DSO, MC and Bar

Born on 9 December 1914 in Bergen, Norway, Max Manus was the son of a Norwegian father and a Danish mother. As a child he lived in Copenhagen and Cuba, returning to Europe in 1930. After the Winter War had broken out in November 1939, Manus travelled to Finland and volunteered to fight the Russians. Returning to Norway on 15 April 1940 with 130 compatriots, shortly after the German invasion, he formed a guerrilla company that operated in Kongsvinger and Brumunddal. This unit eventually disbanded on 15 May 1940.[150]

After Norway's surrender Manus, serving under a Major Helseth, began stockpiling weapons. Following a security breach within his network, the Gestapo confronted him on 16 February 1941.[151] Fearing he knew too much, Manus

> decided to take a risk and, drawing the attention of the six men to some sporting trophies in the room, he quickly jumped through the window. His apartment was on the second floor. He remembers no more until he recovered consciousness in the ULLEVOL Hospital.[152]

Once he managed to get news of his capture to his network, Manus began planning his escape from the hospital. On 13 March 1941 he lowered a fishing line out of the window to a friend waiting below. Onto this Manus' colleagues attached a rope, which he pulled up to his window before climbing down.[153] In order to avoid

> reprisals against the nurse, he had arranged with the doctor that the nurse should receive some facial injection which would cause her face to swell and, in addition, the doctor should discolour the skin in such a way as to make it appear that MANUS had overpowered the nurse.[154]

Following his escape, Manus travelled to the UK via Sweden, Finland, Russia, Turkey, Egypt, South Africa, Trinidad, Canada, arriving in Belfast on 9 December 1941.[155] When he reached Britain his SOE interrogators regarded him as a

> young adventurer, but there is no question at all of his loyalty and one cannot but admire his work and the risks he has taken to avoid falling into the hands of the Gestapo. He has been commissioned into the Norwegian Army ... [and] I recommend that he be released to [SOE] Norway House immediately.[156]

In January 1942 Manus began his training at STS3, Stodham Park, where he was deemed the 'comedian of the party and very popular with the rest of the crowd. He is very keen and intelligent and has also plenty of sound common sense'.[157] After successfully completing this course, Manus was sent to STS24, Inverie House, where he demonstrated an expert knowledge of the weapons and tank traps used in the Finno-Russo war.[158] Manus also attended courses at STS51, RAF Ringway; STS33, The House on the Shore; and STS26, Inverlochy Castle.[159] On 28 February 1943 he began his final stage of training at the Finishing Schools at Beaulieu.[160]

While stationed in the UK Manus began planning an operation against shipping in Norway using canoes and specially constructed charges.[161] On 12 March 1943 Manus and Corporal Gregers Gramm parachuted into Norway east of Oslo. Operation MARDONIUS suffered setbacks almost immediately, as Manus developed a severe bout of pneumonia, and was further delayed by a lack of volunteers, a shortage of suitable targets and a long spell of bright nights. Conditions were finally suitable on the night of 28 April 1943 for an attempt to sabotage shipping in Oslofjord. Despite the fjord being illuminated by the moon, the group managed to place their charges, sinking two ships and damaging a third.[162]

Returning to the UK on 24 May 1943, Manus was posted to STS26 to train students in paramilitary skills. Five months later he was sent to Station 61, Gaynes Hall, as he awaited his return to the field for his next operation.[163] Travelling back to Oslo for Operation BUNDLE, Manus was 'charged with the dual role of continuing ship sabotage when opportunity offered, and particularly, of subverting enemy troops by the distribution of leaflets, posters and other clandestine methods'.[164]

16 Introduction

While in Norway, Manus produced a series of publications that were reported to have had a considerable impact on German morale. He also made several attempts at sabotaging ships that came into his area of operation. One of his successes was to attach a string of limpets to the *Monte Rosa*. The ship sank as she was leaving Oslo harbour with 3,000 German troops aboard. Manus was also involved in a number of other missions including the destruction of aircraft undergoing repairs and the attack on the Vacuum Oil Company storage depot at Sorenga. For his actions in Operation BUNDLE, Manus was awarded a bar to his Military Cross.[165]

One of Manus' most successful missions was the destruction of the transport ship *Donau*. On her arrival in Oslo harbour on 15 January 1945, it was decided that an attempt should be immediately made to sabotage her. Despite ice in the harbour and a search being conducted for a German soldier who had fallen into the water, it was decided to continue with the plan. In order to smuggle the cordex past the guards, Manus and Roy Nielsen wrapped 100 m of the cord around their bodies.[166] As they approached the checkpoint, a pre-arranged diversion was staged:

> It was slippery with ice, and when he came up to the guard, Nielsen, who is over 6 feet, skidded and fell backwards to the great amusement of everyone. As a result the examination of papers was of a very cursory nature.[167]

On entering the site, the pair managed to attach 11 limpets to the side of the *Donau*. As they were leaving, the *Rolanseck* arrived, and they placed their remaining limpet onto her.[168]

At 22:00 on the evening of the attack the *Donau* was sailing past the coast of Drøbak as the charges detonated, sinking her in 25 m of water. The explosion destroyed several hundred vehicles and killed 300 horses and an unknown number of elite Alpine troops. Despite an immediate search of the *Rolanseck*, no devices were found and later the limpet exploded, blowing a hole in the side of the ship.[169]

After completing this mission, Manus escaped Oslo. Arriving in Stockholm on 29 January 1945, he remained there until 1 March 1945, when he was ordered back to Norway.[170] Two months after his return the German forces in Norway surrendered. On 7 June King Haakon VII returned to Oslo accompanied by Manus, who had 'established himself high in the Crown Prince's favour, who regards the trio Fjeld (no.24), Max, and Martin Olsen as the guardians of the Royal Family!'[171]

The operational lives of Max Manus and Albert Robichaud clearly demonstrate the role SOE's infrastructure played in the work of the organisation. Without training, transportation, communications, supplies and a command structure, the outcome of these missions would have been significantly different.

SOE's global headquarters

In order for SOE to operate effectively and coordinate the actions of agents such as Manus and Robichaud, it was essential that the organisation established a global command and control infrastructure. Without this in place, SOE would have lacked the necessary administration to coordinate internal activities and collaborate externally. Throughout the war, SOE's command and control infrastructure was mainly centred on London. Although famously operating out of 64 Baker Street, Marylebone, this was only one office in a much larger network of administrative facilities spread across the city. SOE's offices in 64 Baker Street were established early in the organisation's existence.[172] As the war progressed, and SOE grew, the organisation expanded, taking over additional properties on Baker Street and in the adjoining streets. This location, 2 miles (3.2 km) from SIS's headquarters at 54 Broadway Building, became an important hub in the running of SOE.

Alongside the complex of headquarters buildings centred on Baker Street, SOE concentrated their support infrastructure in four other areas within London. In Bayswater, Earls Court, Belgravia and Fitzrovia SOE established clusters of 'safe houses'. These were generally single rooms located within vetted hotels that could be rented on a nightly basis.[173] In close proximity to each cluster of safe houses, SOE established satellite offices. This arrangement allowed SOE to compartmentalise their activities within London.[174] The organisation's presence within the capital was thus indistinguishable from the daily life of the city.

To coordinate the SOE's global activities, command and control facilities were established by the organisation in, among other places, Cairo, Paris, Moscow, Stockholm, Istanbul, New Zealand, Australia, Switzerland, Crete, Washington, Melbourne and nearly every South American country.[175] In Africa SOE had headquarters and outstations in Durban, Lagos, Kano, Accra, Freetown, Bathurst and Cape Town.[176]

One of the first headquarters established by SOE overseas was in Singapore. The local authorities were informed in early 1941 that a mission would be leaving London by the middle of March for the city. SOE requested that the three or four men and four women of the mission should be supplied by the local authorities with office accommodation comprising 13 rooms, which should be self-contained and furnished with electric fan lighting, desks and telephones.[177] When the senior officers of SOE's Oriental Mission reached Singapore in early May, the local authorities had made few preparations for their arrival. Owing to Japanese advances, the mission was eventually forced to evacuate Singapore by the end of January 1942. The staff were then dispersed to India, Burma, Java and China.[178]

By September 1943 SOE's headquarters in India, known as ME80, was based in Meerut.[179] As this unit was over 40 miles (64.4 km) from the South East Asian Theatre's GHQ in New Delhi, it was necessary for SOE to base a

18   Introduction

liaison staff in the city.[180] The function of ME80 was to direct and administer the whole of SOE's organisation in the region in conformity with directives received from London. In addition, it was responsible for stores, for acquiring and arranging transport, for operating communication facilities and for organising training.[181]

In August 1942 meetings took place in London to discuss SOE's plans for establishing an Advanced Operational Base in North Africa in the event of a successful invasion by the Allies. SOE's Working Committee drew up a charter for the speedy formation of this mission, which was to be known as 'Massingham', on 29 October 1942.[182] The role of this facility was to 'provide a forward base for the continuation and extension of SOE work in Europe ... [and] To carry out such activities and operations as may be required by the Theatre Commander in connection with military operations'.[183]

To ensure that Massingham was self-supporting and could carry out the functions of an operational base, SOE wanted it to contain all necessary support sections, including supply and communications. While planning for this base, it was decided that the Massingham headquarters would be established in the vicinity of Algiers.[184] By early 1942 personnel from this new mission had set up base in a group of villas at Cap Matifou, approximately 15 miles (24.1 km) from Algiers. The unit was brought up to strength in January with the arrival of a staff of drivers, duty men, cooks, orderlies, signal personnel and 11 FANYs. Owing to the unsuitability of the villas at Cap Matifou and the lack of space to expand, Massingham began searching for a new site. On 17 February 1943 the mission relocated to a location 12 miles (19.3 km) to the west of Algiers and established itself in the Club des Pins, a large group of villas surrounded by pine trees and with access to a private beach enclosed by sand dunes.[185] The geographical isolation of this mission meant that the unit had to provide its own social life and recreational activities.[186] As the officers regularly socialised in the regular mess, this led to a 'happy team spirit fostered by the Commandant, who takes an active part and interest in the social life of all ranks [and] maintains very close contact with the progress of work of all sections under his command'.[187]

In January 1944 Allied Forces Headquarters (AFHQ) agreed in principal to the establishment of a central SOE headquarters in the Mediterranean (SOM). This command would also coordinate SOE and OSS(SO) activities and provide transportation and packing facilities to a range of special agencies.[188] By 12 April 1944 SOM aimed to have established its headquarters in the Bari area, Italy, while maintaining a rear administrative HQ in Cairo.[189] SOM was located in four main areas in the Mediterranean Theatre: HQ SOM at Mola di Bari; SOM Admin at Torre a Mare; Rear SOM in Cairo; and SOM Liaison Staff AFHQ at Algiers and, later, Caserta. This geographical dispersal made the periodic inspection of this headquarters by Commander SOM and his staff problematic.[190]

To aid intra-organisational co-operation, a Special Projects Operational Centre (SPOC) was also established in the Mediterranean Theatre. In April

Introduction 19

1944 Massingham was informed of the upcoming invasion of Normandy and an anticipated landing in the South of France. The SPOC originated in the necessity for closer liaison between SOE, OSS and the French authorities in Algiers while preparing for these operations. Owing to the distance between the Club des Pins and Algiers, contact between these organisations was limited. At the time, many of Massingham's section were also understaffed.[191] To address these issues, London agreed that a camp for the SPOC should be constructed in Algiers. At this new site it was planned that 'O.S.S. (S.O.) and S.O.E. Planning Sections, Operational Sections, French Country Sections, Jedburgh and American Operational Groups (O.G's) Planning Staffs and Intelligence Sections should work and live together'.[192]

The SPOC was housed in a camp that consisted of Nissen huts for officers and tents for the other ranks (ORs). Construction occurred quickly and the staff moved in on 15 May 1944. Lieutenant Colonel Anstey, commander of Massingham, took command of the SPOC in conjunction with Colonel Davies of the OSS, while retaining control of Massingham. Staff at the SPOC were divided between nine Nissen huts comprising the Control Hut, the Codes Hut, the Signals Hut, the Operations Hut, the Country Section Field Messages Hut, the Country Section Hut, the RAF Hut, the Jedburgh Hut and the Intelligence Hut.[193]

In view of the progress the Allies had made in France, a decision was taken in early September 1944 to end the work of the SPOC, and their offices closed on September 12. Shortly afterwards, SPOC (Forward) was established in the Hotel Crillon, Avignon, under the command of an American officer, Colonel Baker, with Massingham's Major Searle as second-in-command.[194] The role of SPOC (Forward) was to interview and debrief all agents sent into the South of France by Massingham and to express appreciation for their hard work.[195] In addition, this facility was established to

> enable all agents to regulate their personal difficulties, and generally give them the feeling that although activity had ceased in our theatre of operations, we still had an interest in their future, and would do everything possible in cooperation with the French authorities to assist them in getting further work according [to] their respective tastes and ability.[196]

SPOC (Forward) remained in Avignon until early November, when it was disbanded and its staff returned to the UK.[197]

Notes

1 TNA CAB 301/51 Report to the Minister of Economic Warfare on the Organisation of SOE, p. 1.
2 Nigel West, *Secret War: The Story of SOE: Britain's Wartime Sabotage Organisation* (London, 1992), p. 1.
3 Richard Duckett, *The Special Operations Executive in Burma: Jungle Warfare and Intelligence Gathering in World War II* (London, 2017), p. 5.

20   *Introduction*

4 In this book, infrastructure is being defined as any building, facility, or installation that supported SOE's operations.

5 Owing to the nature of SOE's archives, it has not always been possible to give the full name of the individual being discussed. Full names have been provided when these are known; when the full names are not recorded, the name provided in the primary documents has been used. The place names used throughout this book are as they were at the time SOE was operating.

6 Michael Foot, *SOE: The Special Operations Executive 1940–46* (London, 1993), p. 18.

7 TNA CAB 301/51 Report to the Minister of Economic Warfare on the Organisation of S.O.E., p. 33.

8 TNA FO 1093/155 Special Operations Executive Note by the Secretary of the War Cabinet 22/04/1942, p. 2.

9 Michael Foot, *SOE in France* (London, 1966), p. 14.

10 Mark Seaman, 'A Glass Half Full – Some Thoughts on the Evolution of the Study of the Special Operations Executive', *Intelligence and National Security* 20.1 (2005), p. 28.

11 Nigel Wylie, 'Introduction: Special Operations Executive – New Approaches and Perspectives', *Intelligence and National Security* 20.1 (2005), pp. 1, 5.

12 Wylie, 'Introduction', pp. 1, 2, 5.

13 Seaman, 'A Glass Half Full', p. 29. The quality of the 'in-house' histories varies between authors (Wylie, 'Introduction', p. 2).

14 Seaman, 'A Glass Half Full', p. 30. As a political historian who had worked as a civil servant in the Air Ministry during the war, Mackenzie was ideally suited for this complex task (Seaman, 'A Glass Half Full', p. 30).

15 Seaman, 'A Glass Half Full', p. 30.

16 TNA HS 8/327 WJM/172 24/11/1947, p. 1.

17 William Mackenzie, *The Secret History of SOE: Special Operations Executive 1940–1945* (London, 2000).

18 Seaman, 'A Glass Half Full', p. 30.

19 Foot, *SOE in France*, p. 453.

20 Seaman, 'A Glass Half Full', p. 32.

21 Juliette Pattinson, '"A Story That Will Thrill You and Make You Proud." The Cultural Memory of Britain's Secret War in Occupied France', in *British Cultural Memory and the Second World War*, ed. Lucy Noakes and Juliette Pattinson (London, 2014), p. 134. Shortly after the war, a number of films were made that did much to influence post-war perceptions. See *Carve Her Name with Pride* and *Odette*.

22 Seaman, 'A Glass Half Full', pp. 31, 32, 33.

23 See Tim Carew, *The Korean War: The Story of the Fighting Commonwealth Regiments 1950–1953* (London, 1967); David Halberstam, *The Coldest Winter: America and the Korean War* (London, 2007); Rowland White, *Storm Front* (London, 2012); and Jonathan Walker, *Aden Insurgency: The Savage War in Yemen 1962–67* (London, 2011).

24 See Malcolm Postgate, *Operation FIREDOG: Air Support in the Malayan Emergency 1948–1960* (London, 1992); Eric Smith, *Counter-Insurgency Operations 1: Malaya and Borneo* (Shepperton, 1985); Robert Jackson, *The Malayan Emergency and Indonesian Confrontation: The Commonwealth's Wars 1948–1966* (Barnsley, 2011); Christopher Bayly and Tim Harper, *Forgotten Wars: The End of British Asian Empire* (London, 2007); and Richard Aldrich, 'Legacies of Secret Service: Renegade SOE and the Karen Struggle in Burma, 1948–50', *Intelligence and National Security* 14.4 (1999), pp. 130–48.

25 Basil Liddell Hart, *Defence of the West: Some Riddles of War and Peace* (London, 1950), pp. 53–7.

Introduction 21

26 David Stafford, *Britain and European Resistance 1940–1945: A Survey of the Special Operations Executive with Documents* (London, 1980), p. 5.
27 Richard Deacon, *A History of the British Secret Service* (London, 1969), p. 563.
28 Deacon, *British Secret Service* p. 563.
29 Seaman, 'A Glass Half Full', p. 33, regards Stafford as making as great a contribution to our understanding of the organisation as SOE's official historian, Michael Foot.
30 Stafford, *Britain and European Resistance*, p. 5.
31 Stafford, *Britain and European Resistance*, pp. 5, 7.
32 Seaman, 'A Glass Half Full', pp. 34, 35.
33 Michael Foot, 'Was SOE Any Good?', *Journal of Contemporary History* 16.1 (1981), p. 179.
34 Foot, 'Was SOE Any Good?', p. 177.
35 Wylie, 'Introduction', p. 11.
36 Seaman, 'A Glass Half Full', p. 28.
37 For published material on SOE's activities within specific countries, see Roderick Bailey, *The Wildest Province: SOE in the Land of the Eagle* (London, 2008); Charles Cruickshank, *SOE in Scandinavia* (Oxford, 1986); Foot, *SOE in France*; Michael Foot, *SOE in the Low Countries* (London, 2001); Denis Rigden, *Kill the Fuhrer: Section X and Operation Foxley* (Stroud, 2002); Marcel Ruby, *F Section SOE: The Story of the Buckmaster Network* (London, 1990); David Stafford, *Mission Accomplished: SOE and Italy, 1943–1945* (London, 2011); and Malcolm Tudor, *SOE in Italy 1940–1945: The Real Story* (Newtown, 2011). For research on agents, see Marcus Binney, *The Women Who Lived for Danger: The Women Agents of SOE in the Second World War* (London, 2002); Marcus Binney, *Secret War Heroes: Men of the Special Operations Executive* (London, 2006); Sarah Helm, *A Life in Secrets: The Story of Vera Atkins and the Lost Agents of SOE* (London, 2006); Bruce Marshall, *The White Rabbit: The Secret Agent the Gestapo Could not Crack* (London, 2002); and Henri Raymond, 'Experiences of an SOE Agent in France', in *The Fourth Dimension of Warfare: Vol. 1 Intelligence/Subversion/ Resistance*, ed. Michael Elliott-Bateman (New York, 1970), pp. 111–26.
38 Christopher Murphy, 'SOE's Foreign Currency Transactions', *Intelligence and National Security* 20.1 (2005), pp. 191, 205.
39 Foot, *SOE in France*, p. 449.
40 Duncan Stuart, '"Of Historical Interest Only": The Origins and Vicissitudes of the SOE Archive', *Intelligence and National Security* 20.1 (2005), p. 14.
41 Foot, *SOE in France*, p. 449.
42 Stuart, '"Of Historical Interest Only"', pp. 14–15.
43 Stuart, '"Of Historical Interest Only"', pp. 15, 18.
44 Stuart, '"Of Historical Interest Only"', pp. 14, 15, 18, 20. Among the papers destroyed were the following categories (expressed as number of cabinets): stores and supplies, 20; Middle East, 20; signals and telegrams, 14; training, 14; admin and organisation, 11; Far East, 9; war diaries, 9; French, 7; European Countries general, 6; Scandinavian, 3; Central Europe, 2; Italian, 2; Belgian, 1; and Dutch, 1 (Stuart, '"Of Historical Interest Only"', p. 20).
45 Stuart, '"Of Historical Interest Only"', pp. 14, 15, 18, 20.
46 Seaman, 'A Glass Half Full', pp. 28–9, 36. The selective declassification of files can distort assessments of SOE (Wylie, 'Introduction', p. 5).
47 Eric Howe, *The Black Game: British Subversive Operations against the Germans during the Second World War* (London, 1988), p. 36.
48 Stuart, '"Of Historical Interest Only"', pp. 9, 10.
49 Howe, *The Black Game*, p. 36.
50 Howe, *The Black Game*, p. 38.

22 *Introduction*

51 David Garnett, *The Secret History of PWE: The Political Warfare Executive 1939–1945* (London, 2002), pp. 9–10.
52 Howe, *The Black Game*, pp. 38, 40.
53 Garnett, *The Secret History of PWE*, p. 11.
54 Howe, *The Black Game*, pp. 38, 40. Prior to the outbreak of hostilities, there were concerns within Whitehall over the threat posed by the Luftwaffe to London. To mitigate this risk, government departments began searching for potential safe refuges in the countryside far from the dangers of bombing. Department EH identified Woburn Abbey as suitable for their needs and immediately initiated negotiations with the duke of Bedford's representatives. Leo Russell, a relative of the duke of Bedford, led Department EH's negotiators. Although unwilling to lease the abbey, the duke eventually compromised and allowed the organisation access to the riding school and the stable block (Howe, *The Black Game*, p. 39).
55 Howe, *The Black Game*, pp. 39, 40.
56 TNA HS 8/337 Letter from Hugh Dalton to Lord Reith 02/12/1940, p. 1.
57 TNA HS 8/337 Hugh Dalton to Lord Reith 02/12/1940, p. 2.
58 TNA HS 8/337 Hugh Dalton to Lord Reith 02/12/1940, p. 2.
59 Foot, *SOE*, p. 5.
60 TNA HS 8/305 Recommendations with regard to the control of 'Extra-Departmental' and 'Para-Military' activities, p. 2.
61 TNA HS 8/305 Recommendations with regard to the control of 'Extra-Departmental' and 'Para-Military' activities, pp. 2–3.
62 TNA HS 4/31 Notes on Para-Military Activities 24/06/1939, p. 1.
63 Mackenzie, *The Secret History of SOE*, p. 13.
64 TNA HS 7/27 History of the Research and Development Section of SOE, p. 3.
65 Fredric Boyce and Douglas Everett, *SOE: The Scientific Secrets* (Stroud, 2009), p. 15.
66 TNA HS 7/27 History of the Research and Development Section of SOE, pp. 3, 4, 5.
67 Bernard O'Connor, *RAF Tempsford: Churchill's Most Secret Airfield* (Stroud, 2010), p. 19.
68 TNA HS 7/51 Chapter I: Origin and Early History of the Training Section, p. 1.
69 Foot, *SOE*, pp. 5–6. GS(R) did not expand from two members of staff for the first two years of its existence (Foot, *SOE*, pp. 5–6).
70 Foot, *SOE*, pp. 5–6.
71 Foot, *SOE*, p. 7.
72 TNA HS 4/31 L.2/M/P/3, p. 2.
73 TNA HS 4/31 L.2/M/P/3, pp. 2–3.
74 TNA HS 7/183 Administrative Origins and Early Work of Polish Section, p. 13.
75 TNA HS 7/51 Chapter I: Origin and Early History of the Training Section, p. 3.
76 Foot, *SOE*, pp. 16, 17.
77 Foreign secretary.
78 Colonial secretary.
79 Minister of economic warfare.
80 Permanent secretary for foreign affairs.
81 Private secretary to the permanent secretary for foreign affairs.
82 C, head of SIS.
83 The prime minister's civil assistant, who handled Churchill's relations with the secret service.
84 Foot, *SOE*, p. 18.
85 Dalton quoted in Foot, *SOE*, p. 18.

Introduction 23

86 TNA HS CAB 301/51 Report to the Minister of Economic Warfare on the Organisation of SOE, p. 1.
87 Mackenzie, *The Secret History of SOE*, p. 69.
88 Foot, *SOE*, p. 23. Dalton and Nelson, supported by Jebb, immediately dismissed Grand from SOE. Jebb was responsible for reporting to Halifax on Dalton's activities (Foot, *SOE*, p. 23).
89 Foot, *SOE*, p. 23. Over the course of the Second World War, SOE's internal hierarchy underwent various alterations. Despite these reorganisations, the basic structure remained relatively consistent. Operational control of SOE was in the hands of CD, directly under whom was his deputy, D/CD. The organisation was then arranged into a number of sections whose functions included dealing with security, liaison, research and development, supplies, finance and administration. Sub-sections that dealt daily with activities within mainland Europe were known as the Country Sections. These were tasked with recruiting and arranging the training of their own agents. It was also the responsibility of Country Sections to coordinate, arrange and undertake operations in mainland Europe (TNA HS 8/965 SOE Internal Organisation Summer 1943).
90 Garnett, *The Secret History of PWE*, p. 81.
91 Howe, *The Black Game*, p. 50.
92 Garnett, *The Secret History of PWE*, p. 72.
93 David Stafford, *Churchill and Secret Service* (London, 1997), pp. 4, 7.
94 Stafford, *Churchill and Secret Service*, pp. 173, 188.
95 Stafford, *Churchill and Secret Service*, pp. 6, 237–8.
96 Stafford, *Britain and European Resistance*, p. 151.
97 Stafford, *Churchill and Secret Service*, pp. 6, 237–8.
98 Keith Jeffery, *MI6: The History of the Secret Intelligence Service 1909–1949* (London, 2010), pp. 328, 331, 742.
99 Foot, *SOE*, pp. 18, 22–3.
100 Foot, *SOE*, pp. 37–8, 39–40.
101 Foot, *SOE*, pp. 40–1.
102 Peter Wilkinson and Joan Astley, *Gubbins and SOE* (Barnsley, 2010), pp. 34, 50, 69.
103 Foot, *SOE*, pp. 40–1.
104 TNA CAB 301/51 Report to the Minister of Economic Warfare on the Organisation of SOE, p. 1.
105 Cruickshank, *SOE in Scandinavia*, p. 199.
106 Ray Mears, *The Real Heroes of Telemark: The True Story of the Secret Mission to Stop Hitler's Atomic Bomb* (London, 2003), p. 9.
107 Boyce and Everett, *SOE*, p. 252.
108 Mears, *The Real Heroes of Telemark*, pp. 151–3, 159–64.
109 Rigden, *Kill the Fuhrer*, pp. viii, ix, 2, 3.
110 TNA HS 8/901 SIS and SOE F/3491/134.1 31/03/1942, p. 3.
111 Gill Bennett, 'The Achievements of the Polish Intelligence Service', in *Intelligence Co-operation between Poland and Great Britain during World War II*, ed. Tessa Stirling, Daria Nalecz and Tadeusz Dubicki (Edgware, 2005), p. 441.
112 TNA HS 9/1270/2 27FFC OB.102, p. 1.
113 TNA HS 8/176 From D/F 13/01/1944, p. 1.
114 Jedburghs were three-man international teams of soldiers parachuted into occupied Europe in order to assist the Allied forces who had invaded France in 1944.
115 TNA HS 8/176 From D/F 13/01/1944, p. 1.
116 TNA HS 8/176 RFT/999 13/01/1944.
117 TNA HS 8/176 Para-Military Report, pp. 1–2.
118 TNA HS 8/176 Parachute Training Report – Most Secret, p. 1.

24   *Introduction*

119 TNA HS 8/176 Parachute Training Report – Most Secret, p. 1.
120 TNA HS 8/176 Finishing Report, p. 1.
121 TNA HS 8/176 From D/FB 08/03/1944.
122 TNA HS 8/176 DF/REC/5288 20/04/1944. ROBIN was attached to Operation DULVERTON to cross the English Channel (TNA HS 8/176 5097 03/04/1944).
123 TNA HS 8/176 Operational Orders for Robin 17/03/1944, p. 1. The CHERUB Circuit had been formed to enable the passage of people and messages between Bilbag, Spain, and Bordeaux, France, a distance of approximately 210 miles (337.9 km)
124 TNA HS 8/176 Interrogation of Robichaud, Albert @ Robin (Field Name) 29/04/1944, p. 3.
125 As stricter controls were expected on the Saturday, the decision was taken to travel on the Sunday (TNA HS 8/176 Interrogation of Robichaud, Albert @ Robin (Field Name) 29/04/1944, p. 3).
126 TNA HS 8/176 Interrogation of Robichaud, Albert @ Robin (Field Name) 29/04/1944, pp. 3–4.
127 TNA HS 8/176 Interrogation of Robichaud, Albert @ Robin (Field Name) 29/04/1944, pp. 4–5 and TNA HS 8/176 DF/REC/5288 20/04/1944.
128 TNA HS 8/176 DF/REC/5288 20/04/1944.
129 TNA HS 8/176 Report on Robichaud, p. 1. ROBIN was instructed to visit the bus stop, carrying a newspaper under his arm, where a man would ask him in English for a match; in return, ROBIN was to provide him with a matchbox. This security check ensured both parties knew whom they were dealing with (TNA HS 8/176 Report on Robichaud, p. 1).
130 TNA HS 8/176 Report on Robichaud, pp. 1–2.
131 TNA HS 8/176 DF/OPS/5613 19/05/1944.
132 TNA HS 8/176 DF/OPS/5613 19/05/1944.
133 TNA HS 8/176 Finishing Report 19/05/1944.
134 TNA HS 8/176 FVS/9142 21/06/1944.
135 TNA HS 8/176 Short Three Day Reception Committee Course 26/06/1944.
136 TNA HS 8/176 DF/OPS/5613 19/05/1944.
137 TNA HS 8/176 DF/5944 10/06/1944.
138 TNA HS 8/176 Form CAM.1.A 20/06/1944.
139 TNA HS 8/176 Air Passage 22/06/1944.
140 TNA HS 8/176 Operation Orders for ROBIN 24/06/1944, p. 1.
141 TNA HS 8/176 Interrogation of Robichaud – 28th September 1944, pp. 1–2.
142 TNA HS 8/176 Interrogation of Robichaud – 28th September 1944, p. 2. The guide was actually a French champion skier who was trusted by the Germans and was, therefore, in a position to know troop movements along the road.
143 TNA HS 8/176 Interrogation of Robichaud – 28th September 1944, pp. 2–3.
144 TNA HS 8/176 Interrogation of Robichaud – 28th September 1944, pp. 2–3.
145 TNA HS 8/176 Interrogation of Robichaud – 28th September 1944, pp. 3–4.
146 TNA HS 8/176 Appendix to Interrogation of Robichaud, Albert.
147 TNA HS 8/176 Activity Report of Lt Albert Robichard 15/10/194, p. 6.
148 TNA HS 8/176 CE.10 12/09/1944 and TNA HS 8/176 7099 29/09/1944.
149 TNA HS 9/1270/2 Army Form W.3121, pp. 1–2.
150 TNA HS 9/986/2 4381 MANUS, MAX 13/12/1941, pp. 1, 3.
151 TNA HS 9/986/2 4381 MANUS, MAX 13/12/1941, pp. 3, 4.
152 TNA HS 9/986/2 4381 MANUS, MAX 13/12/1941, pp. 4–5.
153 TNA HS 9/986/2 4381 MANUS, MAX 13/12/1941, p. 5.
154 TNA HS 9/986/2 4381 MANUS, MAX 13/12/1941, p. 5.
155 TNA HS 9/986/2 450/4942 Manus, Max 2/Lt, p. 1.
156 TNA HS 9/986/2 4381 MANUS, MAX 13/12/1941, pp. 1, 7.
157 TNA HS 9/986/2 450/4942 Manus, Max 2/Lt, p. 2.

Introduction   25

158 TNA HS 9/986/2 450/4942 Manus, Max 2/Lt, p. 2.
159 TNA HS 9/986/2 Manus, Max Party 26N, pp. 2–3.
160 TNA HS 9/986/2 Training, p. 1.
161 TNA HS 9/986/2 Fenrik Max Manus, Royal Norwegian Army Recommendation for Award.
162 TNA HS 9/986/2 Fenrik Max Manus, Royal Norwegian Army Recommendation for Award, Remarks. For this, Manus was awarded the Norwegian War Cross with Sword, the highest-ranking Norwegian gallantry decoration, and the British Military Cross.
163 TNA HS 9/986/2 Training, p. 1.
164 TNA HS 9/886/2 Recommendation for the award of a bar to the MC to Fenrik (L/Lieut) Max Manus MC RNA, p. 1.
165 TNA HS 9/886/2 Recommendation for the award of a bar to the MC to Fenrik (L/Lieut) Max Manus MC RNA, pp. 1–2.
166 TNA HS 9/886/2 Recommendation for the award of a bar to the MC to Fenrik (L/Lieut) Max Manus MC RNA, p. 2.
167 TNA HS 9/886/2 Recommendation for the award of a bar to the MC to Fenrik (L/Lieut) Max Manus MC RNA, p. 2.
168 TNA HS 9/886/2 Recommendation for the award of a bar to the MC to Fenrik (L/Lieut) Max Manus MC RNA, pp. 2–3.
169 TNA HS 9/886/2 Recommendation for the award of a bar to the MC to Fenrik (L/Lieut) Max Manus MC RNA, pp. 3–4.
170 TNA HS 9/986/2 Training, p. 1.
171 TNA HS 9/1605/3 Diary of Scandinavian Tour by Colonel JS Wilson OBE pp. 2, 3.
172 Roy Berkeley, *A Spy's London* (London, 1994), p. 173.
173 TNA HS 8/335 London Hotels, pp. 1–3. Each Country Section was allocated specific hotels that could be used as safe houses. SOE also retained a number that they always held in reserve. Pre-war centres of hospitality within London had an influence on the geographical distribution of SOE's safe houses.
174 SOE's safe houses in Belgravia were in close proximity to the offices of various governments in exile and other foreign bodies. This arrangement meant that it was theoretically easy for representatives of these organisations to be involved in the briefing and debriefing of SOE agents.
175 TNA HS 8/200 SOE Council Minutes of Meeting held on Tuesday, March 7th, 1944; TNA HS 8/201 SOE Council Minutes of Meeting held on Tuesday, September 12th, 1944; TNA HS 8/202 SOE Council Minutes of Meeting held on Friday, February 2nd, 1945; TNA HS 8/202 SOE Council Minutes of Meeting held on Wednesday, August 22nd, 1945; TNA HS 8/202 SOE Council Minutes of Meeting held on VE-Day, 8th May, 1945; TNA HS 1/207 No. 104 Mission to Australia and New Zealand, p. 1; TNA HS 8/209 Australia 28/11/1944; TNA HS 1/234 Letter to AD from AKL JC/29/M 08/11/1945 p.1; TNA HS 7/73 SO in Latin America – its past history, present resources and future possibilities 02/06/1942, p. 1; and TNA HS 7/199 Switzerland: Berne post, pp. 1, 4. SOE's headquarters in Cairo were established to aid operations in the Middle East. As there was no central Mess and offices were dispersed throughout the city, communication between officers and sections was impeded (TNA HS 7/169 Visit to Massingham, Cairo, Maryland, Jungle and Naples by L/IT 23rd February/31st March, 1944, p. 18). By February 1945 SOE in Cairo was 1,200 strong, of whom 740 were British (TNA HS 8/202 SOE Council Minutes of Meeting held on Friday, February 2nd, 1945).
176 TNA HS 3/11 Draft Telegrams to High Commissioner of Union of South Africa 20/12/1941; TNA HS 3/11 Memorandum SOE East African Mission 17/12/1941, p. 1; TNA HS 3/73 Proposed re-organisation of the Franck Mission

26 *Introduction*

in the British West African Colonies Memorandum 12.7.41, p. 2; and TNA HS 3/73 Directive for SOE Southern African Mission February 1943, p. 1. In 1943 A/DW requested names of persons who might be suitable for holding administrative posts in Madagascar (TNA HS 8/198 SO Council, Minutes of the 46th Meeting, held on 11.5.42, p. 2).

177 TNA HS 1/207 Cypher Telegram to Governor Straits Settlements 26/02/1941. The offices should also cover approximately 500 ft^2 (46 m^2).

178 TNA HS 1/207 History of SOE Oriental Mission, pp. 1, 2, 7. By July 1945 SOE was operating a number of bases within China, including at Kunming and Chungking. In November 1944 it was proposed that staff at the base in Kunming should be housed in tents and temporary mud huts (TNA HS 1/131 Proposals for the formation of a resistance movement in China. The composition and functions of such a resistance movement and its coordination with allied military operations 07/11/1944, p. 4). By September 1944 a Chinese Coast Section had also been established to run agents in the region of Hong Kong. As a result of Japanese advances, the base was forced to withdraw to Iahang from Kweilin (TNA HS 1/168 Role of SOE in China 21/09/1944, p. 1). SOE's Force 136's headquarters in China was located at Chungking (TNA HS 1/131 Nominal Rolls 31/07/1945, p. 3). Financial approval for the formation of this base was granted in April 1942 (TNA HS 8/198 Notes on a Meeting of the SO Council, held on 2.4.42, p. 1). In February 1945 the offices in Chungking were accommodating a delegation tasked agreeing with the Chinese the formation of an Anglo-Chinese guerrilla organisation (TNA HS 8/202 SOE Council Minutes of Meeting held on Tuesday, February 20th, 1945). Originally designated No. 1 Advance Base, Force 136, Kunming, and No. 2 Advance Base, Force 136, Chungking, in July 1945 they were eventually renamed as ME 93 (Kunming) and HQ ME 93 respectively (TNA HS 1/131 Directive to OC, ME 93 (Kunming) 10/07/1945, p. 1).

179 TNA HS 1/229 SOE – Far East Group Plans/130/1322 September 1943, p. 1. Force 136's headquarters also operated out of a number of small offices in Bombay and Madras (TNA HS 1/229 SOE – Far East Group Plans/130/1322 September 1943, p. 1). The Properties Section also based staff in Delhi, Calcutta, Jessore, Ceylon and Poona (TNA HS 1/276 Staff Requirements Props/1/162 06/03/1945, pp. 1, 2).

180 TNA HS 1/281 Report on visit to India, Middle East and North Africa SD/376 06/01/1944, p. 1. Delhi was also home to FANY Admin HQ (TNA HS 8/209 FANY Administrative Staff – India 30/08/1944).

181 TNA HS 1/229 SOE – Far East Group Plans/130/1322 September 1943, p. 1. In June 1945 plans were being developed to transfer SOE's main base to Rangoon, which would involve moving everything forward from Calcutta. At the same time, SOE was considering moving their headquarters from Kandy to Singapore once the latter had been recaptured (TNA HS 8/202 SOE Council Minutes of Meeting held on Tuesday, 19th June, 1945).

182 TNA HS 7/169 Part II Conception of Massingham and Its Formation, p. 1.

183 TNA HS 7/169 Part II Conception of Massingham and Its Formation, p. 1. Massingham's responsibilities were to work with France, Corsica, Sardinia and Italy, while SOE Cairo was to work into the Balkans (TNA HS 8/199 Record of agreement reached at meeting held 22:00 hrs 14th August, 1943, pp. 1–2).

184 TNA HS 7/169 Part II Conception of Massingham and Its Formation, p. 2. As the strategic situation developed, it was proposed that the headquarters would move or additional sub-bases would be established. The Advanced Party sent to North Africa to set up Massingham did not include anyone with prior knowledge or experience of Algiers. The group felt that if an officer who

knew the area was involved in setting up Massingham the selection of the final site would have been quicker and much simpler (TNA HS 3/64 Massingham 22/03/1943, p. 1).

185 TNA HS 7/169 Part II Conception of Massingham and Its Formation, pp. 5–6. The beach was ideal for Massingham's Training Section.

186 TNA HS 7/169 Visit to Massingham, Cairo, Maryland, Jungle and Naples by L/ IT 23rd February/31st March, 1944, p. 18.

187 TNA HS 7/169 Visit to Massingham, Cairo, Maryland, Jungle and Naples by L/ IT 23rd February/31st March, 1944, p. 18.

188 TNA HS 7/61 HQ SOM History and Problems, pp. 1, 6.

189 TNA HS 3/160 Control of Operations 24/03/1944, p. 1. Force 399, SOE's mission to Albania, also operated from Bari (TNA HS 5/34 Albanian Military Mission in Italy AFHQ/776/Q(Maint) 26/03/1945, p. 1). In March 1945, when Force 399's Bari base was closing down, it comprised of four officers and approximately 26 ORs (TNA HS 5/34 Albanian Military Mission in Italy AFHQ/776/Q(Maint) 26/03/1945, p. 1). One of the main roles of Force 399 at Bari was to collect Albanian nationals who were resident in Italy during the war and return them to Albania. To achieve this, Force 399 borrowed requisitioned premises from SO(M) and operated them as a transit camp that could accommodate approximately 60 individuals (TNA HS 5/34 Memorandum for Lt Col Alan Palmer 16/01/1945, p. 1).

190 TNA HS 7/61 HQ SOM History and Problems, p. 8.

191 TNA HS 7/169 Part V SPOC, p. 1.

192 TNA HS 7/169 Part V SPOC, p. 1. Both Massingham's and the OSS's Signal Stations, in addition to the packing stations and stores depots, were to remain where they were, but the rest of SOE and OSS efforts and materials were to be pooled at the SPOC.

193 TNA HS 7/169 Part V SPOC, pp. 1–2. The Codes Hut coded and decoded all messages between Massingham and the South of France. Staff of this hut were transported from the Club des Pins each day. The Signals Hut enabled communications between the SPOC and Massingham via a teleprinter line. It was the role of the Operations Hut, which was staffed by both British and American personnel, to mount operations in liaison with the RAF. In the Country Section Field Messages Hut, all messages to the field were written. This hut also coordinated the distribution of responses. The Country Section Hut housed the British and American local heads of the French Section.

194 TNA HS 7/169 Part V SPOC, pp. 3, 4.

195 TNA HS 7/169 Part General report on debriefing of Algiers agents at SPOC Avignon, p. 1.

196 TNA HS 7/169 Part General report on debriefing of Algiers agents at SPOC Avignon, p. 1.

197 TNA HS 7/169 Part V SPOC p. 4 and TNA HS 7/ Debriefing Centre – Avignon 11 September – 25 October 1944, p. 1.

References

Archives

The National Archives (TNA), London

CAB 301/51: Hanbury Williams report on the Special Operations Executive (SOE).

FO 1093/155: Special Operations Executive (SOE) organisation: relations between SOE and the Secret Intelligence Service (SIS).

28 *Introduction*

HS 1/131: M.E.93; Hong Kong volunteers; European personnel.

HS 1/168: Organisation and coordination.

HS 1/207: History of SOE Oriental Mission; Killery Mission.

HS 1/229: Organisation and co-ordination; SEAC stores.

HS 1/234: Visits; FELO; stores and despatch; HQ Australia ME100; recruits; liquidation.

HS 1/276: War establishments (Trincomalee Training school, American mission, South and West Africa, Chungking mission, Remorse, HQ India, Calcutta sub-mission).

HS 1/281: Military establishments: 143 (Air Liaison Section) to 145 (Radar, India).

HS 3/11: East African mission: terms of reference and general organisation.

HS 3/64: Formation of MASSINGHAM mission.

HS 3/73: West African missions; SOE in Nigeria; CHARTER of Franck mission; SOE/SIS meeting; US observers in Vichy territories.

HS 3/160: Cairo: operational directives; charter and directives from COS and Combined COS.

HS 4/31: Czech bureau: escape, para-military and political organisations.

HS 5/34: Bari HQ military mission; Force 399 personnel.

HS 7/183: Polish section history.

HS 7/199: Switzerland: Berne post.

HS 7/27: SOE Research and Development section 1938–45.

HS 7/51: Training section 1940–45; industrial sabotage training 1941–44.

HS 7/61: History of HQ SOM (Special Operations Mediterranean) by Lt Col Beevor and Lt Col Pleydell Bouverie; 15th army group liaison mission to German C-in-C, south west by Colonel H M Threlfall.

HS 7/73: Review of SO activities in Latin America.

HS 8/176: Circuits and missions: Individual missions: A Robichaud.

HS 8/198: Committees: SOE Council minutes.

HS 8/199: Committees: SOE Council minutes.

HS 8/200: Committees: SOE Council minutes.

HS 8/201: Committees: SOE Council minutes.

HS 8/202: Committees: SOE Council minutes.

HS 8/209: Committees: War Establishment Board.

HS 8/305: Propaganda: Propaganda.

HS 8/327: Liaison: Foreign Office.

HS 8/335: Organisation and administration: Staff.

HS 8/337: Organisation and administration: Property.

HS 8/901: Correspondence with Right Honourable Anthony Eden.

HS 8/965: London headquarters: symbols and organisation charts.

HS 9/1270/2: Albert ROBICHAUD – born 18.02.1916.

HS 9/1605/3: John Skinner WILSON – born 20.05.1888.

HS 9/986/2: Max MANUS – born 09.12.1914.

Secondary sources

Aldrich, Richard. 'Legacies of Secret Service: Renegade SOE and the Karen Struggle in Burma, 1948–50', *Intelligence and National Security* 14.4 (1999), pp. 130–48.

Bailey, Roderick. *The Wildest Province: SOE in the Land of the Eagle* (London, 2008).

Bayly, Christopher and Harper, Tim. *Forgotten Wars: The End of British Asian Empire* (London, 2007).

Bennett, Gill. 'The Achievements of the Polish Intelligence Service', in *Intelligence Co-operation between Poland and Great Britain during World War II*, ed. Tessa Stirling, Daria Nalecz and Tadeusz Dubicki (Edgware, 2005).

Berkeley, Roy. *A Spy's London* (London, 1994).

Binney, Marcus. *The Women Who Lived for Danger: The Women Agents of SOE in the Second World War* (London, 2002).

Binney, Marcus. *Secret War Heroes: Men of the Special Operations Executive* (London, 2006).

Boyce, Fredric and Everett, Douglas. *SOE: The Scientific Secrets* (Stroud, 2009).

Carew, Tim. *The Korean War: The Story of the Fighting Commonwealth Regiments 1950–1953* (London, 1967).

Cruickshank, Charles. *SOE in Scandinavia* (Oxford, 1986).

Deacon, Richard. *A History of the British Secret Service* (London, 1969).

Duckett, Richard. *The Special Operations Executive in Burma: Jungle Warfare and Intelligence Gathering in World War II* (London, 2017).

Foot, Michael. *SOE in France* (London, 1966).

Foot, Michael. 'Was SOE Any Good?', *Journal of Contemporary History* 16.1 (1981), pp. 167–81.

Foot, Michael. *SOE: The Special Operations Executive 1940–46* (London, 1993).

Foot, Michael. *SOE in the Low Countries* (London, 2001).

Garnett, David. *The Secret History of PWE: The Political Warfare Executive 1939–1945* (London, 2002).

Halberstam, David. *The Coldest Winter: America and the Korean War* (London, 2007).

Hart, Basil Liddell. *Defence of the West: Some Riddles of War and Peace* (London, 1950).

Helm, Sarah. *A Life in Secrets: The Story of Vera Atkins and the Lost Agents of SOE* (London, 2006).

Howe, Eric. *The Black Game: British Subversive Operations against the Germans during the Second World War* (London, 1988).

Jackson, Robert. *The Malayan Emergency and Indonesian Confrontation: The Commonwealth's Wars 1948–1966* (Barnsley, 2011).

Jeffery, Keith. *MI6: The History of the Secret Intelligence Service 1909–1949* (London, 2010).

Mackenzie, William. *The Secret History of SOE: Special Operations Executive 1940–1945* (London, 2000).

Marshall, Bruce. *The White Rabbit: The Secret Agent the Gestapo Could not Crack* (London, 2002).

Mears, Ray. *The Real Heroes of Telemark: The True Story of the Secret Mission to Stop Hitler's Atomic Bomb* (London, 2003).

Murphy, Christopher. 'SOE's Foreign Currency Transactions', *Intelligence and National Security* 20.1 (2005), pp. 191–208.

O'Connor, Bernard. *RAF Tempsford: Churchill's Most Secret Airfield* (Stroud, 2010).

Pattinson, Juliette. '"A Story That Will Thrill You and Make You Proud." The Cultural Memory of Britain's Secret War in Occupied France', in *British Cultural Memory and the Second World War*, ed. Lucy Noakes and Juliette Pattinson (London, 2014).

Postgate, Malcolm. *Operation FIREDOG: Air Support in the Malayan Emergency 1948–1960* (London, 1992).

Raymond, Henri. 'Experiences of an SOE Agent in France', in *The Fourth Dimension of Warfare: Vol. 1 Intelligence/Subversion/Resistance*, ed. Michael Elliott-Bateman (New York, 1970).

30 *Introduction*

Rigden, Denis. *Kill the Fuhrer: Section X and Operation Foxley* (Stroud, 2002).

Ruby, Marcel. *F Section SOE: The Story of the Buckmaster Network* (London, 1990).

Seaman, Mark. 'A Glass Half Full – Some Thoughts on the Evolution of the Study of the Special Operations Executive', *Intelligence and National Security* 20.1 (2005), pp. 27–43.

Smith, Eric. *Counter-Insurgency Operations 1: Malaya and Borneo* (Shepperton, 1985).

Stafford, David. *Britain and European Resistance 1940–1945: A Survey of the Special Operations Executive with Documents* (London, 1980).

Stafford, David. *Churchill and Secret Service* (London, 1997).

Stafford, David. *Mission Accomplished: SOE and Italy, 1943–1945* (London, 2011).

Stuart, Duncan. '"Of Historical Interest Only": The Origins and Vicissitudes of the SOE Archive', *Intelligence and National Security* 20.1 (2005), pp. 14–26.

Tudor, Malcolm. *SOE in Italy 1940–1945: The Real Story* (Newtown, 2011).

Walker, Jonathan. *Aden Insurgency: The Savage War in Yemen 1962–67* (London, 2011).

West, Nigel. *Secret War: The Story of SOE: Britain's Wartime Sabotage Organisation* (London, 1992).

White, Rowland. *Storm Front* (London, 2012).

Wilkinson, Peter and Astley, Joan. *Gubbins and SOE* (Barnsley, 2010).

Wylie, Nigel. 'Introduction: Special Operations Executive – New Approaches and Perspectives', *Intelligence and National Security* 20.1 (2005), pp. 1–13.

2 Training

When operating in hostile territory some form of training is conducive to an agent's survival. Appreciation of a society's culture, laws and language enables an individual to 'pass' and avoid suspicion.[1] To ensure that students received the most accurate information regarding life in occupied countries, information gathered from the debriefing of returning agents was fed into the training programme provided by SOE.[2] The probability of operational success was also influenced by an agent's knowledge of weapons, tactics and concealment.

Immediately after the creation of SOE in July 1940, it became clear that if the organisation was to achieve its purpose, it had to have access to a continuous stream of trained agents. The organisation's predecessors, however, had placed little importance on the value of training. In 1940, SOE was effectively starting with a blank canvas.[3] The task of developing this training programme befell Major Davies. Within weeks of joining SOE from Military Intelligence (Research) (MI(R)) in the autumn of 1940, Davies had completed his paper outlining the new regime. Immediately adopted by SOE, the broad training principles he developed remained relatively unchanged over the course of the war. Under Davies' scheme, UK-based students would receive instruction at Special Training Schools (STSs) organised into a four-tier system: Preliminary Schools, Paramilitary Schools, Finishing Schools and Holding Schools.[4] The STSs were designed to act as a 'set of sieves' that, theoretically, allowed only the most competent students to graduate as agents.[5]

By the time of SOE's disbandment in 1946, the schools had devised a flexible training regime, indispensable to those operating abroad.[6] Over the course of the Second World War, the organisation ran an estimated 13,500 'courses' for 6,800 students of various nationalities. At its peak, the Training Section employed 1,200–1,400 officers, non-commissioned officers (NCOs) and other ranks (ORs).[7] Training was not, however, restricted to SOE's field agents. On 5 November 1941, a memo informed the heads of all sections that '[i]t has been agreed by C.D. [the head of SOE] and the Daily Council that all newly joined officers of S.O.E., and other officers who have not yet taken a comprehensive training course, should do so in the future'.[8] This intensive

DOI: 10.4324/9781315180106-2

32 Training

seven-day course was designed to cover nearly all aspects of life as an agent operating within an enemy-occupied country.[9]

To provide training in clandestine warfare techniques, SOE employed an eclectic group of individuals,[10] specifically seeking out instructors who were not shackled by traditional military thinking.[11] Among those employed were the Sandringham estate's gamekeeper, who taught fieldcraft; John Wedgwood, of the pottery family; Bill Brooker, a European Nestlé salesman; Paul Dehn, a Sunday newspaper film critic; and Johnny Ramenski, an ex-convict released from prison by SOE.[12] Individuals with specialist skills were also engaged as instructors. Major Eric Sykes, the personification of a country rector,[13] and William Fairbairn, both former police officers in Shanghai, 'the dirtiest bloodiest most corrupt city in the world',[14] were employed to teach close combat, knife fighting and pistol shooting.[15] Agents returning from the field were also often reassigned as instructors.[16]

People from all walks of life – enlisted soldiers, housewives, refugees or academics, to name just a few – were considered for enrolment into SOE's training programme. Before an individual was called for interview, a background check was conducted. Once approved, the candidate would be invited to London to meet one of the Country Section's recruiting officers.[17] These interviews provided the recruiter with an opportunity to assess if the candidate 'were a suitable chap to undertake this kind of work'.[18]

Following selection, the new recruits were despatched to the Preliminary Schools. At these STSs, the instructors focused on basic physical fitness, map reading and elementary firearm handling.[19] Basic demolition, elementary wireless communication, fieldcraft and close combat were also included in the syllabus.[20] As a number of the organisation's recruits lacked any previous military experience, these STSs also provided an introduction to the skills necessary for life operating within hostile territory and prepared recruits for more complex training.[21] By 19 April 1941 the Paramilitary Schools commandant was already of the opinion that 'No.1 Special School [Brock Hall] deserve great credit for the manner in which the students had been prepared for their Paramilitary ... In fieldcraft and guerrilla warfare they are excellent'.[22]

The Preliminary Schools were designed 'to test out the student['s] ... "guts" ... [and to] weed out those who are in any way unsound'.[23] At STS5, Wanborough Manor, SOE agent William Abbott recalled that the training was of a 'very elementary nature ... where the selection was made ... before they knew too much'.[24] The further along the training tiers a prospective agent progressed, the greater the security risk they posed if they were eventually deemed unsuitable for clandestine work.[25] SOE's Preliminary Schools, therefore, acted as a form of student assessment.[26] Keen for students to quickly progress within the training regime, Country Sections often criticised Preliminary Schools, however; the three- to four-week delay imposed by elementary training at the STSs was deemed an inconvenience.[27]

Students who failed to make the grade were potential security risks for SOE. In an attempt to mitigate the dangers they posed, a facility was established at Inverlair known as the 'ISRB (Inter Services Research Bureau) Workshop', or 'The Cooler'. It was here that individuals removed from the training programme were 'detained' until they no longer presented a threat to the organisation's security.[28] By 1943 the number of students being failed by the instructions was overwhelming this facility[29] and it was decided that the selection process needed an overhaul.

At this time, the newly appointed director of training, Lieutenant Colonel Woolrych, shared the Country Sections' concerns that students spent too long on preliminary instruction.[30] In 1943 SOE decided to replace the Preliminary Schools with a Students Assessment Board (SAB).[31] This new scheme was based on the War Office Selection Board for Officers. The finalised plan for the new selection board was presented to Gubbins by March of that year. By the following month, the necessary arrangements had been made to replace the Preliminary Schools. Lieutenant Colonel Charley, from the Security Section, was selected to be the president of SOE's new SAB. Accommodation for the board was found at Preliminary School STS4, Winterfold, which was renamed STS7.[32] On 5 April 1943 all regional heads and Country Sections were informed that the Preliminary Schools were no longer accepting applicants.[33] The following month, the SAB welcomed its first party of prospective students.[34]

Prospective students, who were still selected by the Country Section's recruiting officer,[35] were sent to STS7 for four days of interviews and physical and psychological tests.[36] On arrival, every candidate was interviewed by either the board's president or deputy president. This allowed the SAB to form its own opinion of the prospective student. The tests that followed allowed the board to assess a wide range of characteristics, including the individual's stability, personality, intelligence, memory, courage, stamina and self-reliance. Once the recruit had completed the assessments, a final board was held. At this, all staff involved in testing were present to offer their opinion of the candidate. The Country Section also sent a representative who stated the type of work to which the prospective agent might be assigned. After all views had been heard, the president gave their ruling as to the suitability of the candidate.[37] Results of the tests were kept at STS7 so that it was possible to

modify the tests where necessary. It was also of value when an agent, as a result of his [or her] experience was in need of psychiatric treatment, which was carried out as far as possible by the psychiatrists of the SAB.[38]

The replacement of the four-week preliminary course with the four-day SAB placated the concerns of the Country Section. Some elements within SOE were now, however, worried that students spent insufficient time undergoing instruction. To address these apprehensions, the Training Section extended the syllabus at the Paramilitary Schools. Despite this, the length of time prospective agents spent at the STSs was still reduced. By introducing the SAB, SOE managed to increase the number of students the STSs could handle by releasing the Preliminary Schools for more pressing training requirements.[39]

34   Training

The introduction of the SAB saw a marked decrease in the number of agents rejected from training. Country Sections were also more satisfied with the new system. There were some in SOE who felt that the SAB caused a 'bottleneck' that held up their operations, and a number of applications were made for candidates to be excused from attending the SAB. In the autumn of 1944, SOE began to reduce dramatically the scope of their training programme and the SAB was closed on 16 November of that year. SOE, however, retained the services of one of the board's psychiatrists and a sergeant to administer remedial treatment to returning agents.[40]

Once a student had graduated from either the Preliminary Schools or the SAB they relocated to the Scottish Highlands for an intensive three- to four-week course in paramilitary instruction.[41] At these STSs prospective agents were taught fieldcraft, survival skills, map reading and living off the land.[42] By 1941 the syllabus had expanded to include weapons training, demolitions, grenade throwing, wireless telegraphy (W/T), close combat and long route marches.[43] Instructors at these schools ensured that the students were pushed both mentally and physically. Before breakfast each morning, students had to complete a series of physical exercises. The rest of the day was spent in lectures and attending practical courses. Extended exercises were also developed that were designed to train students in self-sufficiency. Instructors would drop the students off in the middle of the highlands with dummy explosives and a predefined 'target'. While planning and preparing for the attack, they were expected to survive by poaching and foraging.[44]

At every stage of the training programme exercise was an important component of the syllabus. Physical fitness was useful not only for living a clandestine life but also for preparing students for the stresses involved in parachuting. The exercises, focused on tumbling, rope work, crossing of obstacles and hill work, were designed to make the students supple and strengthen their torso and ankles. Without the correct physical conditioning, a bad landing during a parachute descent might lead to a medical discharge. The physical training culminated in assault courses established at SOE's Paramilitary Schools. These involved a series of specially designed hurdles, topographical obstacles and targets that had to be engaged with various weapons. Each course was different, but they were all designed around narratives. Students were scored on time taken, shooting accuracy and their ability to tackle the various obstacles. These courses provided the instructors with a valuable opportunity to assess the determination and stamina of the prospective agents.[45]

Physical training was also important for an agent's safety. Being able to fight off an attacker was a skill that all of SOE's students were taught. To train students in hand-to-hand combat, instructors would suspend a 'dummy' from a pulley system. Following a series of attacking moves on their 'adversary', a student would be expected to get the dummy into a head lock. This would release the dummy, causing the pair to fall to the ground. The 'fight' continued on the floor until the student had 'killed' their opponent. Once they had grasped the basics, students would have to attack their instructors, who were dressed in German uniforms.[46]

As it was unlikely that an agent would only ever be involved in one-on-one combat, instructors also taught techniques to fend off multiple attackers. In a square 10 ft × 10 ft (3.04 m × 3.04 m), six dummies were suspended from overhead supports. On entering the space, students had to attack all the targets using a variety of different techniques. To complete this successfully, students were expected to defeat their 'opponents' in under a minute, which would leave them physically drained.[47]

Besides hand-to-hand combat, SOE instructed their students in the use of personal firearms. In order to provide this training, the organisation, in 1941, acquired the services of Captain William Fairbairn, assistant commissioner of the Shanghai Municipal Police Reserve and Training Branch.[48] While in Shanghai he had devised a more natural way of shooting based on the movement of the body. Students were taught to fire to kill instinctively and without hesitation.[49] It was drilled into them that:

a You will always fire from the crouch position – you will <u>never</u> be in an upright position.
b You have <u>no time</u> to adopt any fancy stance when killing with speed.
c You have <u>no time</u> to use the sights.[50]

To assist in firearms instruction, a series of specialised targets and ranges was devised.[51] These were designed so that students could be instructed on a one-to-one basis. The first stage of training involved individuals engaging with the 'Recruit Target'. This was the size of an adult male, painted field grey and had an aiming mark located on the stomach. As this target was placed 3 yards (2.74 m) from the student, it was impossible for them to miss. This enabled the instructors to easily correct faults in their technique. As a student gained confidence and experience, the ranges became increasingly difficult. SOE employed 'Gallows Targets' designed to be placed in trees or on platforms, while 'Spray Targets' were developed for students being instructed in the use of sub-machine guns.[52]

Through the erection of screens on the ranges, the instructors could create 'alleyways' in which targets were hidden. The screens were constructed by hanging wire between posts arranged along both sides of the range. Split sandbags were then draped over the suspended cables. Obstacles such as doorframes could also be incorporated into the passageways created by the screens. To enhance the realism of the training, targets were attached to mechanisms that made them mobile. These targets were designed to appear in awkward locations, forcing the student to shift position while engaging. As only one student could use the range at a time, 'Firing Bays' were constructed nearby. These enabled those awaiting their turn on the range the opportunity to practise their shooting. The bays, which were 5 yards (4.57 m) long, were constructed from turf, railway sleepers or sandbags.[53]

36   Training

SOE's most advanced range was the 'stalk course'. This was designed not only to test the student's proficiency with weapons but also to assess their fieldcraft skills.[54] The course was constructed in such a manner that it sprang targets onto students unexpectedly, 'so that he [or she] reacts almost without thinking. He [or she] must be forced to move fast in killing a target and prevented from deliberate aiming'.[55]

Students were also taught how to clear buildings of enemy soldiers. This training was delivered in a facility known within SOE as a 'fighting house'. Originally developed as a 'mystery house' by Fairbairn during his time in Shanghai, this structure incorporated pop-up targets, firecrackers and an assortment of other hazards.[56] These facilities were designed to prepare students for the challenges and stresses of indoor fighting. Instructions produced by STS103 for the construction of a fighting house stated that, owing to a shortage of material and labour, the structure should be only single storey. Ideally, three fighting houses were grouped together to form a single complex. Fences, lamp posts, pavements and gardens would be added to increase the realism of the training scenario. Overlooking the complex was a control tower or observation point.[57] From their vantage point, instructors could observe the progress of individual students and provide feedback based on their performance.

On entering the complex a student was immediately on their guard. Targets, which could be either operated by the instructors using pulleys and weights or triggered automatically, could appear anywhere: they might 'run' between buildings, appear at windows or be waiting in ambush outside a cleared building. Sound effects were also employed to give the impression that people were moving around the interior of the structure. The fighting houses were also constructed with internal partitions, enabling the instructors to vary the training exercises. It was also possible to move the furniture and reposition targets to alter the scenario.[58]

In addition to the land-based training offered at the Paramilitary Schools, SOE provided instruction in 'paranaval' activities. Students were trained in simple navigation, elementary sailing, boat maintenance, the use of underwater containers, beach reconnaissance and visual signalling.[59] To aid the instructors, a number of small vessels were made available by SOE in lochs near the Paramilitary Schools.[60] Paranaval training, however, was a source of criticism and regarded as 'impracticable'.[61]

After successfully completing the paramilitary course, students were sent to Beaulieu, Hampshire, for six weeks of 'finishing'.[62] The Finishing Schools, also known as Group B, had their origins in the autumn of 1940. To provide this final stage of training, SOE required a number of suitably sized buildings conveniently located around a property that could become a central headquarters.[63] Surrounding Beaulieu Manor was a range of properties of various sizes that were ideal for accommodating students.[64] At these STSs, prospective agents were taught how to 'pass' everyday scrutiny when living in enemy territory.[65]

Following their arrival at the Finishing Schools, prospective agents received a lecture on the facilities' security regulations, including a strict ban on leaving the confines of the STS.[66] Despite these regulations, students regularly wandered off.[67] At the schools prospective agents were taught robbery, burglary, forgery, 'black' propaganda, blackmail, cyphers, pigeon handling and the use of invisible inks.[68] Students also received instruction in 'the German army and party organisation ... how to recognise different types of German troops ... plus a certain amount of background of German methods'.[69]

To ensure that students received practical instruction, the Finishing School tutors devised three types of course:[70] indoor, outdoor and 96-hour schemes. Indoor, or 'Y', exercises offered students the opportunity to practise topics such as concealment and body searches, which had previously been covered in lectures. Similarly, 'X' schemes allowed students to practise their training outdoors.[71] Extended outdoor exercises lasting 96 hours were also organised by the Finishing Schools. These were designed to test a student's ability to 'survive' in enemy territory. Prospective agents were dispatched to nearby towns or cities with the objective of reconnoitring a predetermined target.[72] To aid in the 'attack', the 'agent' had to make contact with a known 'sympathiser' who was

> favourable to the cause. The student [then] has to ... give him a definite job in the organisation, and train him not only for this job but also in general security precautions. In addition he [or she] has to arrange clandestine communications with the contact.[73]

While on the exercise the students were placed under police surveillance. Even if they managed to lose their tail, the agent would eventually be 'arrested' and subjected to an interrogation.[74] Second Lieutenant T Brooks recalled:

> About two o'clock in the morning we were woken up by batmen and mess waiters we recognised but dressed as German troops with tin hats on and rifles with bayonets. We were thrown out of bed, told to wrap ourselves up in our blankets and marched out barefoot across the parade ground into the garage where *Sturmführer* Follis was wearing his SS uniform. We were told to stand up and were harangued in broken Kruat, which became English, and taken through our training cover stories and I played it straight ... This was a very valuable experience.[75]

Once the student had completed finishing training, they were sent to one of SOE's Holding Schools, which were established to accommodate agents while they awaited deployment.[76] Holding Schools acted as 'pools in which trained agents could be held in conditions of comparative security and in which undue deterioration of their physical condition could be avoided'.[77] Originally, SOE intended to segregate students by nationality, but as the

38 *Training*

numbers of agents of each Country Section fluctuated over time[78] it was not feasible to allocate specific Holding Schools to the different sections.[79]

Despite this, SOE allocated Fawley Court, Buckinghamshire, as accommodation for Norwegian agents. Concerns were raised by November 1941, however, over the suitability of this property for holding agents destined for Norway. The topography and climate of the Home Counties were not providing the agents with sufficient challenges, adversely impacting their operational readiness. To ensure that they maintained their pre-deployment conditioning, the Norwegian Holding School relocated to Aviemore, Scotland.[80]

Accommodating agents in Holding Schools was routinely criticised by some within SOE. Many felt that it was difficult to effectively plan work programmes for agents held at these facilities. It was also the preference of Country Sections to accommodate their agents in London so that they could easily attend pre-operational briefings.[81] By August 1942 SOE decided that Holding Schools required closer supervision. The task of overseeing them was given to Major Spooner, commandant of STS45, who was subsequently promoted to lieutenant colonel and appointed as inspector of schools. Spooner's remit was to ensure not only a high standard of instruction within the Holding Schools but also that students' training was coordinated throughout their career.[82]

Despite Spooner's appointment, criticism of Holding Schools did not cease. In December 1942 it was brought to the attention of General Ingr that morale among the Czechoslovakian agents accommodated at STS46, Chichley Hall, was deteriorating.[83] Colonel Moravec was tasked with investigating these reports and, although he determined that morale was good, there was a lack of military discipline at the school. It was his opinion that the reports were due to 'the fact that these men had been too long at STS46'.[84] SOE's own investigation concluded that the deterioration was the result of the Czechoslovakian headquarters failing to develop an operational programme. The decline in morale was attributed to the agents' complete lack of direction.[85]

Holding Schools were also criticised for failing to develop innovative training programmes. This was attributed, however, to the Country Sections' negative attitude towards these facilities. In an attempt to improve the situation, the Training Section, in collaboration with the Country Sections, began making changes to the Holding Schools. Throughout 1942 and 1943, the elderly commandants of these schools were replaced with younger, more dynamic officers in an attempt by SOE to introduce new, unorthodox training techniques to these STS.[86]

One Holding School that generally avoided criticism was STS45, Hatherop Castle. At this facility, 'a comprehensive and graduated programme of training was put into practice, due mainly to the energy and foresight of Major Spooner and to the co-operative attitude of the Danish Country Section'.[87] STS45 developed the principle that a student's advanced training should revolve around the Holding School. From these facilities, they would attend specialised courses at other schools but return to STS45 to consolidate their knowledge and integrate it into their mission-orientated training plan.[88]

With the formation of the SAB in 1943, SOE combined the remnants of the Preliminary Schools with the Holding Schools to form 'Operational Holding Schools'.[89] Despite this reorganisation, there was still little co-operation between the schools and the Country Sections, which persisted in withdrawing their students at short notice. The uncertainty over the length of time students would spend at these facilities made the development of a training programme difficult. Training provided by the Operational Holding Schools was shaped around the anticipated role of the student and the previous instruction they had received, being tailored to address weaknesses that had been identified by the agent's instructors.[90]

The syllabus offered at Holding Schools included an 'extended' exercise. Moravec felt that these schemes, however, 'encouraged the [Czechoslovakians] students to sit about in pubs and did little to improve either their conspirative skill or their morale'.[91] By January 1943 Moravec had changed his opinion and could now see the benefits of extended exercises.[92] When the Operational Holding Schools were formed, these exercises were replaced with the 'Group C Continuation Schemes', designed to test group dynamics. To succeed in the scheme students would have to employ the full range of skills they had learnt during their training.[93]

With the end of the war in sight, SOE decided by autumn 1944 to disband their Paramilitary Schools. To ensure that they continued to offer the course run by these STSs, the Operational Holding Schools inherited their syllabuses. As the nature of the war was also changing, SOE felt it was no longer necessary to supply the resistance with support staff. What was now required were professionals who could lead and organise the activities of guerrilla forces. SOE, therefore, began increasing its recruitment of officers with experience of modern warfare. As the military situation within Europe was changing on a daily basis, the training regime had to become even more flexible. In addition, students were now being rushed through the programme, with some courses lasting only seven days. Following the liberation of France and Belgium, Operational Holding Schools ran paramilitary courses only on an *ad hoc* basis.[94]

To prepare students for the specific role they would play while deployed, SOE established numerous Specialist Schools in the UK. These STSs covered a range of topics including industrial sabotage, radio communication, organising reception committees and microphotography.[95] Before students were released for active duty, they each had to complete a specialist course.[96]

SOE's first specialist school was Station XVII, Brickendonbury.[97] Originally founded by Section D, SOE used this facility as an industrial sabotage school and renamed it STS17. The aim of this STS was to teach students the most effective way of disabling machinery.[98] On its formation there was no previous experience on which the staff could base their instruction. It was

40 *Training*

necessary, therefore, for STS17 to start from scratch and develop suitable methods of sabotage and then build a suitable training programme. Instructors also had to design the courses so that they were accessible to students with limited engineering knowledge. Despite these issues, staffing shortages and the necessity of providing multilingual instruction, the work of STS17 was deemed 'surprisingly good'.[99]

By August 1944 STS17's instructors had tailored three training packages for different abilities. The basic course, intended for students with no prior technical experience, lasted three weeks. For those prospective agents tasked with sabotaging a specific industry, the school provided specialist courses that lasted from one to seven days. Operational courses, which lasted from two to seven days, were designed for those students preparing to attack a particular target. To provide hands-on experience, instructors organised fieldtrips to engineering works, factories and other installations that the students might encounter while operating abroad. The handling and examining of real-life equipment became an invaluable teaching aid.[100]

To support those students being trained in demolition, instructors installed machinery and equipment at the STSs on which they could practise. In the grounds of many schools, for example, railway tracks were laid.[101] At STS43, Audley End, Essex, the Polish Section even had access to a disused Valentine tank. This allowed the *cichociemni* agents to practise their techniques for destroying armoured vehicles.[102] At SOE's school in Algiers, known as Massingham, a captured Heinkel He 111 and another enemy plane were made available for training purposes.[103] When it was not feasible for the instructors to provide the real artefact, models were made available. In preparation for Operation GUNNERSIDE, SOE arranged for the manager of the Vemork Heavy Water Plant to be smuggled out of Norway.[104] Based on the information he provided, a scale model of the factory's machinery was constructed at STS17.[105] This not only was an excellent training resource for the agents but also enabled the engineers to custom make the explosives for the operation.[106]

As training in explosives was conducted at STSs in the UK, facilities were required to safely store these items when not in use. At STS63, Warnham Court, five purpose-built explosives stores were constructed. The security of these buildings was, however, questionable. Between 8 and 11 May 1945, 700 No. 8 detonators were removed from one of these stores.[107] After a series of investigations, the missing items were eventually found in the possession of four local teenagers.[108]

One of the most important individuals in a resistance network was the wireless operator. It was only through these agents that operations could be organised and coordinated with SOE. As this position was also regarded as one of the most dangerous, it was essential that the right calibre of students was selected for W/T training.[109] As early as possible, instructors tried to identify prospective agents who demonstrated a 'combination of intelligence, courage and discretion, plus the necessary degree of physical fitness' to attend the wireless schools.[110] SOE quickly appreciated that '[s]ecret signallers are as

Training 41

different from ordinary W/T operators as race-horses are from cart-horses'.[111] Instruction, therefore, had to be tailored to the specific needs of clandestine wireless operators: students were to be instructed not only in the use of radios but also in how to evade German direction finders. As the time available for W/T training was limited, it was essential that the Training Section closely coordinated their activities with the Operations Section.[112]

To provide a realistic training experience, instructors organised long-distance signalling schemes. On one such exercise, held on 21 March 1944, two radio operators were despatched to Birmingham and Newcastle. At their designated 'safe houses', the pair had to communicate back to 'base', STS52, and their 'control station', STS47.[113] Until 25 April 1944, students on these exercises were unaccompanied. Following this date, Holding Schools replaced the safe houses from which the students communicated with STS52. Before they arrived, the STS commandant was informed of the exercise, allowing them time to arrange for a signal officer to supervise. One benefit of observing the students was that it ensured the safe return of the wireless equipment on completion of the scheme.[114] Students often wanted the sets they had trained on to accompany them on deployment,[115] as familiarity with their equipment reduced the likelihood of surprises when operating in enemy-occupied territory.

Once agents were ready for the field they required transportation to their area of operation. From 1942 the principal mode of transport utilised by SOE was aeroplanes. It was, therefore, essential that students were instructed in the use of parachutes. Within the UK the RAF's Parachute Training Squadron at RAF Ringway, Manchester, provided this training.[116] This unit welcomed 'with open arms the men [and women] that SOE sent them'.[117] As more and more of SOE's students were despatched to RAF Ringway, eventually the organisation required their own accommodation to house them.[118] By the end of the war, Dunham House, STS51a, Fulsham Hall, STS51b, and York House, STS51c, were all billeting SOE's students undergoing training at RAF Ringway.[119]

Quick to appreciate the unique conditions under which SOE's agents would be parachuting, instructors at Ringway adapted their training syllabus. As the students would be jumping alone, often at night, to an unknown reception committee, they experienced a heightened state of nervous tension prior to exiting the aircraft. To combat this, instructors aimed to raise the confidence and morale of SOE's students. As SOE would also send multinational groups to RAF Ringway, training had to be offered in multiple languages on a one-to-one basis.[120]

The training of agents was not, however, restricted to STSs located in the UK. Initially, it was the intention of SOE that the director of training in England would be responsible for the organisation's global network of training facilities. Owing to the failure to enforce this directive, the majority of the overseas schools operated independently of the Training Section in the UK. As they received little guidance from the UK, local

42 Training

SOE commanders took on the responsibility for setting up and developing training establishments based on their own needs. Any subsequent attempts by London to impose control were seen as interfering in their sphere of responsibility.[121]

When overseas schools were first established, SOE initially sent out instructors from the Training Section in England to provide training in the organisation's methods. Over time, as the facilities became more established, they began recruiting staff locally. It was only in cases when a particular specialist was required, or when there was a lack of suitable candidates, that the overseas STS looked further afield. The final decision as to whether the school was to employ officers sent from England lay with the local commander. Despite the Training Section's lack of control over the overseas schools, they did continue shipping copies of syllabuses to them, although these did not always reach their destination.[122]

The first school established abroad was opened in December 1940 at Haifa, Israel.[123] Known as ME102, the training facility was located in an old police barracks on Mount Carmel. Here, students received instruction in sabotage, handling explosives and foreign weapons. Eight-week courses on the use of radios were also offered. This culminated in an exercise during which students were left in the middle of the desert with a broken radio. They would be collected only once they had fixed the set.[124] Instruction in the use of parachutes was also provided nearby, at RAF Ramat David.[125] The students who attended ME102 were being prepared by SOE to work in the Balkans and the Middle East.[126]

Training in the Mediterranean also occurred on the coast of North Africa. Founded in November 1942,[127] following Operation TORCH, SOE established their largest school in Africa near Algiers. Known as 'Massingham', students sent there were prepared to operate mainly in the South of France and Italy.[128] In the early days of this facility, Major Bruce and Captain Gubbins, who had been tasked with establishing the base's Training Section, were kept very busy, as they had no sergeant instructors or armourers. In early 1943 Massingham moved to the Club des Pins, approximately 12 miles (19.3 km) to the west of Algiers. At this new location the Training Section finally had room to instruct their students. In addition to an indoor firing range, the instructors laid out a series of ranges in the sand dunes.[129] Scrap metal, railway lines and aeroplane fuselages were all sourced and used in practical demolition instruction.[130] Lectures were given in one of the complex's villas and stores for explosives and weapons were established. At Massingham a Nissen hut was also erected, which SOE converted into a 'museum' in which were various British and foreign weapons, SOE devices, booby traps, demolitions stores and enemy uniforms. Not only was the museum used during students' training, but it was also valuable when dignitaries visited the facility. During the visit of 'His Majesty the King ... [to Massingham] in the summer of 1943 he spent a long time in the museum and showed great interest in everything, particularly a specimen tin of "Itching Powder"'.[131]

In February 1943 Major Wooler started training students in the use of parachutes at Massingham. Ground training occurred within the complex and aircraft fuselages were provided to assist the instructors. The sand dunes surrounding the Club des Pins were used as the drop zone. Wooler was joined by Major Rucker from the Office of Strategic Services (OSS) two months after he started parachute training. Together, they ran a combined parachute school that eventually became a solely OSS venture.[132]

The training on offer at Massingham was expanded in June 1943 with the creation of the Naval Training Establishment. Based in a small fishing shack at Cabanon Loulou, just outside the Club des Pins, this facility offered four-day courses in landings, embarkations and the use of rubber dinghies and folboats.[133]

Massingham also trained students in W/T. One of the villas at the Club des Pins was converted to enable 16 students to receive instruction on radios using STS52's syllabus. As the majority of the students who attended these courses had prior knowledge of Morse code and electricity, the training offered was more tailored to the individual than back in the UK. As demand for wireless operators increased in early 1944, more students were sent for training. To cope with this expansion, a preliminary W/T training school was established away from the Club des Pins at Moretti Plage. Known as Camp 14, this facility could accommodate 15–20 students for two weeks' initial instruction before returning to Massingham. This not only relieved the pressure on the instructors but also acted as a filter, identifying candidates unsuitable for clandestine work.[134]

Until May 1943 finishing training was also provided at the Club des Pins. Following the arrival of Major Brooker at Massingham, a new school was established in a children's summer holiday camp at Chrea. Brooker, with the assistance of Captain Crosby of the OSS, offered finishing courses at the newly formed Camp 6. Students would attend this facility for instruction lasting between ten days and three weeks, depending on how long the Country Section could spare the individual.[135] In August 1943 the OSS took over control of Camp 6 and converted it into a combined paramilitary and finishing school. This forced SOE to once again provide finishing training at the Club des Pins. For security reasons, Massingham preferred to segregate agents undergoing the finishing courses from other students. To limit the interactions of students at different stages of their training, those receiving finishing instruction were accommodated in a separate villa from the rest. In addition, they were under the constant supervision of a security NCO and had to eat at different times from the other students.[136]

Until October 1943 agents who had completed their training but were awaiting deployment were held at the Club des Pins. As this was far from ideal, Massingham decided to establish a separate Holding School at Cabanon Loulou. Several fishing cabins were requisitioned to accommodate up to 20 agents. This facility was run by the French Section and used to brief agents prior to deployment. Revisionary training, lectures and firing practice were also provided.[137]

44 Training

Following the Allied invasion of Italy, some of the training responsibilities of Massingham were transferred to liberated areas of this country.[138] By November 1943 SOE's missions in Italy, known as 'Maryland', had established a parachute training school at San Vito dei Normanni, 8 miles (12.9 km) west of Brindisi, while paramilitary instruction was provided at a facility on the coast at Castello di Santo Stefano,[139] 2 miles (3.2 km) from Monopoli. The 'Castle' was situated on an outcrop that overlooked a small bay surrounded by small caves and inlets. At this school the instructors constructed three small arms training ranges and a battle course that combined scaling cliffs and subterranean passages.[140] Training in W/T was also offered at a facility located at La Selva, 10 miles (16.1 km) to the south of Monopoli. For agents who had completed their training, holding facilities were also established in Italy.[141]

In July 1944 the Training Section that remained at Massingham, with the exception of ground parachute instruction, relocated to a camp at Palm Beach. The new site in Algeria, located between Staouéli and Zeralda and known as Camp 25, could accommodate all training officers and instructors. Demolitions and firing practice were conducted on the beach and a W/T school was established in one of the Nissen huts. Training continued at Camp 25 until September 1944, when the school was closed down. At this time, Massingham's Training Section returned to the Club des Pins for disbandment.[142]

Massingham was not the only school established by SOE in Algeria. By November 1942 a second training facility was under construction in this country. Based at Mahouna Camp, Guelma, and known as 'Brandon', this facility acted as a training base and storage depot. Brandon was official disbanded on 30 June 1943.[143]

In Africa, SOE constructed schools in Nyasaland, Kenya, Nigeria and South Africa to provide training to local agents.[144] In West Africa, students were prepared for paramilitary operations, including attacks on vulnerable points in Vichy West Africa.[145] In September 1942 SOE had been operating a school in Olokomeji, Nigeria, for at least ten months.[146] At around the time this facility was being set up another school was being formed in the Gold Coast at Nanwa.[147] In November 1942 plans were also being drawn up to establish a new training facility in Sierra Leone.[148] Training in Africa was also provided at a school located in Umdoni Park in South Africa. At this facility students were instructed in unarmed combat, small arms and elementary demolitions. The quality of the training was, however, inadequate, as the staff had themselves only completed a course at SOE's Scottish STSs. It was the desire of the South African Mission to replace this facility with a school nearer Cape Town established on the lines of the Beaulieu Finishing STSs.[149]

Training facilities were also operated by SOE in the South East Asian Theatre of Operation. On the arrival of SOE's Oriental Mission in Singapore in 1941, the organisation set about trying to find a suitable location for a training base.[150] The local military authorities offered the Mission the island of Pula Uban for their school. As the island was covered in dense jungle and stagnant pools of water, increasing the risk of malaria, SOE deemed it unsuitable. It was clear to the Mission that the local military authorities had little interest in assisting their search, so they set about finding their own site.[151] Eventually a suitable location was found at Tanjong Bali, approximately 20 miles (32.2 km) from Singapore.[152] The facility, named STS101, was centred on a large ornamental bungalow and gave instructors access to a wide range of training environments, including the sea, mangrove swamps and a number of small jungle-covered islands off-shore. The military authorities granted permission for SOE to requisition the site and the Mission moved in on 26 June 1941.[153]

STS101's curriculum included demolitions, sabotage, unarmed combat, weapons handling, communications, navigation and fieldcraft.[154] The school's instructors considered local military installations as ideal targets when designing realistic training scenarios. Those bases attacked by STS101's students, however, regularly complained about the school's activities to General Headquarters (GHQ).[155] Because of a ban by the governor of Singapore on training people of Asian descent, STS101's students were initially all Europeans. It was not until December 1941 that the school began instructing a considerable number of Malayan Chinese to work behind Japanese lines.[156] STS101 continued training students throughout the Malayan Campaign until the Japanese reached Singapore.[157]

Following the Fall of Singapore, the majority of STS101's staff joined the Indian Mission. As SOE had no schools in the region at this time, the Mission loaned the instructors to the army.[158] The first training facility in India was established in July 1942 at Kharakvasla on the shore of Lake Fife, near Poona.[159] Originally known as the 'Guerrilla Training Unit' and later renamed the Eastern Warfare School (India) (EWS(I)), the facility was set up to provide instruction in paramilitary activities. To assist in the training, a detached camp was established at Singarh Fort, 3.5 miles (5.6 km) from the lake and at an altitude of 2,000 ft (610 m).[160]

On 7 January 1943 command of EWS(I) was transferred to Lieutenant Colonel GF Ingham Clark. In his first year at the school Clark expanded the accommodation and training facilities by constructing a number of new satellite camps.[161] By January 1944 EWS(I)'s paramilitary training was dispersed over a number of locations, including a maritime camp at Cochin and a jungle camp at Belgaum. Courses lasted ten weeks and the schools could accommodate up to 200 recruits every two months. Attached to EWS(I) was also a wireless wing offering four-month courses for 24 students. On completion of their training the agents were accommodated in the school's holding camps near Poona until required in the field.[162]

Throughout 1942 and until the spring of 1943, SOE's instructors in India predominately focused on preparing students for a post-occupational role in Assam and East India: sabotage, with and without explosives, was prevalent in the syllabus. With the halting of the Japanese advance on India's eastern border, SOE began preparing for an offensive role. This transition was gradual, as the organisation had to penetrate the Japanese Occupied Territory and

46 *Training*

establish contact with resistance forces. As the Country Sections could not provide a clear picture of future operations, training could not be effectively organised. In 1943 SOE opened two additional training facilities in India: the Eastern Warfare School (Bengal) (EWS(B)), Calcutta, and the Eastern Warfare School (Ceylon) (EWS(C)), Trincomalee. Throughout this year, the training offered by the schools suffered from a shortage of instructors. As there was also no standard route for selecting prospective agents, the facilities had no control over student intake. The Country Section's conducting officers also often interfered with the training regime by altering the programmes.[163]

In an attempt to address the issues faced by the schools, the Indian Training Section organised a conference in August 1943. This resulted in Standing Instructions being agreed that outlined the relationship between Country Sections and the schools.[164] Those attending the conference also settled on the roles of the three schools. EWS(I) and EWS(C) were both tasked with paramilitary instruction, with the former preparing agents for Burma, Siam and French-Indo China and the latter focusing on Malaya. It was decided that although EWS(B) would provide some paramilitary training it would mainly instruct students in psychological warfare.[165]

Following the conference, work also began on establishing a 'filter' based on the SAB run by SOE's UK Training Section. As the majority of SOE's potential recruits arrived in India via Bombay, EWS(I) was deemed the most suitable location for the filter. This new part of the selection process developed into a seven-day course that included a 'settling-in' period during which potential recruits could adjust to camp life, and a number of tests. The filter continued in this format until August 1944, when the number of potential students sent on the course started to decline. At this stage in the war the majority of SOE's new recruits were being handpicked from the military. In November of that year, SOE sent specialists from England to staff the Indian filter. Despite finding very little wrong with the course, they suggested changes that reduced the length of the filter, for a party of 12, from one week to an average of four days.[166] It was decided in January 1945 that all new personnel joining SOE's mission in India had to attend the filter before they could commence further training.[167]

By May 1945 the function of the EWS(I) was to ascertain the suitability of recruits for clandestine operations. After passing through the filter process the school then graded the personnel and allocated them a role in the organisation. Students then received instruction in paramilitary activities, demolitions, weapons, jungle warfare and the basics of small boat handling, navigation and beach landings. Specialist industrial sabotage training was also offered by the instructors at EWS(I).[168] The school also acted as 'a rehabilitation centre for the accommodation of personnel returning from the field and their refresher training prior to returning to operations'.[169]

Despite recruits undertaking a filter course at EWS(I), not every student was suitable for clandestine work. Those who failed to complete their training were deemed a security risk and sent to the school's 'Cooler' at 'B' Camp. This was eventually replaced with a system whereby unsuccessful students were sent to remote parts of the Madras Presidency. There they would stay with planters until they were no longer felt to be a security risk.[170]

The second of SOE's schools in India was established in May 1943. Under the command of Captain JFF Crossley, and originally known as the EWS(B), it was renamed the School of Eastern Interpreters (SEI) in January 1944.[171] The SEI cover name 'was so effective in its immediate environs that on one occasion an Indian gentleman wrote for the prospectus as he wished to send his son there!'[172] The school was based in a villa located in secluded grounds on the banks of the Hooghly River, at Alam Bazaar, 12 miles (19.3 km) from the centre of Calcutta.[173] Between September and October 1943, the EWS(B) was enlarged and the staff were joined by Major Vibert and Captain Powell-Evans from Beaulieu. This enabled the instructors to replace the *ad hoc* training with standardised courses based on the finishing syllabus developed in the UK. The enlargement of the EWS(B) meant that the school could provide basic and more in-depth programmes of training that both incorporated aspects of psychological warfare.[174] By January 1944 the school had also developed a six-week course on intelligence work that could accommodate 12 students at a time.[175] At the end of the war SEI offered training in a wide range of topics, including cover stories, subversive living, propaganda and photography.[176]

SOE's India Mission opened a third school in June 1943 at Koddiyar Bay, Trincomalee, on the east coast of Ceylon. ME25, also known as EWS(C), was founded to provide students with their final stage of training. The syllabus at this school was based on that developed by the EWS(I), although there were some adjustments to suit the different region. In addition, it was intended that the facility would despatch agents to the field by sea. EWS(C) was originally established for the Malay Country Section and students destined for south Burma and the Siam coast and islands.[177] Not only was the living accommodation at EWS(C) deemed to be good, but the facility also had the capacity to segregate students of different political leanings.[178]

There were, however, concerns expressed over the suitability of Trincomalee as a training base. The main worries were those of the naval forces using the base, who disliked SOE operating small submersible craft in the area, especially as the chief threat to this major naval facility was Japanese midget submarines. Concerns over the presence of rocks offshore were also raised internally. These were felt to be dangerous obstacles for students undergoing submersible training at the facility.[179]

In 1944 the Royal Navy decided to take over the site of EWS(C) in Trincomalee as they wanted to expand their own facilities. As the school was vital to the work of SOE they were forced to acquire the first suitable camp that became available for its re-establishment. The new site was a former Royal Artillery camp at Horana, 28 miles (45.1 km) south-east of Colombo, which could not only accommodate 750 people but was also close to the Ceylon

48 *Training*

Country Sections HQ. Due to the size of the camp, SOE used the facility both as a depot and for providing the final instruction for all paramilitary parties. The establishment of this new base coincided with a reorganisation of training in India from two parallel programmes based at EWS(I) and EWS(C) into a single stream. Under the new structure, EWS(I) would be responsible for basic paramilitary training, while EWS(C) would handle advanced operational instruction. In November 1944 the facility at Horana was further divided into two wings offering, respectively, individual and collective training.[180]

At EWS(C), a signals training section was also established. It was their responsibility to provide all advanced operational W/T instruction to paramilitary parties and 'Jedburgh' teams. The instruction was 'over and above' the standard para-military training these personnel received. EWS(C) was equipped to teach leaders and key members of a team a wide range of topics, including codes and ciphers, meteorological reports, operational message writing and coordinating air drops.[181] The school was eventually closed on 6 December 1945.[182]

Specialist instruction in signalling was also initially provided by ME9, located at Meerut, approximately 40 miles (64.4 km) north-east of Delhi.[183] By October 1943 the pressures on training faced by this school led to SOE decentralising W/T instruction. Training wings were established at each of the paramilitary schools in India that could provide students with three to four months of basic instruction. These courses were designed to prepare students for a final operational training course that was retained by ME9.[184] For those students who were to go on to work in forward propaganda units, SOE established the Indian Forward Broadcasting Unit (IFBU) Training Camp. This facility also acted as a holding and rehabilitation camp for personnel returning from the field.[185]

Holding camps were essential for accommodating students awaiting despatch to the field in the South East Asian Theatre. Strain was placed on these facilities in 1944, when large numbers of students had completed their training but few were deployed. In response, the Malay Country Section acquired a number of bungalows at Avissawella, Ceylon, in January 1944 to act as a holding facility. Students attending this camp undertook refresher training and jungle exercises organised by an instructor supplied by the Training Section.[186] Agents in the South East Asian Theatre were also held at ME90 Special Operations Holding Camp (Ceylon) at Kosgoda, officially known as Force 136 Recce Unit, at ME87 Colombo Holding Camp (VIC), and at ME96 Holding Camp Jessore at Fagu.[187]

In order to train their students in the use of parachutes, in January 1943 the Indian Mission arranged with the Indian Parachute Training School, Chaklala, to instruct their students. To oversee the training, SOE obtained a bungalow on the outskirts of Pindi and an office on the airfield to house their liaison officer. This officer also gave lectures to the students and organised night schemes on the clandestine reception of personnel and stores.

Training 49

During 1943 students were generally only sent for parachute training once they had been allocated a mission that required transportation by plane. In early 1944 these courses were incorporated into a student's standard training, as the use of parachute had become more commonplace in the South East Asian Theatre.[188]

In October 1944 an airfield in South East Asia was finally allotted to special duty operations. RAF Jessore also became home to SOE's Force 136's packing station and a parachute-training wing known as ME89. To instruct students in the art of parachuting, ground equipment was installed in a small hangar on the airfield.[189] Owing to accommodation constraints, until March 1945 only 25 students at any one time could undergo instruction at this facility.[190] When more housing was made available the airfield operated at full capacity, providing instruction to 45 new recruits every week until 1 November 1945.[191]

For the first six months instructors at RAF Jessore relied on Special Duty Squadrons to provide aircraft for practice drops. Although this meant the aircrews gained important operational experience, the school could not always rely on aircraft being available for training purposes.[192] In addition to training students in how to parachute, RAF Jessore provided instruction on reception committee procedure and the dropping and disposal of containers.[193] Shortly after the allocation of RAF Jessore to Special Duties, a Radar wing was attached to the school. Although this placed an additional strain on the number of aircraft available for training purposes, it instructed students in the use of Eurekas and S-Phones.[194]

Despite the best efforts of SOE's Training Section in the South East Asian Theatre, this unit did not escape criticism. Many agents operating in Burma felt that they were inadequately prepared for intelligence-gathering activities.[195] Some instructors were also criticised for having no practical experience in the field.[196] The Training Section was also criticised, as the environment, topography and vegetation of the areas used by their schools were unlike the jungles in which the agents operated.[197] Only courses run by the parachute school at RAF Jessore received universal praise.[198]

Training in India developed along similar lines to that in the UK. Initially providing *ad hoc* instruction in 1942, the training programme developed into a comprehensive system that could be tailored for individual agents. In India the main administrative difficulty faced by the Training Section was the vast distances between facilities and the inevitable effects these had on communications, control and the movement of people and supplies. The section was also faced with delays and slow construction when expanding and developing their schools. It was as a result of these challenges that SOE established a handful of large training units.[199]

The only school operated by SOE in North America was located in Canada. Discussions began in the summer of 1941 over the possibility of establishing this facility. By October, a site had been found near Toronto and SOE had devised the syllabus and constitution of the school. Known as both STS103

50 Training

and Camp X, the school welcomed its first students in December 1941. The school was housed in a specially constructed camp that allowed it to be expanded and adapted as required. It was the purpose of this facility to train men and women who had been recruited in Canada. In addition, the school was intended to assist US Secret Intelligence and Special Operations, which could not be done on American soil as they had yet to enter the war. Although STS103 was run by SOE's New York Mission, the director of training in England controlled the training activities and appointed the commandant and instructors. The school's syllabus focused primarily on instructing Canadian students in paramilitary activities, as the rest of their training was provided in the UK. Finishing courses and propaganda training, however, were offered to American students who attended the facility. In addition, advanced instruction was provided to those Americans who were tasked with establishing their own schools back in the USA.[200] By the end of the Second World War STS103 was just one of a global network of schools developed by SOE to instruct agents in clandestine warfare. As demonstrated here, facilities providing customisable training packages were established from North America to South East Asia.

Notes

1 'Passing' refers to the ability of an agent to act naturally within occupied territories so as not to draw attention to themselves.
2 Agents in France, for example, could have compromised their cover if they attempted to order a 'café noir'; as milk was rationed, coffee was always served black (Elizabeth Vigurs, 'The Women Agents of the Special Operations Executive F Section – Wartime Realities and Post War Representations' (unpublished PhD thesis, University of Leeds), p. 59).
3 W Mackenzie, *The Secret History of SOE: Special Operations Executive 1940–1945* (London, 2002), p. 729.
4 Mackenzie, *The Secret History of SOE*, pp. 729–30.
5 Michael Foot, *SOE: The Special Operations Executive 1940–46* (London, 1993), p. 79.
6 Mackenzie, *The Secret History of SOE*, p. 735.
7 Mackenzie, *The Secret History of SOE*, p. 734.
8 TNA HS 8/334 DA/OR/2444 05/11/41 Programme for officers of SOE, pp. 1–2.
9 TNA HS 8/334 DA/OR/2444 05/11/41 Programme for officers of SOE, pp. 1–2.
10 Cyril Cunningham, *Beaulieu: The Finishing School for Secret Agents 1941–1945* (London, 2005), p. 63.
11 Stuart Allan, *Commando Country* (Edinburgh, 2010), p. 174.
12 Roderick Bailey, *Forgotten Voices of the Secret War: An Inside History of Special Operations during the Second World War* (London, 2008), pp. 49, 58; Kim Philby, *My Silent War: The Autobiography of a Spy* (London, 2003), p. 30; and Cunningham, *Beaulieu*, pp. 63, 65, 66, 70, 72.
13 Bailey, *Forgotten Voices of the Secret War*, pp. 49, 58.
14 IWM Interview Pilkington, William 16854 00.52.
15 Bailey, *Forgotten Voices of the Secret War*, pp. 49, 58.

16 TNA HS 9/986/2 Training, p. 1.
17 Juliette Pattinson, *Behind Enemy Lines: Gender, Passing and the Special Operations Executive in the Second World War* (Manchester, 2011), pp. 26, 27.
18 IWM Interview Mackenzie, Archibald George Dunlop 11949 05.00.
19 Foot, *SOE*, p. 80 and Bailey, *Forgotten Voices of the Secret War*, p. 45.
20 TNA HS 6/961 MZ/OR/1004 Appendix F, pp. 1–2.
21 Patrick Yarnold, *Wanborough Manor: School for Secret Agents* (Guildford, 2009), p. 21.
22 TNA HS 6/961 19/04/1941 Course 23D.
23 TNA HS 6/961 MZ/OR/1004 Appendix F, p. 1.
24 IWM Interview Abbott, George William 4843 11.00.
25 Foot, *SOE*, pp. 59, 79. Students eventually rejected by SOE would have gained a knowledge of their peers, instructors, techniques and potential targets.
26 One technique employed by the STSs to assess the character of their students was to ply them with alcohol (Ruby, *F Section SOE*, p. 80). Following a lecture on the security concerns related to excessive drinking, instructors would take the students to a local bar. Security officers would then provide the recruits with free drinks to test their willpower and observe their inebriated state (Pattinson, *Behind Enemy Lines*, pp. 52–3).
27 Mackenzie, *The Secret History of SOE*, p. 730.
28 Mackenzie, *The Secret History of SOE*, p. 730.
29 TNA HS 7/51 History of the Training Section of SOE, p. 18.
30 TNA HS 7/51 History of the Training Section of SOE, p. 18.
31 Mackenzie, *The Secret History of SOE*, p. 730.
32 TNA HS 7/51 History of the Training Section of SOE, pp. 18–19.
33 TNA HS 8/792 MCD/884 08/04/1943.
34 TNA HS 7/51 History of the Training Section of SOE, pp. 18–19.
35 TNA HS 7/51 History of the Training Section of SOE, p. 18.
36 Mackenzie, *The Secret History of SOE*, p. 730.
37 TNA HS 7/51 History of the Training Section of SOE, pp. 19, 20–1.
38 TNA HS 7/51 History of the Training Section of SOE, p. 21.
39 TNA HS 7/51 History of the Training Section of SOE, p. 18.
40 TNA HS 7/51 History of the Training Section of SOE, pp. 20, 21–2.
41 Foot, *SOE*, p. 80. In 1939 the Defence Regulation empowered by the Emergency Powers (Defence) Act designated the whole of north-west Scotland, above the Great Glen, as a 'Protected Area'. Although this was established to protect the strategically sensitive coastline at Scapa Flow, it also provided security for clandestine training occurring in the locality (Allan, *Commando Country*, p. 35 and Stuart Allan, 'Individualism, Exceptionalism and Counter Culture in Second World War Special Service Training', in *Waterloo to Desert Storm: New Thinking on International Conflict, 1815–1991*, Scottish Centre for War Studies, Glasgow University, conference 24–25 June 2010 (Glasgow, 2010), pp. 2, 6). SOE's link to the Scottish Highlands originated in 1940. Following a failed operation to Sognefjord in Norway, Lieutenant Colonel Bryan Mayfield and Captain William 'Bill' Stirling, in collaboration with MI(R), established an irregular warfare school at Inverlochy Castle (Allan, 'Individualism', p. 6 and Allan, *Commando Country*, p. 37).
42 Allan, 'Individualism', p. 6; Allan, *Commando Country*, p. 37; and Pattinson, *Behind Enemy Lines*, p. 64.
43 TNA HS 6/961 MZ/OR/1004 Appendix F, p. 3 and IWM Interview Chalmers-Wright, Fergus Camille Yeatman 8188 08.40.
44 Bailey, *Forgotten Voices of the Secret War*, pp. 49–50.
45 TNA HS 7/56 I2, p. 1.

52　*Training*

46　TNA HS 7/56 I4, pp. 1, 6.
47　TNA HS 7/56 I4, p. 5.
48　Charles Melson, 'Introduction', in *The World's First SWAT Team: WE Fairbairn and the Shanghai Municipal Police Reserve Unit*, ed. Leroy Thompson (London, 2012), p. 4.
49　Denis Rigden, *Kill the Fuhrer: Section X and Operation Foxley* (Stroud, 2002), p. 379.
50　TNA HS 7/56 I5, p. 4.
51　TNA HS 7/56 I5, pp. 6, 11–2, 14–15, 28. Firearm practice was not always conducted on specialised ranges. At STS52, Thame Park, sand-filled boxes were placed in the miniature firing range located within the recreation room. These were designed to limit the damage to the walls (TNA HS 6/961 STS/TR/41 16/08/41).
52　TNA HS 7/56 I5, pp. 6, 11–12, 14–15, 28.
53　TNA HS 7/56 I5, pp. 11–12, 15, 28.
54　TNA HS 7/56 I5, p. 13.
55　TNA HS 7/56 I5, p. 13.
56　Allan, *Commando Country*, p. 53.
57　TNA HS 7/56 I5, p. 34.
58　TNA HS 7/56 I5, pp. 34, 36.
59　TNA HS 8/792 HHH/683 05/04/1942.
60　TNA HS 8/792 MZ/2019 24/04/1941.
61　TNA HS 8/792 From D/NAVY to M 16/06/1942.
62　Pattinson, *Behind Enemy Lines*, p. 69.
63　This arrangement allowed SOE to segregate the students by nationality while pooling instructions (Cunningham, *Beaulieu*, p. 18).
64　TNA HS 8/960 SOE Special Schools at Beaulieu, Hampshire October 1942, p. 1.
65　Nigel West, *Secret War: The Story of SOE: Britain's Wartime Sabotage Organisation* (London, 1992), p. 85.
66　TNA HS 7/52 Security Talk.
67　It was the responsibility of SOE's security officers to monitor conversations in local pubs and to return to the school any students they found outside the STSs (Cunningham, *Beaulieu*, p. 5).
68　Cunningham, *Beaulieu*, pp. 43, 63, 109 and TNA HS 7/52 Introduction to Course A.1, pp. 1–2.
69　IWM Interview Threlfall, Henry McLeod 8238 25.15.
70　TNA HS 7/52 Introduction to Course A.1, p. 1.
71　TNA HS 7/52 Exercises, p. 1.
72　TNA HS 7/52 Exercises, pp. 1–2.
73　TNA HS 7/52 Exercises, p. 2.
74　TNA HS 7/52 Exercises, p. 2.
75　Bailey, *Forgotten Voices of the Secret War*, p. 60.
76　Mackenzie, *The Secret History of SOE*, p. 731.
77　TNA HS 7/51 History of the Training Section of SOE Chapter X, p. 50.
78　Mackenzie, *The Secret History of SOE*, p. 731.
79　TNA HS 7/51 History of the Training Section of SOE Chapter X, p. 49.
80　TNA HS 7/174 Norwegian Section History 1940–45, p. 26.
81　Mackenzie, *The Secret History of SOE*, p. 729.
82　TNA HS 7/51 History of the Training Section of SOE Chapter X, p. 50.
83　TNA HS 4/1 MX/CZ/1393, p. 3.
84　TNA HS 4/1 MX/CZ/1393, p. 4.
85　TNA HS 4/1 MX/CZ/1393, p. 4.

Training   53

86 TNA HS 7/51 History of the Training Section of SOE Chapter X, pp. 50–1.
87 TNA HS 7/51 History of the Training Section of SOE Chapter X, p. 50.
88 TNA HS 7/51 History of the Training Section of SOE Chapter X, pp. 50–1.
89 TNA HS 7/51 History of the Training Section of SOE Chapter X, p. 51. These schools were also known as Group C.
90 TNA HS 7/51 History of the Training Section of SOE Chapter X, pp. 51, 52.
91 TNA HS 4/1 MX/CZ/1393, p. 4.
92 TNA HS 4/1 MX/CZ/1446, p. 1.
93 TNA HS 7/51 History of the Training Section of SOE Chapter X, p. 52.
94 TNA HS 7/51 History of the Training Section of SOE Chapter X, pp. 52–3.
95 Mackenzie, *The Secret History of SOE*, pp. 732–3.
96 TNA HS 8/792 MCD/884 08/04/1943.
97 TNA HS 7/51 History of the Training Section of SOE Chapter I, p. 2.
98 Gordon Rottman, *World War II Allied Sabotage Devices and Booby Traps* (Oxford, 2010), p. 30.
99 TNA HS 8/370 Report on the Development of Industrial Sabotage Training at STS17, pp. 1, 3, 6, 11–12.
100 TNA HS 8/370 Report on the Development of Industrial Sabotage Training at STS17, pp. 3, 6, 11–12.
101 Cunningham, *Beaulieu*, p. 43.
102 Ian Valentine, *Station 43: Audley End House and SOE's Polish Section* (Stroud, 2006), p. 76.
103 IWM Oral History Hargreaves, Harry 12158 28.00.
104 Fredric Boyce and Douglas Everett, *SOE: The Scientific Secrets* (Stroud, 2009), p. 252.
105 Charles Cruickshank, *SOE in Scandinavia* (Oxford, 1986), p. 200.
106 Boyce and Everett, *SOE*, p. 252.
107 TNA HS 4/228 Report on the 'Breaking Into' of an Explosive store, and the loss of 700 No. 8 detonators at STS63. No. 8 detonators were commercial non-electric blasting caps.
108 TNA HS 4/228 In continuation of my report submitted on 17 May 1945.
109 TNA HS 8/357 Wireless Communications, p. 1.
110 TNA HS 8/357 Wireless Communications, p. 1.
111 TNA HS 8/357 Wireless Communications, p. 1.
112 TNA HS 8/357 Wireless Communications, p. 1.
113 TNA HS 7/35 Exercise BLUFF Signal Instruction No. II, p. 1.
114 TNA HS 8/360 D.SIGS/1536.
115 TNA HS 8/357 DCDO/1220 17/08/1942.
116 TNA HS 6/961 MZ/SP/1047 28/02/1941. RAF Ringway was also used by SOE for its other airborne requirements. Training was provided at this airfield to air-crews in the dispatch of containers (TNA HS 4/173 ADDP/609 26/04/1942). Trials in container dropping were also conducted at RAF Ringway. On 26 October 1941, for example, a trial had to be postponed owing to a technical fault with the Halifax (TNA HS 4/173 Notes on Visit to Ringway – 26th October 1941).
117 TNA HS 7/174 SOE History of the Norwegian Section 1940–44, p. 17.
118 TNA HS 8/435 History of the Training Section Chapter VI, p. 30. SOE gener-ally tried to acquire properties large enough to accommodate the students sent to the facility for training. This was not always possible, however. At STS42, Thame Park, Oxfordshire, there were, for example, issues over accommodation during 1941. In August of that year Major THH Grayson expressed concerns with regard to the SCONCES winter accommodation. It was deemed no longer feasible to provide their students with tents erected in the estate. As the provi-sion of bunk beds or the conversion of the recreation room into barracks was felt

54 *Training*

to be impractical, plans were devised to construct a hut near the ablution bench (TNA HS 6/961 STS/TR/41 16/08/41).

119 TNA HS 8/435 History of the Training Section Chapter VI, p. 30.
120 TNA HS 8/435 History of the Training Section Chapter VI, p. 30.
121 TNA HS 7/51 History of the Training Section of SOE Chapter XV Overseas Training Schools, p. 74.
122 TNA HS 7/51 History of the Training Section of SOE Chapter XV Overseas Training Schools, p. 74. Staff would still be sent to training schools abroad when a specialist instructor was required but could not be sourced locally. In 1945 the director of training, Colonel Spooner, did try to exert more control over the schools abroad. Although this was not effectively implemented, it did lead to an increase in liaison.
123 TNA HS 7/51 History of the Training Section of SOE Chapter XV Overseas Training Schools, p. 76.
124 IWM Oral Purvis, Robert William Berry 12195 REEL 1 04.00; IWM Oral Irwin, Basil William Seymour 9772 REEL 1 14.00; IWM Oral Mason, Raymond Thomas 12037 REEL 2 28.00; and IWM Oral Kerevan, Benjamin 9723 REEL 1 25.00.
125 IWM Oral Mason, Raymond Thomas 12037 REEL 3 00.30.
126 TNA HS 7/51 History of the Training Section of SOE Chapter XV Overseas Training Schools, p. 76.
127 Martin Thomas, 'The Massingham Mission: SOE in French North Africa, 1941–1944', *Intelligence and National Security* 11.4 (1996), p. 696; and Thomas Wales, 'The "Massingham" Mission and the Secret "Special Relationship": Co-operation and Rivalry between the Anglo-American Clandestine Services in French North Africa, November 1942–May 1943', *Intelligence and National Security* 20.1 (2005), p. 44.
128 TNA HS 7/51 History of the Training Section of SOE Chapter XV Overseas Training Schools, p. 76.
129 TNA HS 7/169 Part VI Recruiting and training in Algiers, p. 1 and IWM Oral History Hargreaves, Harry 12158 REEL 1 28.00.
130 TNA HS 7/169 Part VI Recruiting and training in Algiers, p. 1. When the Signals Station expanded the demolition practice had to be moved along the beach, as it was interfering with their equipment. Paramilitary courses were also run at Massingham. During their training students would have to live off the land while planning an 'attack' on a local military installation (TNA HS 7/169 Part VI Recruiting and training in Algiers, p. 1).
131 TNA HS 7/169 Part VI Recruiting and training in Algiers, p. 1.
132 TNA HS 7/169 Part VI Recruiting and training in Algiers, p. 3.
133 TNA HS 7/169 Part VI Recruiting and training in Algiers, p. 5; and IWM Oral Croft, Noel Andrew Cotton 14820 REEL 3 02.40. The Naval Training Base was closed in the middle of October 1943 (TNA HS 7/169 Para-naval work in the Western Mediterranean, p. 4).
134 TNA HS 7/169 Part VI Recruiting and training in Algiers, p. 6.
135 TNA HS 7/169 Part VI Recruiting and training in Algiers, p. 4. Tension generally existed between the Country and Training Sections as the former was anxious to limit the time agents spent in finishing training.
136 TNA HS 7/169 Part VI Recruiting and training in Algiers, p. 4.
137 TNA HS 7/169 Part VI Recruiting and training in Algiers, p. 5.
138 TNA HS 7/51 History of the Training Section of SOE Chapter XV Overseas Training Schools, p. 76.
139 David Stafford, *Mission Accomplished: SOE and Italy, 1943–1945* (London, 2011), p. 58.

Training 55

140 TNA HS 7/169 Visit to Massingham, Cairo, Maryland, Jungle and Naples by L/ IT 23rd February/31st March, 1944, p. 14. Special Operations (Mediterranean) also ran nine holding houses within Italy (TNA HS 3/163 HQ SOM Directive No. 13 Training and Holding Houses under FREEBORN Conditions SD/62 30/04/1945, p. 2).

141 Stafford, *Mission Accomplished*, p. 58.

142 TNA HS 7/169 Part VI Recruiting and training in Algiers, p. 6.

143 TNA HS 7/67 The "Brandon" Mission in the Tunisian Campaign, pp. 5, 14.

144 TNA HS 8/198 Notes on a Meeting of the SO Council, held on 36.3.42, p. 2; TNA HS 3/11 General; mission to Portuguese East Africa; account of operations in Africa An Account of SOE Operations in Africa, p. 1; TNA HS 3/11 East African mission: terms of reference and general organisation Memorandum SOE East African Mission 17/12/1941, p. 1; and TNA HS 3/73 General 29/08/1941 and TNA HS 3/83 Report on visit to South Africa 04/02/1943, p. 18.

145 TNA HS 8/198 Notes on a Meeting of the SO Council, held on 26.3.42, p. 2; and TNA HS 3/73 West Africa. Students were also prepared to operate as mounted levies on the frontiers (TNA HS 3/73 West Africa).

146 TNA HS 3/74 SOE Missions in West and East Africa 26/09/1942, p. 2.

147 TNA HS 3/73 Proposed re-organisation of the Franck Mission in the British West African Colonies Memorandum 12.7.41, p. 1; and TNA HS 3/74 Report on Frawest Mission 11/11/1942, p. 14.

148 TNA HS 3/74 Report on Neucols Mission 16/11/1942, p. 19; and TNA HS 3/74 Report on Frawest Mission 11/11/1942, p. 14.

149 TNA HS 3/83 Report on visit to South Africa 04/02/1943, p. 18.

150 TNA HS 1/207 History of SOE Oriental Mission, p. 2.

151 Richard Gough, *SOE Singapore 1941–42* (London, 1985), p. 28.

152 TNA HS 1/207 History of SOE Oriental Mission, p. 6.

153 Gough, *SOE Singapore 1941–42*, pp. 28–9.

154 Charles Cruickshank, *SOE in the Far East* (Oxford, 1983), p. 16.

155 Gough, *SOE Singapore 1941–42*, p. 32.

156 TNA HS 1/207 History of SOE Oriental Mission, pp. 6–7.

157 Gough, *SOE Singapore 1941–42*, p. 137.

158 Cruickshank, *SOE in the Far East*, p. 16.

159 Richard Duckett, *The Special Operations Executive in Burma: Jungle Warfare and Intelligence Gathering in World War II* (London, 2017), p. 79.

160 TNA HS 7/115 Force 136 Training Historical, p. 1.

161 TNA HS 7/115 Force 136 Training Historical, pp. 1, 2.

162 TNA HS 1/281 Report on visit to India, Middle East and North Africa SD/376 06/01/1944, pp. 2–3.

163 TNA HS 7/115 Force 136 Training Historical, pp. 1, 2–3.

164 TNA HS 7/115 Force 136 Training Historical, p. 3. The conference also agreed on the centralisation of the control of training and the necessary documentation required on each student.

165 TNA HS 7/115 Force 136 Training Historical, p. 3.

166 TNA HS 7/115 Force 136 Training Historical, pp. 3–4.

167 TNA HS 1/280 Filter 02/01/1945, pp. 1, 2, 3.

168 TNA HS 1/281 Force 136 Establishments Summary of Functions 06/05/1945, p. 4.

169 TNA HS 1/281 Force 136 Establishments Summary of Functions 06/05/1945, p. 4.

170 TNA HS 7/115 Force 136 Training, p. 8.

171 TNA HS 1/281 Report on visit to India, Middle East and North Africa SD/376 06/01/1944, p. 1.

172 TNA HS 7/115 Force 136 Training Historical, p. 8.

56   *Training*

173 TNA HS 7/115 Force 136 Training Historical, p. 2 and Cruickshank, *SOE in the Far East*, pp. 16–17.
174 TNA HS 7/115 Force 136 Training Historical, p. 3.
175 TNA HS 1/281 Report on visit to India, Middle East and North Africa SD/376 06/01/1944, p. 2.
176 TNA HS 1/281 Force 136 Establishments Summary of Functions 06/05/1945, p. 4.
177 TNA HS 7/115 Force 136 Training Historical, pp. 2, 4. EWS(C) was advantageously located in an area with a climate similar to that of the areas in which its students would be deployed (TNA HS 7/115 Force 136 Training Historical, p. 2).
178 TNA HS 7/115 Force 136 Training Historical, p. 2; and TNA HS 1/234 Report on visit to India and Australia, p. 4.
179 TNA HS 1/234 Report on visit to India and Australia, p. 4.
180 TNA HS 7/115 Force 136 Training Historical, pp. 7–8. EWS(C) was also responsible for a number of holding camps, including ME87 Colombo Holding Camp, ME90 Special Operations Holding Camp (Ceylon) and ME96 Holding Camp Jessore (TNA HS 1/281 Force 136 Establishments Summary of Functions 06/05/1945, p. 3). Throughout 1944 schools in India were reinforced by instructors from SOE's UK STSs. This resulted in a high esprit de corps and technical efficiency. To adapt to Far Eastern conditions, every officer had to complete the course and undergo Basic Jungle Training before they could teach (TNA HS 7/115 Force 136 Training Historical, p. 4).
181 TNA HS 1/281 Force 136 Establishments Summary of Functions 06/05/1945, p. 1.
182 TNA HS 1/276 Telegram 4158 06/12/1945. After the fall of Rangoon and before the Japanese surrender plans were developed to create a school in Burma modelled on EWS(C). The war ended before this facility could be established (TNA HS 7/115 Force 136 Training Historical, pp. 13).
183 Cruickshank, *SOE in the Far East*, p. 17.
184 TNA HS 7/115 Force 136 Training, p. 7.
185 TNA HS 1/281 Force 136 Establishments Summary of Functions 06/05/1945, p. 3.
186 TNA HS 7/115 Force 136 Training Historical, pp. 6–7.
187 TNA HS 1/276 SOE India Organisational Chart, TNA HS 1/278 Cipher telegram from Delhi No. 920 29/07/1944 and TNA HS 7/115 Organisation of Training – November 1944/1945. Force 136 was SOE's general cover name for operations in the South East Asian Theatre of Operation from early 1945.
188 TNA HS 7/115 Force 136 Training Historical, pp. 1–2, 4.
189 TNA HS 7/115 Force 136 Training Historical, p. 10.
190 TNA HS 7/115 Force 136 Training Historical, pp. 10–11. Parachute training continued at Chaklala until the capacity of Jessore increased.
191 TNA HS 7/115 Force 136 Training Historical, pp. 10–11.
192 TNA HS 7/115 Force 136 Training Historical, p. 11.
193 TNA HS 1/281 Force 136 Establishments Summary of Functions 06/05/1945, p. 3.
194 TNA HS 7/115 Force 136 Training Historical, pp. 10–11. At Jessore a loftsman was also employed to provide students instruction in the handling of messenger birds (TNA HS 1/275 War Establishments – Military Establishment No. 9 SE/8 18/09/1944, p. 4).
195 Cruickshank, *SOE in the Far East*, pp. 19–20. Intelligence-gathering was the initial focus of many agents operating in Burma.
196 Cruickshank, *SOE in the Far East*, pp. 19–20.
197 TNA HS 7/105 Report on Operation "Heavy" by Major CB Jones GSO(11) Burma Country Section, p. 2.
198 Cruickshank, *SOE in the Far East*, pp. 19–20.
199 TNA HS 7/115 Force 136 Training, p. 1.
200 TNA HS 7/51 History of the Training Section of SOE Chapter XV Overseas Training Schools, p. 75.

Training 57

References

Archives

The National Archives (TNA), London

HS 1/207: History of SOE Oriental Mission; Killery Mission.

HS 1/234: Visits; FELO; stores and despatch; HQ Australia ME100; recruits; liquidation.

HS 1/275: War establishment: No 9 Signals.

HS 1/276: War establishments (Trincomalee Training school, American mission, South and West Africa, Chungking mission, Remorse, HQ India, Calcutta sub-mission).

HS 1/278: Military establishments: 83 (Kunming Advance Base) to 91 (Field Propaganda Units).

HS 1/280: Military establishments: 95 (Marine Research Training Centre) to 100 (HQ Australia), 121, 122 and 141.

HS 1/281: Military establishments: 143 (Air Liaison Section) to 145 (Radar, India).

HS 3/11: East African mission: terms of reference and general organisation.

HS 3/73: West African missions; SOE in Nigeria; CHARTER of Franck mission; SOE/SIS meeting; US observers in Vichy territories.

HS 3/74: West African missions; SIS and SOE; Prof Cassin's report; Franck mission (NEUCOLS and FRAWEST); US cooperation.

HS 3/83: South Africa Mission: reorganisation of SOE; draft directive for mission; prohibited areas adjoining Portuguese East Africa.

HS 3/163: Mediterranean Group: Moli di Bari HQ; operational directives to country sections and stations.

HS 4/1: British-Czechoslovak negotiations on SOE; OSS and Soviet activities.

HS 4/228: Lists of personnel at STS 63; security; postings; administration.

HS 6/961: Training for SCONCE (Spanish Republican refugees in UK): to be re-infiltrated into Spain in event of German invasion.

HS 7/34: Section I signals.

HS 7/51: Training Section 1940–45; industrial sabotage training 1941–44.

HS 7/52: SOE group B training syllabus.

HS 7/56: Lecture folder STS 103: Part 2 minor tactics and fieldcraft, demolitions and physical training syllabus.

HS 7/67: BRANDON west African mission.

HS 7/105: Burma country section: reports on individual operations by staff and operational officers.

HS 7/115: Force 136: SOE training in India 1942–45.

HS 7/169: MASSINGHAM: Special Projects Operational centre (SPOC); operation in Corsica; BALACLAVA naval section; para-naval work.

HS 7/174: Norwegian section 1940–45.

HS 8/198: Committees: SOE Council minutes.

HS 8/357: Equipment supplies and requirements.

HS 8/360: Communications: Organisation of Communication.

HS 8/370: Recruitment and training: Industrial sabotage training (STS 17).

HS 8/435: Histories: SOE training section 1940–45.

HS 8/792: Naval establishment training ship 'orca'.

HS 8/960: War Office: Special training schools.

HS 9/986/2: Max MANUS – born 09.12.1914.

58   *Training*

Imperial War Museum (IWM), London

Abbott, George William (Sound Archive interview number 4843).

Chalmers-Wright, Fergus Camille Yeatman (Sound Archive interview number 8188).

Croft, Noel Andrew Cotton (Sound Archive interview number 14820).

Hargreaves, Harry (Sound Archive interview number 12158).

Irwin, Basil William Seymour (Sound Archive interview number 9772).

Kerevan, Benjamin (Sound Archive interview number 9723).

Mackenzie, Archibald George Dunlop (Sound Archive interview number 11949).

Mason, Raymond Thomas (Sound Archive interview number 12037).

Pilkington, William (Sound Archive interview number 16854).

Purvis, Robert William Berry (Sound Archive interview number 12195).

Threlfall, Henry McLeod (Sound Archive interview number 8238).

Secondary sources

Allan, Stuart. *Commando Country* (Edinburgh, 2010).

Allan, Stuart. 'Individualism, Exceptionalism and Counter Culture in Second World War Special Service Training', in *Waterloo to Desert Storm: New Thinking on International Conflict, 1815–1991*, Scottish Centre for War Studies, Glasgow University, conference 24–25 June 2010 (Glasgow, 2010).

Bailey, Roderick. *Forgotten Voices of the Secret War: An Inside History of Special Operations during the Second World War* (London, 2008).

Boyce, Fredric and Everett, Douglas. *SOE: The Scientific Secrets* (Stroud, 2009).

Cruickshank, Charles. *SOE in the Far East* (Oxford, 1983).

Cruickshank, Charles. *SOE in Scandinavia* (Oxford, 1986).

Cunningham, Cyril. *Beaulieu: The Finishing School for Secret Agents 1941–1945* (London, 2005).

Duckett, Richard. *The Special Operations Executive in Burma: Jungle Warfare and Intelligence Gathering in World War II* (London, 2017).

Foot, Michael. *SOE: The Special Operations Executive 1940–46* (London, 1993).

Gough, Richard. *SOE Singapore 1941–42* (London, 1985).

Mackenzie, W. *The Secret History of SOE: Special Operations Executive 1940–1945* (London, 2002).

Melson, Charles. 'Introduction', in *The World's First SWAT Team: WE Fairbairn and the Shanghai Municipal Police Reserve Unit*, ed. Leroy Thompson (London, 2012).

Pattinson, Juliette. *Behind Enemy Lines: Gender, Passing and the Special Operations Executive in the Second World War* (Manchester, 2011).

Philby, Kim. *My Silent War: The Autobiography of a Spy* (London, 2003).

Rigden, Denis. *Kill the Fuhrer: Section X and Operation Foxley* (Stroud, 2002).

Rottman, Gordon. *World War II Allied Sabotage Devices and Booby Traps* (Oxford, 2010).

Stafford, David. *Mission Accomplished: SOE and Italy, 1943–1945* (London, 2011).

Thomas, Martin. 'The Massingham Mission: SOE in French North Africa, 1941–1944', *Intelligence and National Security* 11.4 (1996), pp. 696–721.

Valentine, Ian. *Station 43: Audley End House and SOE's Polish Section* (Stroud, 2006).

Vigurs, Elizabeth. 'The Women Agents of the Special Operations Executive F Section – Wartime Realities and Post War Representations' (unpublished PhD thesis, University of Leeds).

Wales, Thomas. 'The "Massingham" Mission and the Secret "Special Relationship": Cooperation and Rivalry between the Anglo-American Clandestine Services in French North Africa, November 1942–May 1943', *Intelligence and National Security* 20.1 (2005), pp. 44–71.

West, Nigel. *Secret War: The Story of SOE: Britain's Wartime Sabotage Organisation* (London, 1992).

Yarnold, Patrick. *Wanborough Manor: School for Secret Agents* (Guildford, 2009).

3 Research and development

Besides preparing agents for missions, SOE issued them with equipment specifically designed for their role. Over a period of several years, the organisation's Research and Development Section developed, improved and manufactured a wide range of equipment designed for clandestine warfare.[1] This section also devised disguises that allowed weapons and stores to be smuggled into the field and moved around enemy territory. Many of the devices developed by SOE remained classified for many years following the end of the Second World War.[2]

The work of the Research and Development Section was built on earlier efforts and inventions created by the War Office and other branches of the British secret services, among them Section D.[3] Research conducted by this section was often subcontracted out, especially to Mr Bailey, who was based at University College London. Contracts were also placed with the Royal Arsenal, Woolwich; the British Scientific Instrumental Research Association; the Royal Society; Imperial Chemical Industries; and Shell Oil.[4] The practice of commissioning external research was continued by SOE. University scholars, members of the armed forces and the private sector were all employed by the organisation to aid in the research and development of new equipment. By December 1941 SOE had appointed Professor Norrish from the University of Cambridge to undertake research into incendiaries. Although there were concerns that Norrish's research might prove a failure, the preliminary results were encouraging.[5] Dr Reich of Imperial College was also commissioned by SOE to undertake research on their behalf. His work focused on the development of a new volatile compound that potentially had twice the power of any contemporary explosive.[6]

Until 1941, SOE's Research and Development Section was a relatively small part of the organisation, but as increasing demands were placed on the unit during the following year the section had to expand rapidly. By the end of 1942 the resulting reorganisation was complete and the section had taken its final form.[7] To accommodate this expansion, SOE acquired new facilities to assist the research they conducted at sites that had been inherited from the organisation's predecessors.

DOI: 10.4324/9781315180106-3

Research and development 61

The main facility used by SOE's Research and Development Section was The Frythe, Hertfordshire. Requisitioned on 26 August 1939, Section D acquired The Frythe Residential Private Hotel to house the organisation's Radio Communication Division.[8] Section D also used the property to store their records, safe from the dangers of London, and to house the staff required to look after these files, as well as the organisation's Drawing Office and Planning Department. In the event of enemy activity forcing Section D's staff from London, the former hotel was also intended as the organisation's evacuation centre.[9]

Following the transfer of The Frythe to SOE the facility became known as Station IX. Initially, SOE continued running the research and development establishment along the same lines as had Section D. This included maintaining the plans to use the site as an evacuation centre in the event their staff had to leave London.[10] Arrangements were also put in place to use the facility as accommodation for some of SOE's staff who worked in the capital. Each morning at 07:45 a shuttle bus would leave Station IX for the organisation's offices in London, making the return journey at 17:15 sharp. At this time, SOE maintained strict working hours and required staff to have left their office by 17:00 each day.[11] It was also expected that 'once a week [every officer and secretary should] ... take a Luncheon from 13.00 to 14.30 hours to enable them to see friends, [and] do shopping'.[12]

In early 1941 SOE began exploring various schemes for the reorganisation of the Research and Development Section. One proposal involved relocating all of SOE's research staff to The Frythe.[13] At this time, the organisation housed a small Technical Department nearby at Aston House, which was known within SOE as Station XII. Under the plans drawn up for the reorganisation of the Research and Development Section, Aston House's technical department would move to Station IX.[14] Station XII would then focus its efforts on production, routine inspection, packing and the despatch of stores. On 9 June 1941, following the appointment of Professor Dudley Newitt MC, formerly of Imperial College London, as director of scientific research, this reorganisation was put into effect.[15] As a result of this, The Frythe's laboratories and workshops were formed into six new sections: Operations (including large-scale trials); Explosives (including fuzes, switches and delays); Incendiaries, Flares, Smokes; Technical Sabotage; Bacteriology and Toxicology; and Camouflage (including home-made devices).[16]

Over the course of the Second World War SOE's scientists and engineers developed a wide range of equipment for clandestine warfare. These included explosives, incendiaries, small arms, motorcycles, electricity generators, wireless sets, itching powder and stimulants.[17] On first arriving at Station IX, John Brown, who was attached to SOE from the Royal Corps of Signals, was confronted with a device sitting outside mess hall that appeared to be a huge searchlight. Following further enquiries, he was informed that it was an

> experimental loudspeaker sonic device to focus high power sound energy on the enemy across no man's land to drive him mad with supersonic

62 Research and development

sound. And I remembered wondering what kind of mad house I had got into because everything I came across seemed to me to be to be way out ideas, science fiction.[18]

To accommodate the expansion of Station IX as a result of the reorganisation, SOE erected 'temporary' structures in the grounds of The Frythe.[19] These prefabricated, single-storey felt-roofed wooden huts typically measured 35 ft × 15 ft (10.67 m × 4.57 m). Partitions were used to create smaller workspaces, with each building typically organised into two laboratories, a specialist room and two small offices. To ensure that these huts were heated, a steam boiler plant was constructed in the grounds of Station IX.[20]

While reorganising their Research and Development Section, SOE determined that Station IX's Wireless Section was in urgent need of expansion. On 26 June 1941 the director of research, development and supply (AD/Z) requested an increase in the number of mechanics at Station IX. These personnel were to be employed in running trials on SOE's new 'micro-wave telephonic duplex communication ground-to-air set' and the 'D-Phone'. As the Secret Intelligence Service (SIS) had recently been granted an additional 18 engineers, AD/Z felt his demand for three electrical mechanics trained in the handling of precision bench machinery was not unreasonable.[21] At the time of the reorganisation, SOE was concerned that the Axis powers might infringe international law by using chemical and biological weapons. Provisions were, therefore, made available in case the Research and Development Section had to start working in this field.[22]

To support the work of the sections based at Station IX, SOE provided their staff with access to a photographic department and machine, and carpenters' and sheet metal shops.[23] In late 1941 the responsibility for servicing Station IX's laboratories was allocated to a newly formed Engineering Section. This unit was also tasked with the manufacturing of small mechanisms and devices as and when required by the facility's designers. The Engineering Section was given the authority, during periods when their workload was light, to independently develop clandestine equipment.[24] The quality, precision and speed of Station IX's engineers' work often received praise from other members of the facility. While based at The Frythe, one of John Brown's tasks was to fit a radio set into a briefcase. To aid him in his work, Brown made full use of the staff of the Engineering Section, who had set up their workshop in the conservatory of the main house. Brown provided the handpicked instrument makers and precision mechanics a freehand sketch of his design, and they had completed the finished, 'beautifully made', article by the time it took him to have lunch.[25]

At the beginning of 1941 the Engineering Section operated from a single small shop of 600 ft^2 (55.7 m^2). As the work of this department increased over the year, it was necessary to expand the amount of space allocated to them at Station IX. SOE, therefore, constructed an additional carpenters' shop and a sheet metal shop of 1,200 ft^2 (111.5 m^2). In 1942 the Engineering Section was allocated a further 2,400 ft^2 (223 m^2) of space at The Frythe. From four members of staff in August 1942, Station IX's Engineering Section had grown to 160 by September 1944. Over the same period, the unit's workshops had expanded by 19,600 ft^2 (1,820.9 m^2).[26]

Engineering workspace was also made available to staff working on specific projects. Following the entry of the Soviet Union into the war in June 1941, the German battleship *Tirpitz*, which was stationed in the Baltic, became an increasing concern to the Allies.[27] SOE's believed the solution was to develop a one-man attack submarine.[28] Known as the 'Welman', the craft was the brainchild of Colonel John Dolphin.[29] Following successful trials of the prototype, SOE decided to look into the possibility of mass producing the submarine. To allow the first 20 craft to be built while contracts were arranged with external companies, SOE constructed hangars with a footprint of 5,000 ft^2 (465 m^2) in the grounds of Station IX in which the Welman could be built.[30]

In 1943 SOE began another expansion of the departments within their Research and Development Section. As there was insufficient space at The Frythe to accommodate this growth, the Supplies Board decided on 12 August to relocate the Radio Communication Division (RCD). This unit was selected as it was anticipated that the workload of the RCD would significantly increase in support of Operation OVERLORD. The RCD, therefore, required more space to expand than was available at Station IX. It took the Property Section until 4 October to identify suitable premises for the RCD at Allensor's Joinery Works, Watford. Almost immediately on acquiring the site SOE embarked on a programme of alterations to get the factory ready. On completion of the work in January 1944 the RCD relocated and all radio research ceased at Station IX.[31]

In 1944 the capabilities of The Frythe were enhanced with the construction of another new specialist facility. Known as the 'Thermostat Hut', it was designed to provide a number of constant-temperature environments.[32] The new laboratory provided SOE's engineers and scientists with the necessary apparatus to study the effects of global climatic conditions on their prototypes. Inside the building, SOE provided their staff with a wide array of equipment, including compressed air, vacuum and hydrostatic pressure test apparatus, an analytical and plating laboratory and the five thermostats.[33] For part of the war the responsibility of maintaining the apparatus within the Thermostat Hut was given to John van Riemsdijk. When he took over this role, van Riemsdijk discovered that his predecessor had neglected their duty, as

> much of the apparatus was in a half complete state, and of the usable equipment 50% was out of order. There were at that time no wiring diagrams or descriptions to guide him in the work of restoring it to its former condition.[34]

The work undertaken by the staff at Station IX was, therefore, not always to a high standard.

64   *Research and development*

In the same year SOE decided to increase the number of engineers and designers they obtained from the army and RAF. As there was no spare accommodation at Station IX at this time, SOE undertook extensive refurbishment of the stable block to make it fit for habitation. Unfortunately, on 29 January 1944 a fire swept through this building, gutting three-quarters of the structure. Instead of repairing the damage, SOE arranged for some of their staff to be billeted nearby in the houses of civilians.[35]

Within the grounds of Station IX SOE made facilities available to their staff for the testing of a wide range of different prototypes. To support the scientists and engineers working on maritime equipment, a large tank was constructed within the estate.[36] By 18 February 1945 SOE had also managed to acquire the fuselage of a Stirling bomber, which they installed in the grounds of Station IX. This gave the engineers developing air delivery mechanisms opportunities to test their designs in an actual aircraft. One set of trials conducted in the fuselage assessed prototype conveyors and methods for increasing the mobility of packages in an aircraft. During these trials, one solution tested was the loading of stores onto lightweight wooden 'toboggans', which allowed two despatchers to unload 1,760 kg of supplies in 11 seconds.[37] Staff at The Frythe were also provided with facilities to conduct experiments on explosive devices. To the south of the main house, the terraced gardens were excavated and extended to create a test range. In order that staff could observe the experiments, a concrete bunker fitted with bombproof windows was constructed to one side of the range.[38]

In March 1945, with the end of the war in sight, control of Station IX was transferred from SOE to the Admiralty's Department of Miscellaneous Weapon Development. As this department had no use for The Frythe's chemical laboratories, SOE maintained a presence onsite to operate and ensure the upkeep of these facilities.[39]

SOE also collaborated with external organisations to design new equipment. In order to develop new radio sets, SOE worked closely with the Polish military. At an Anglo-Polish meeting held at the Hotel Rubens, London, on 29 April 1943 Colonel Sulislawski, of the Polish Ministry of National Defence, presented a draft agreement that paved the way for Polish-led wireless research.[40] Under this agreement, the Polish General Staff planned to convert their existing Military Wireless Research Unit (PMWR), based at Stanmore, into a self-reliant organisation with increased research and production capacity. These proposals were supported by SOE and it was agreed that the PMWR board of directors would be comprised of six Polish representatives, two SIS personnel, someone from the Telecommunications Research Establishment (TRE) and two members of SOE.[41]

Following the approval of the Polish General Staff's plans, the Ministry of Works began constructing workshops in the grounds of Wykeham House, Gordon Avenue, Stanmore.[42] To fund this and the research and development conducted by the PMWR, the unit was provided with a yearly budget of £59,580.[43] The responsibility for designing new wireless prototypes befell the PMWR's Laboratory and Research Section.[44] To support the staff at Wykeham House, by 16 May 1945 the PMWR encompassed a laboratory and general administrative offices, two workshops, which included mechanical and electrical assembly, inspection facilities and general stores. Inside the mechanical workshop machine tools were provided that enabled the unit to manufacture small runs of radio sets.[45] Between May 1943 and June 1945, the PMWR manufactured 1,800 wireless sets in addition to their continuing work on research and development.[46]

Once prototypes had been developed either internally or through SOE's collaborations, it was important that field trials were conducted on the equipment. If tests were not conducted under realistic conditions design flaws could have been overlooked. Despite the Research Section employing a trials officer, there was no requirement that new devices had to undergo trials until August 1943. It was at this time that SOE established a Trials Subsection within their Operational Research Section. All new equipment now had to undergo a complete set of clearly defined tests before it could be issued.[47]

The majority of these trials were conducted at facilities that were already operated by SOE. For example, testing of new containers designed for air dropping was initially conducted at RAF Ringway.[48] Later on, SOE moved all trials associated with packing and air dropping to Station 61, Gaynes Hall, Cambridgeshire. Some tests, however, were also conducted by the Special Parachute Section, Henlow, or the RAF's operational squadrons based at RAF Tempsford. The Balloon Development Establishment, Cardington, also placed a balloon at the disposal of SOE for drop tests.[49]

Wireless equipment developed at either Station IX or by the PMWR was often trialled between SOE's training facilities and other locations across the UK.[50] During one series of tests in early 1945, Sergeant Creaton, of the Royal Signals, was tasked with evaluating the English Midget Mains Receiver and the Polish Midget Mains Transceiver. Creaton was ideally suited to conduct these trials as he had

> been responsible, for more than a year, for the technical training of all students at S.T.S. 52 and has, consequently, a wide knowledge of the ability of the student to handle radio equipment, and it was on the understanding that he would review ... from the students' point of view.[51]

To conduct the tests on the midget receivers and transmitters, Creaton travelled to Thurso in the Scottish Highlands and then communicated back to a home station.[52]

For certain items of equipment, it was not feasible for SOE to conduct trials at facilities they already operated. Following the allocation of £3,000 in March 1942 to support the development of the Welman, SOE had to start searching for a new site that was suitable for testing submersible vehicles. Eventually the organisation settled on Queen Mary's Reservoir, Staines, and

66   Research and development

the new facility became known as Station VIII. By October 1942 SOE was ready to conduct their first trials of the Welman on this large body of water.[53]

In order to support the trials that were conducted on Queen Mary's Reservoir, it was necessary that SOE provided their staff with certain infrastructure.[54] To lower the submersibles into the reservoir specially designed cradles had to be constructed. Workshops were also erected on the banks of the reservoir so that SOE's engineers could make alterations to the submersibles onsite. At the time of the building work at Station VIII, security concerns were being raised within SOE over the employment of casual civilian contractors. In late 1942 SOE, with the knowledge and approval of the Ministry of Works and War Office, established a mobile construction unit. Formed of Royal Engineers, the new unit, known as the Mobile Construction Unit (MCU) 77, was tasked with the designing and construction of all new building work required by SOE.[55]

By July 1943 the development of the Welman had reached a stage whereby it was necessary for SOE to conduct open water trials. To support these tests, the organisation planned to establish a base at Fishguard, in south-west Wales. The director of Local Defence and the director of Naval Intelligence, however, both expressed concerns over SOE's choice of location. At the time, Fishguard was the patrol base for ships responsible for searching maritime traffic that sailed between Ireland and the Iberian Peninsula. As both areas harboured pro-German sympathisers, it was assumed that Fishguard was under enemy surveillance. As the town was also not located within a 'Protected Area', it would not have been possible to hide the trials from observers.[56] Eventually, after much deliberation, all objections to Fishguard were dropped and SOE took over the second floor of the Great Western Hotel for their staff. This provided accommodation for 15 of the organisation's officers, with the remainder of the staff billeted in the hotel's annexe and nearby naval huts.[57]

Known as Station IXc, SOE's facility at Fishguard was ideally suited for the open-water trials of submersibles. The bay provided SOE's engineers with a sheltered body of water in which they could calibrate the submarines before entering the Irish Sea. Fishguard's pre-existing port infrastructure was also key to the safe handling and movement of SOE's submersibles into and out of the water.[58] Once SOE had established Station IXc, the organisation used the facility to conduct other trials besides those on submersibles, including those on direction finders for ships and the free dropping of supplies in conjunction with S-Phone homing sets.[59]

Despite the vast majority of SOE's research and development occurring within the UK, some overseas facilities conducted their own work on an *ad hoc* basis. The Indian Mission, for example, established the Marine Research and Training Centre at Trincomalee, Ceylon, which was partly tasked with conducting research into boats and navigational aids.[60] To support the work of the engineers, the facility was provided with a number of workshops, stores and hangars.[61] By developing equipment overseas, SOE's engineers and scientists could ensure that the devices were tailored to local conditions.

Notes

1 Roderick Bailey, *Secret Agent's Handbook: The Top Secret Manual of Wartime Weapons, Gadgets, Disguises and Devices* (London, 2008), p. 9. SOE's catalogue of devices was finally published in 2008 (Bailey, *Secret Agent's Handbook*, p. 181).
2 Bailey, S*ecret Agent's Handbook*, pp. 12–13.
3 Bailey, S*ecret Agent's Handbook*, p. 9. One of the most important designs SOE inherited from Section D was the 'Pencil Time Fuze'. This was to become the standard time delay fuze utilised by the secret services throughout the war (TNA HS 7/27 History of the Research and Development Section of SOE, pp. 1–3).
4 TNA HS 7/27 History of the Research and Development Section of SOE, pp. 1–3.
5 TNA HS 8/334 Services Directorate and 'U' Section ADZ/OR/730 25/12/1941, p. 1.
6 TNA HS 8/334 Services Directorate and 'U' Section ADZ/OR/730 25/12/1941, p. 1.
7 TNA HS 7/27 History of the Research and Development Section of SOE, p. 1.
8 Fredric Boyce and Douglas Everett, *SOE: The Scientific Secrets* (Stroud, 2009), p. 15; and TNA HS 7/46 Radio Communication Division, p. 1.
9 TNA HS 8/334 Letter to Jebb 05/08/1940.
10 TNA HS 8/334 Emergency Evacuation covering 64, Baker Street, Michael House and 5, Porchester Gate 21/04/1941, p. 3.
11 TNA HS 8/334 Office Hours 15/10/1940.
12 TNA HS 8/334 Office Hours 15/10/1940.
13 TNA HS 7/27 History of the Research and Development Section of S.O.E., p. 7.
14 TNA HS 8/334 Letter to Jebb 05/08/1940.
15 TNA HS 7/27 History of the Research and Development Section of S.O.E., p. 7.
16 TNA HS 7/27 History of the Research and Development Section of S.O.E., p. 8.
17 See Boyce and Everett, *SOE*; and TNA HS 7/27 Appendix A DMN/7366 List of Devices Developed by the Engineering Section, pp. 1–2.
18 IWM Oral History 11035 Brown, John Isaac Godfrey REEL 1 18.00.
19 TNA HS 7/27 SOE History Experimental Station 6 (War Dept.) – otherwise known as Station XII, p. 1.
20 Boyce and Everett, *SOE*, p. 16.
21 TNA HS 8/358 ADZ/XX/510 26/06/1941.
22 TNA HS 7/27 History of the Research and Development Section of S.O.E., p. 8.
23 TNA HS 7/27 History of the Research and Development Section of S.O.E., p. 8.
24 TNA HS 7/27 Appendix E Research and Development Organisation: Short History of Engineering Section Station IX since August, 1941, p. 1.
25 IWM Oral History 11035 Brown, John Isaac Godfrey REEL 1 20.20.
26 TNA HS 7/27 Appendix E Research and Development Organisation: Short History of Engineering Section Station IX since August, 1941, pp. 1, 3.
27 Edward Thomas, 'Norway's Role in British Wartime Intelligence', in *Britain and Norway in the Second World War*, ed. Patrick Salmon (London, 1995), p. 124.
28 Boyce and Everett, *SOE*, p. 123. SOE's solution was, however, not unique. Prior to the summer of 1940 the British army had begun work on a miniature submarine. During July control of the project transferred to the Admiralty. It took the Admiralty a further two years of development before they placed their first order for 12 'X-Crafts' (Paul Kemp, *Underwater Warriors* (London, 1999), pp. 152, 153).
29 Kemp, *Underwater Warriors*, p. 160.
30 TNA HS 7/27 Appendix E Research and Development Organisation: Short History of Engineering Section Station IX since August, 1941, p. 2. By 20 July 1943 two-man Welmans were being manufactured at The Frythe (TNA HS 8/799 Two Man Welman for Training SM.04353/432 20/07/1943). While undertaking

68   *Research and development*

trials on the submersible it became apparent that the submarine contained design flaws. During an attack run, for example, there was simply far too much for a single person to effectively accomplish. Furthermore, by being alone, the operator was denied the moral support of another crew member (Kemp, *Underwater Warriors*, p. 160). Despite growing concerns within SOE about the operational shortcomings of the Welman, work on the submersible continued (TNA HS 8/798 Report on Capabilities of Welman Craft, pp. 1–4). SOE also began work designing a submersible capable of delivering supplies to an enemy coastline. This submersible, known as the 'Welfreighter', had a surface range of 400 miles (643.7 km) travelling at seven knots and 20 miles (32.2 km) submerged at three knots. It could also accommodate two passengers and carry 1,000 lbs (453.6 kg) of freight (TNA HS 8/801 ADL/542 Welfreighter Specifications 29/12/1942). Concerns were also raised within SOE about the Welfreighter, as it did not appear to have any advantages over a motor gun boat (MGB) and rubber dinghy (TNA HS 8/799 Naval Section Staff Minute Sheet Subject: 2-man Welman 10/08/1943).

31 TNA HS 7/46 Radio Communication Division, pp. 23, 24, 30, 31.
32 Boyce and Everett, *SOE*, pp. 16, 90. The five thermostats installed in this building could produce constant temperature environments between −20 °C and 40 °C (IWM Document 12893 Operation and Maintenance Manual for the Thermostat Hut at Station IX, 1945, pp. 4, 11, 12, 13, 14, 16).
33 IWM Document 12893 Operation and Maintenance Manual for the Thermostat Hut at Station IX, 1945, pp. 4, 11, 12, 13, 14, 16. The hut was constructed from 0.36-m-thick brickwork, roofed with corrugated asbestos and arranged into five rooms (IWM Document 12893 Operation and Maintenance Manual for the Thermostat Hut at Station IX, 1945).
34 IWM Document 12893 Operation and Maintenance Manual for the Thermostat Hut at Station IX, 1945, p. 2.
35 TNA HS 7/46 Radio Communications Division, pp. 30, 31.
36 IWM HU 56775 A Motorised Submersible Canoe (MSC) in full buoyancy condition; and IWM Oral History 13244 Bennette, Harvey Ryding REEL 2 14.30. The tank was 16 ft (4.88 m) deep, 20 ft (6.10 m) long and 8 ft (2.44 m) wide.
37 TNA HS 7/50 DHE/A/5032 Air Supply Research Problems under Investigation. Summary No. 6. Progress to February 18th, 1945, p. 2. Concerns were expressed over the security implications of scattering toboggans across the drop zone. These would clearly indicate that supplies had been dropped in the area (TNA HS 7/50 DHE/A/5032 Air Supply Research Problems under Investigation. Summary No. 6. Progress to February 18th, 1945, p. 2).
38 Boyce and Everett, *SOE*, p. 16. In order to provide a safe environment in which the explosives could be stored on site, single-storey magazines were constructed in the grounds of The Frythe. These were built of Fletton bricks and roofed with reinforced concrete. Reached via a sloping concrete ramp, the structures were surrounded by a Fletton brick retaining wall (Helen Ashworth and David Hillelson, 'The Frythe, Digswell Hill, Welwyn, Herts: Archaeological and Historic Building Impact Assessment' (unpublished report, 2011), p. 17).
39 TNA ADM 277/1 Miscellaneous Weapon Development Department – Admiralty – 1940–45: A History of the Department, A Survey of its Projects and A Key to its Technical Histories, p. 9.
40 TNA HS 4/186 Minutes of Anglo/Polish Meeting held at Hotel Rubens on 29/4/43, p. 1.
41 TNA HS 4/186 An agreement between the Polish General Staff and S.O.E. concerning the Polish Military Wireless Research Unit Stanmore, (P.M.W.R.), p. 1.

It was also agreed at the meeting that all material purchased by the PMWR had to be approved by SOE (TNA HS 4/186 Minutes of Anglo Polish Meeting held at the new factory, Wyckham House, Stanmore on Thursday, 25th March, 1943 at 15:00 hours, pp. 1, 2).

42 TNA HS 7/183 Appendix G Polish Military Wireless Research Unit, p. 1. These workshops had a footprint of 10,000 ft^2 (929 m^2) (TNA HS 7/183 Appendix G Polish Military Wireless Research Unit, p. 1). Under the Anglo-Polish agreement, the security of the PMWR at Wykeham House was provided by SOE in conjunction with the SIS (TNA HS 4/186 Minutes of Anglo Polish Meeting held at the new factory, Wyckham House, Stanmore on Thursday, 25th March, 1943 at 15:00 hours, pp. 1, 2).

43 TNA HS 4/187 Report on the Activities of PMWR for the Year 1943–44, pp. 6–7. This budget was partly financed by SOE.

44 All the scientific and technical officers of the PMWR had received a university education (TNA HS 7/183 Appendix G Polish Military Wireless Research Unit, p. 1).

45 TNA HS 7/183 Appendix G Polish Military Wireless Research Unit, p. 1.

46 TNA HS 4/187 Sets manufactured by PMWR from 01/05/1945 to 08/06/1945. To assemble and test the wireless sets developed and manufactured by the PMWR, an Electrical Assembly Workshop was established at Wykeham House. This workshop could achieve an output of 8,000 working hours per month. Once the wireless sets were assembled, an Inspection Section undertook final checks before they were issued (TNA HS 7/183 Appendix G Polish Military Wireless Research Unit, p. 1).

47 TNA HS 7/27 History of the Trials Section, 1943–44, p. 1.

48 TNA HS 4/173 Notes on visit to Ringway – 26th October 1941, p. 1.

49 TNA HS 7/50 History of SOE Air Supply Research Section, p. 13.

50 TNA HS 8/336 System for Research, Demand and Supply of Radio Equipment required by SOE CD/644907/01/1944, p. 1.

51 TNA HS 4/187 HJB/18/52/4054 12/04/1945.

52 TNA HS 4/187 HJB/18/52/4054 12/04/1945. Trials of the new 'Squirt' transmitter were also conducted in Scotland (TNA HS 7/46 Radio Communication Division, p. 21). A 'squirt' transmitter was a wireless set that could compress an average 15-minute message into a couple of seconds (Boyce and Everett, *SOE*, p. 218).

53 Boyce and Everett, *SOE*, pp. 123, 126, 132.

54 IWM Oral History 13244 Bennette, Harvey Ryding REEL 2 09.30.

55 TNA HS 7/15 Properties Section History, p. 6.

56 Boyce and Everett, *SOE*, pp. 142–3. The Helford Estuary in Cornwall was suggested as an alternative to Fishguard. This was dismissed by the head of Military Branch II, Naval Intelligence, as the number of cross-channel operations they conducted was to intensify. Increased military activity in the region could attract the enemy's attention.

57 Boyce and Everett, *SOE*, pp. 142–3.

58 Fishguard was also connected to the national railway network allowing for the easy transportation of Welmans to the site.

59 TNA HS 7/46 History of SOE Air Supply Research Section, p. 34; and TNA HS 7/50 Radio Communication Division, p. 12.

60 TNA HS 1/280 Marine Research and Training Centre G.74/193 02/08/1944.

61 TNA HS 1/280 Requirements for despatch camp and Marine Research and Training Centre Trincomalee 19/08/1944, p. 1. The hangars at the Marine Research and Training Centre could accommodate four Welfrighters, 25 Sleeping Beauties, 150 Canoes Mk1A, 40 Canoes Mk3 or Mk6, 250 Y Dinghies, 100 Wheelwrights or Landing Craft Rubber (small) and 50 Outboard motors.

70   *Research and development*

References

Archives

The National Archives (TNA), London

ADM 277/1: History of the department, a survey of its projects and a key to its technical history.

HS 1/280: Military establishments: 95 (Marine Research Training Centre) to 100 (HQ Australia), 121, 122 and 141.

HS 4/173: Aircraft and airfields: foreign crews for SOE air operations.

HS 4/186: Polish military wireless research unit Stanmore; correspondence and minutes of board meetings; Anglo-Polish wireless meetings.

HS 4/187: Polish military wireless research unit Stanmore; correspondence and minutes of board meetings; Anglo-Polish wireless meetings.

HS 7/15: D FIN/2 section: FANY pay and allowances; properties section.

HS 7/27: SOE Research and Development section 1938–45.

HS 7/46: E section 1940–45; radio communications division; false document section; supplies organisation.

HS 7/50: Planning and supply of air dropping equipment 1941–45.

HS 7/183: Polish section history.

HS 8/334: Organisation and administration: Staff.

HS 8/336: Organisation and administration: Staff.

HS 8/358: Communications: Relations with SIS.

HS 8/798: Policy: consideration of operational use of Welman craft.

HS 8/799: Welman craft: training of two-man Welman.

HS 8/801: Welman craft: specifications, drawings and photographs.

Imperial War Museum (IWM), London

12893 Private Paper: Operation and Maintenance Manual for the Thermostat Hut at Station IX, 1945.

Bennette, Harvey Ryding (Sound Archive interview number 13244).

Brown, John Isaac Godfrey (Sound Archive interview number 11035).

HU 56775 A Motorised Submersible Canoe (MSC) in full buoyancy condition.

Secondary sources

Ashworth, Helen and Hillelson, David. 'The Frythe, Digswell Hill, Welwyn, Herts: Archaeological and Historic Building Impact Assessment' (unpublished report, 2011).

Bailey, Roderick. *Secret Agent's Handbook: The Top Secret Manual of Wartime Weapons, Gadgets, Disguises and Devices* (London, 2008).

Boyce, Fredric and Everett, Douglas. *SOE: The Scientific Secrets* (Stroud, 2009).

Kemp, Paul. *Underwater Warriors* (London, 1999).

Thomas, Edward. 'Norway's Role in British Wartime Intelligence', in *Britain and Norway in the Second World War*, ed. Patrick Salmon (London, 1995).

4 Supply

Once SOE had approved equipment for use by their agents, it was essential that the organisation could manufacture and prepare the devices ready for transportation to the field. Without an efficient and reliable supply chain, SOE's ability to arm resistance groups would have been negatively impacted. Although the organisation had to coordinate and contract external companies to manufacture some of their more specialised items, SOE depended on the RAF, Royal Navy and British Army to supply them with standardised equipment. SOE managed to come to an agreement with the branches of the armed forces that any request for supplies originating from the organisation would be met with no questions.[1] To ensure that the supplies requested from the military arrived on time, the heads of SOE's departments were expected to provide notice of upcoming operations. This allowed those in SOE responsible for supplies, Section E, to prioritise the allocation of equipment.[2] Sometimes the demands SOE placed on military channels outstripped the armed forces' ability to supply equipment. In an effort to ensure that the organisation had sufficient stockpiles of explosive charges in advance of Operation OVERLORD, SOE had to arrange for the transfer of Royal Ordnance Factory Elstow, Bedfordshire, to their control.[3]

By July 1944 SOE expected that a request from their Section E should be fulfilled by the military within days. At this stage of the war, the armed forces regarded requests for equipment from SOE as urgent and required in the 'quickest possible time'.[4] To ensure the supplies were delivered to the correct location, Section E enlisted the assistance of the War Office to arrange road transportation. On one occasion, when 1,600 tons of ammunition was urgently required by SOE, the stores were despatched by two special ammunition trains. Although the delivery of large quantities of supplies by purposely allocated trains was an efficient way of moving equipment, the rail network was not always reliable for moving individual parcels.[5] SOE discovered that sending equipment 'by passenger train to a London terminus was not a good idea as so many parcels and cases arrived at the same time that it took Railway staff a considerable time to locate packages intended for us'.[6]

Military supplies that could be obtained from the armed forces only partly contributed to SOE's equipment requirements. To help meet the operational

DOI: 10.4324/9781315180106-4

72 *Supply*

demands of the organisation, SOE contracted work from various private businesses scattered throughout the UK and allied nations. These companies supplied both the raw materials and, occasionally, the finished product. It was the responsibility of SOE's Section E to oversee the production of supplies and the delivery of raw materials.[7] Although most companies were willing to co-operate with SOE, which issued contracts under the auspices of the War Office, some were reluctant to 'supply any goods ... unless they still bore their trade name'.[8] To aid SOE in creating relationships with private businesses, Section E's staff generally contracted companies they have worked with before the outbreak of the war. Not only could the quality of the work of these companies be guaranteed, but experience demonstrated that these businesses asked fewer questions of the nature of SOE's contracts. On the whole, the companies employed by the organisation undertook their work with 'great enthusiasm'.[9] Without the support of the private sector, SOE felt that it 'would have been impossible to carry on'.[10]

Not all of SOE's supplies had to be sourced from external organisations. Facilities were available at both Station IX, The Frythe, and Station XII, Aston House, that allowed SOE's staff to manufacture prototypes and undertake small-batch production. At Aston House these were done in the machine and carpenters' shops, as well as in the miniature filling factory, constructed in the grounds.[11] SOE did not manufacture equipment exclusively at The Frythe or Aston House. In June 1942 the organisation's Wireless Production Unit relocated their manufacturing process from Station IX to the Bontex Knitting Mills, Wembley.[12] In addition to producing sets for SOE, this unit was contracted by the Ministry of Supply to produce wireless sets to the value of hundreds of thousands of pounds.[13]

Production of certain sensitive items also had to be kept in-house, including the forging of documents. The site selected by SOE to house their forgers was Briggins, Essex, which became known as Station XIV. Originally, the forgers shared the facility with the students of Special Training School (STS) 38, but by 1 April 1942 SOE had relocated the school to Audley End[14] and the forgers were able to significantly increase the size of their printing works. At its peak, the Forgery Section employed 50 members of staff, the majority of whom were ex-convicts.[15] Pamela Niven, a First Aid Nursing Yeomanry (FANY) who served with SOE, recalled that the staff at Briggins were 'Fantastic forgers ... they were extremely efficient and always very dapper and very courteous'.[16] Over the course of the war, the Forgery Section produced in excess of 275,000 documents.[17]

One of the most secretive aspects of SOE's manufacturing process was the camouflaging of equipment so that it might 'pass' in occupied territory. By November 1941 the organisation was employing only a single camouflage expert. It soon became apparent that the work of this one member of staff could not meet SOE's operational demands. In order to increase their capacity to camouflage equipment, a small camouflaging facility was established in the grounds of The Frythe in January 1942. Within weeks of being set up, the department had already outgrown the facilities at Station IX. As workspace with a larger footprint was required, SOE decided to take over part of the Victoria and Albert Museum, Kensington, for their camouflaging activities. The staff installed in the museum were responsible for the production of devices that could be used to conceal arms, explosives, operational money, codes, documents, radio transmitters and receivers during transit. Only a few months later, in June 1942, the Camouflage Section had to relocate once more to the Thatched Barn on the Barnett bypass.[18] Known as Station XV, this facility provided SOE sufficient space to expand their Camouflage Section as operational requirements demanded.[19] Although the camouflaging of items could now occur on a large scale at Station XV, the facilities at the Victorian and Albert Museum were retained by SOE to design prototype camouflage schemes and to liaise with agents.[20]

The staff at Station XV were all either artistic or had received training in the arts. Tinsmiths and screen printers would work together to produce tins of tomatoes or peaches, which would be filled with grenades and detonators.[21] When tyre bursters with the appearance of rocks were being manufactured, Station XV received geological samples from the field so that the explosive device would blend into the area in which it was to be deployed. Feedback on the camouflaged equipment was sent to Station XV from agents returning to the field; staff would occasionally be informed that 'such and such load got through and done its job', but if anything was intercepted, 'we never did it again'.[22] The raw materials that Station XV's staff had access to were the 'best … that could be obtained from all over the world to use as we wished in any way we wished and if it was wasted it didn't matter. The finest of cloth to do uniforms with and everything was the very very best'.[23]

Once SOE had arranged for equipment to be manufactured and camouflaged, it was necessary for supplies to be stored until they were required in the field. The main depot operated by SOE during the Second World War was Station XII, at Aston House. Until February 1941 the operational demands placed on SOE's supplies were limited. It was during this month that the Auxiliary Units placed an order with Aston House for 1,000 'mixed parcels'.[24] The equipment that made up these parcels was housed in a number of small structures that had been constructed in close proximity to the main house. At this time, SOE did not implement the segregation of explosive groups at Station XII, nor did the staff follow regulations for the safe storage of dangerous material.[25] Despite some concerns over how these stores were handled, SOE soon accumulated a floating stock of several tons of high explosives, incendiaries and other equipment at Aston House.[26]

Following the appointment of Professor Dudley Newitt as SOE's director of scientific research on 9 June 1941, there was a period of organisational restructuring. During this reorganisation The Frythe was tasked with focusing on research and development, while Aston House became responsible for the production and storage of supplies.[27] The latter was to remain SOE's primary depot until the end of the Second World War. Despite the central role

74 *Supply*

Station XII now had in supplying agents in the field, the conditions in which the facility kept explosives and incendiary devices were not addressed. Issues surrounding how SOE handled and stored equipment came to a fore on 2 January 1942.[28] While Aston House's staff were attending a New Year's party at The Frythe, the facility's incendiary magazines caught fire.[29] In the aftermath of this disaster, SOE undertook a review of the Station XII's storage facilities. The organisation also removed all surplus stores from Aston House and sent them to STS41, Fawley Court, Oxfordshire, for storage. Storage of equipment that remained at Aston House was improved by the construction of a number of elephant shelters in the grounds of the facility.[30]

The fire at Aston House occurred at a time in the war when it became apparent to SOE that the organisation's storage capacity required substantial expansion.[31] As a temporary measure, SOE was granted access to a significant portion of the 84 Command Ammunition Depot, Sandy, Bedfordshire, in July 1942.[32] Plans were also made for an extensive building programme at Station XII, including new stores, incendiary and explosive storage, accommodation for explosive filling and a light engineering workshop. By early 1943 building work at Aston House was nearing completion, which allowed SOE to increase staffing levels at this facility. At the end of the war approximately 600 people were employed at Station XII to handle the organisation's stores.[33]

Among the new staff recruited by SOE for Aston House were a number of personnel from the Royal Army Ordnance Corps. Under the guidance of these specialists, Station XII implemented a more efficient system of stores accounting.[34] Although this process was based on standard operating procedure, some slight modifications had to be introduced to cope with the specialist nature of certain items in SOE's inventory. The personnel from the Royal Army Ordnance Corps also segregated SOE's stockpile of explosives into their various classifications and ensured that the proper safe distances between buildings were maintained.[35]

Although Station XII acted as SOE's main supply depot in the UK, the organisation operated a number of other facilities in the country for the handling of small arms. During the early stages of the war, small arms were stored in the dining room of The Frythe and in an armoury that was constructed in the grounds of this facility.[36] Some weapons were also held nearby in the North Road Garage, Welwyn.[37] By February 1941 SOE's Small Arms Section had the capacity to send a single consignment of 20 tons of arms to Norway.[38] Within five months, the increasing demands being placed on the armouries at The Frythe and the North Road Garage could no longer be met by these facilities and in August 1941 SOE decided to relocate their small arms storage to the nearby Bride Hall.[39]

Owing to the perceived threat posed by the Fifth Column, 'secrecy was of paramount importance' when selecting a new site of operation. Located 'miles from anywhere', Bride Hall, known as Station VI, was the perfect secret service 'hide-out'.[40] In the grounds of Bride Hall were also two spacious barns that were ideally suited to the needs of SOE's Small Arms Section.[41]

Supply 75

On establishing themselves at Station VI, SOE tasked their staff with repairing, servicing and testing all the weapons required by the organisation.[42] To aid them in their work the Small Arms Section constructed a firing range 30 yards (27.4 m) long in the grounds of Bride Hall. Over the operational life of this facility, 100,000 pistols destined for the European resistance passed through Station VI.[43]

Before the supplies held in SOE's depots could be shipped to the field, they had to be packed into containers to help protect them in transit. During 1940 this was carried out at RAF Henlow.[44] Although one of Britain's busiest airfields, and home to the RAF's Special Parachute Section, SOE managed to find some space for filling packages and storing and packing parachutes.[45] Initially, SOE packed equipment into panniers in a small office under extreme security on the airfield.[46] Over time, and as needs demanded, SOE expanded the footprint of their workspaces to cover 8,000 ft^2 (743 m^2).[47]

On 5 June 1941 SOE and RAF representatives met to discuss the future coordination of the two organisation's parachute requirements. As it was felt that time and petrol was being wasted by both SOE and the RAF in the storing and packing of special parachutes, it was proposed that rooms in Richmond Terrace, London, should be requisitioned for this purpose.[48] The limited capacity of these rooms to allow SOE to expand their packing operations meant the move never materialised, however.[49]

On 2 October 1941, four months after the meeting between SOE and the RAF, the former moved some of their packing operations out of RAF Henlow and into the stable block of Audley End House, Essex. At the time, SOE was using the facility to train Polish agents. As there was limited space at Audley End into which the packing section could expand, the packers could not keep pace with SOE's expanding operation requirements. Just six months after moving to Audley End, the packing section relocated to a facility that had been specifically assigned to their unit.[50]

The move of SOE's Packing Section to Gaynes Hall, Huntingdonshire, known as Station 61, was an important development in the organisation's UK supply chain. Space was now available to develop an efficient facility dedicated to preparing supplies for transportation to the field. Shortly after moving into their new accommodation at Station 61, SOE's packers devised the contents for a series of standardised containers.[51] The introduction of standardised packages and the increasing staffing numbers at this facility enabled SOE's packers to expand their annual output of 2,176 containers in 1943 to 56,464 in 1944.[52] Despite the effort of the staff at Station 61, they were informed that they 'can't fill enough [packages]. The demand is insatiable it doesn't how many you packed there won't be enough'.[53]

With increasing demands placed on Gaynes Hall, it was essential that the facility expanded to keep up with the workload. In the summer of 1943 SOE implemented a programme of building work at Station 61 to increase its capacity to pack containers. This involved the construction of six large packing sheds, two magazines, one assembly shed, two container stores and a new

76 *Supply*

camp to accommodate the staff.[54] During their shifts packing containers, SOE would lock their staff into the buildings.[55] In the summer months this caused distress, as the buildings were

> scorching hot and we were locked in and we were dehydrated. And they only unlocked the door to allow us to go to the canteen for a drink for say 10 or 15 minutes. You couldn't drink it in that time and there was a long queue anyway. So we investigated and we found that the second gate which was permanently locked had a little building plank near to it which when pushed under the gate lifted the locked gate a foot or two ... so we now staggered our morning and afternoon tea breaks. We kept up production but used our common sense. Which was lacking on this army camp. The only man in charge inside the working compound was a sergeant who was working with us and the other disabled RAF soldiers.[56]

Despite increasing staffing numbers, standardised containers and sufficient workspace, the quality of the packers' work was occasionally criticised. On 9 February 1943 Colonel Chichaeff of the Soviet Armed Forces complained about the 'inefficient work at Station 61 in an alleged mixing up on one occasion of containers for agents destined for Holland and Belgium respectively'.[57] The Court of Enquiry determined that the mistake was the result of

> labels on the containers [that] must have become detached and been substituted either between the packing office and the aerodrome or at the aerodrome itself ... [Consequently,] the whole procedure in respect of despatch of containers was overhauled and there now exists no possibility of such a substitution occurring in the future.[58]

In November 1943 SOE realised that Gaynes Hall did not have sufficient capacity to develop a container reserve for the planned upcoming invasion of mainland Europe. It was decided that the organisation would send one of their most experienced packers to Messrs Carpet Trades Ltd of Kidderminster. The packer would be tasked with instructing the employees of this company in the packing of Sten, Bren and Rifle containers. These packages were chosen as there was a great demand for these weapons and the containers could be packed by unskilled labour.[59] Following the training of the staff at Messrs Carpet Trades, SOE placed an initial order with this company for the packing of 4,000 containers. This was increased at a later date to 18,500 packages.[60]

In 1944 the capacity to supply the European Resistance from the UK was enhanced. By this stage in the war the American Office of Strategic Services (OSS) was ready to assist SOE in preparing packages for dispatch to the field. To prepare the OSS for this complex task, a number of their officers and non-commissioned officers (NCOs) were attached to Gaynes Hall in February 1944 to observe SOE's operational procedures. Within a month,

SOE was happy that the staff seconded to Station 61 were ready to work independently. To enable the OSS to pack equipment for the European Resistance, these newly trained staff moved into a new facility at Holme, Peterborough, known as 'Area H'.[61]

Despite the training and support SOE provided to the OSS,

> all special containers continued to be packed at Station 61, the only reason being that years of experience counted in the packing of specials, the most difficult task being to get the correct centre-of-gravity and still ensure the maximum pay-load.[62]

Only the easiest containers were allocated to the OSS to be packed at Area H.[63] Arrangements were also made so that if they 'ran into any snags and run into them they did, one of St. 61's [Gaynes Hall] Officers would go over to Area H and help to put them on the right road again'.[64]

In the build-up to Operation OVERLORD SOE began exploring ways to supply the French Resistance with a greater quantity of medical equipment.[65] As an immediate response to this supply issue, SOE requested that the War Office supply them with 102 special 'Medical Units'. Each of these units had the capacity to treat 15,000 casualties. SOE also arranged with the deputy assistant director of medical services of the Airborne Division for additional medical equipment. By August 1943 SOE had placed orders for 100 tons of medical stores. In order that the medical supplies were packed in time for the anticipated invasion, SOE decided to establish a specialised medical packing station, which was known as ME10.[66] Within weeks of August 1943, ME10 was up and running and ready to begin work.[67]

To support their worldwide operations, SOE established supply dumps around the globe. In the Mediterranean, the organisation's main depot was located at 'Camp 8'.[68] This facility was based 7 miles (11.3 km) from Massingham and was well camouflaged from aerial observation by extensive tree coverage. By the end of March 1944, the depot was handling so many supplies that the camp had become congested with stores and sheds. In this situation explosives and ammunition were kept in close proximity, and in the event of a detonation, either accidental or through enemy action, it was predicted there would be a serious loss of life and equipment. Although the camp was surrounded by wire, it was found that this provided little protection against the local population, who crawled under it at night to steal arms and stores. Despite the overcrowding and lack of security, an inspection of the depot in March 1944 reported that Camp 8's workshops and bulk stores were well laid out and allowed staff easy access to supplies.[69]

Following the review of Camp 8, the personnel conducting the inspection visited Italy and SOE's new Camouflage School being established in a former factory 2 miles (3.2 km) south of Monopoli on the Brindisi road. In setting up this facility, the staff, some of whom had been trained at SOE's Station XV, were taking full advantage of the excellent opportunities offered by the

78 *Supply*

internal layout of the old factory building. Only minimum alterations to doorways and partitions were required before the site satisfied all of SOE's requirements. The inspectors believed that, on its expected completion in May 1944, the Camouflage School would be self-contained unit with all the necessary workshops, stores and magazines. The facility also had sufficient living accommodation and messes for all the personnel and guards required for the operation of the school.[70]

The purpose of this new base in Italy was to assist and support the work of SOE's Force 133's Camouflage and Technical Unit in Cairo.[71] Staff at the school in Monopoli were tasked with designing and manufacturing small quantities of special stores for both specific and general operations. In addition, the school was responsible for meeting the personal camouflage needs of agents. While the unit in Cairo would supply operations in the Western Mediterranean, the new Monopoli unit would be responsible for issuing stores and equipment to Italy and Algiers.[72]

Depots were also established by SOE to support operations in the South East Asian Theatre of Operation. In 1942, the organisation's Indian Mission began developing storage facilities at Jubbulpore. Known as GSI(K) Depot, the staff initially operated out of buildings located in the city's arsenal. As space was at a premium, because SOE was allocated only a small number of the arsenal's magazines, the depot's office was located in the corner of one of these explosive stores.[73] Supplies also had to be kept in huts and laid in the bottom of trenches that were then covered by tents and tarpaulins. During the early days of GSI(K) Depot, the packing of equipment ready for transportation to the field occurred in a requisitioned cow shed. This was eventually replaced by a small two-room structure that acted as both a packing shed and office.[74]

As operational requirements placed increasing demands on GSI(K) Depot, the facility had to grow. To accommodate the stores, six brick 'godowns' measuring 70 ft × 30 ft (21.3 m × 9.1 m) and roofed with asbestos sheets were constructed.[75] As part of this construction programme, a number of workshops were also erected. The design and building of these new facilities was personally supervised by the chief ordnance officer of the Jubbulpore Arsenal, Lieutenant Colonel Beamiss. Under Beamiss, the building work was completed in a fraction of the anticipated time and at a much lower cost than projected. His designs also proved to provide ample protection during the monsoon.[76]

During the early days of the Jubbulpore depot, the number of packers employed by the facility was just 15. As the work at the depot increased the level of staffing was doubled. The packing staff at GSI(K) Depot were split into two teams, each of which was given a daily quota of containers to be packed. To ensure that the correct equipment was packed into each container, boards were displayed in the workshops listing the contents of each type of package. Each time a new type of package was introduced the staff would be given a demonstration and a record was made of the time it should take them to complete the task.[77] On an average day, the teams at Jubbulpore could pack and

Supply 79

crate 100 containers ready for despatch. This output was generally sufficient to meet SOE's operational requirements in the theatre.[78]

During 1943 SOE's main depot at Jubbulpore and an overflow site at Ferozepur issued stores to the two main despatch centres, located at Calcutta and the other in Ceylon, and supplies to the three Training Schools.[79] As the organisation began increasing their clandestine activities in South East Asia, it became apparent that the capacity of SOE's Indian Mission to handle supplies would need to expand. To assist in this growth, Lieutenant Colonel LJC Wood, together with Majors Moneypenny and Munro, Captain Press and Lieutenants Rawson and Wampach, departed England late in 1943 to set up a new depot in India. It was intended that this new facility would serve as the main supply centre, as well as being a workshop and development base and a special packing centre for the theatre of operation. Following a tour of India, the group decided to locate the new base in the Poona area.[80] This was an ideal location for the new Special Forces Development Centre (SFDC), as it was near a port and with easy access to the national railway network.[81]

Following financial approval from the UK, work began on constructing the SFDC in early 1944 under the direction of the commander Royal Engineers, Poona. It was anticipated that the site would be ready by 1 April of that year. The contract for the work was given to the Hindustan Construction Company, but owing to transportation difficulties and a shortage of materials they were granted an extension to complete the work. Eventually, the SFDC was ready to receive its first members of staff in July 1944.[82]

The facilities at the SFDC were arranged over two areas. On one of these sites, four storage sheds measuring 90 ft × 40 ft (27.4 m × 12.2 m) were erected for the storage of clothing, food and small arms. This area also contained three 90 ft × 30 ft (27.4 m × 9.1 m) structures that housed the SFDC's offices, the medical stores, and the Arms Inspection and Test Workshop. In the facility's Magazine Area seven incendiary sheds, each capable of holding 5 tons of equipment, were constructed. SOE also erected two small packing sheds, a magazine that could hold 10 tons of nitro–glycerine-based explosives and one small arms ammunition shed measuring 180 ft × 40 ft (54.9 m ×12.2 m).[83] SFDC also had access to a command post and three converted gun sites that were licenced to hold 50 tons of explosives and ammunition.[84] In order to display the range of equipment available to Force 136, SFDC opened a small 'museum' at the facility.[85] Surrounding the whole of the SFDC was a security fence, with security areas within the SFDC protected by a further barbed-wire fence 8 ft (2.4 m) high and perimeter lighting.[86]

In order to adapt standard stores for use by SOE's Force 136, the SFDC established a Workshop Section and a Development Section in January 1944. The Development Section comprised of five sub-units: Section A dealt with war-like stores; Section B with rations, medical supplies, camp and personal equipment; Section C with camouflage and packing; Section D with air despatch; and Section E with mechanical items, while it was the function of the

80 *Supply*

Workshop Section to manufacture small quantities of operational stores and to develop prototypes.[87]

By December 1944 the operational pressures placed on SFDC meant that the depot needed to expand.[88] As part of the planned building work, the facility requested a lecture room, which could be used for dances, as well as a boat testing tank and a swimming pool, but these all were turned down. Permission was given, after much persuasion, for the construction of a canteen. Once completed, the new structure was still too small to accommodate all ranks.[89] The bureaucratic process meant that the expansion was delayed by six months.[90]

Although it was originally intended that the SFDC would be the main depot in the theatre and Jubbulpore's activities would be transferred to the site, SOE's Force 136 never closed the GSI(K) Depot.[91] Control of the depot at Jubbulpore did, however, pass to SFDC's QC Branch, which was responsible for provisions and stores control. At the time that control of the depot passed to the SFDC, the facility at Jubbulpore had grown significantly. For certain items of equipment, GSI(K) Depot held Force 136's entire stock. Although SFDC was in charge of supplies in the theatre, the depot did not always have a clear picture of Force 136's supply consumption. This was partly due to the vast quantities of equipment still held by the GSI(K) Depot, but also because there were a number of other small depots throughout India that supplied South East Asia.[92] Owing to these issues, it was difficult for SFDC to plan for Force 136's equipment requirements.[93]

The SFDC also developed close working relationships with the local military and civil authorities. An ammunition factory at Kirkee not only supplied the depot with considerable quantities of equipment but were also willing to manufacture rush orders based on prototypes and drawings supplied by the SFDC. The SFDC also issued contracts for the manufacture of equipment to Messrs Kemp and Co. and The Metal Box Company of India.[94] Contracts were also placed with The Overseas Supply Company for the preparation and supply of foodstuff in bulk. This company was also willing to erect new factories for the processing of food with no guarantee of the quantity of supplies or the period over which they would be required.[95]

One of the functions allocated to the SFDC was to pack the packages and containers for Force 136's air operations. Built into the original plans for the site was the capacity for the SFDC to expand their packing facilities as required. To assist this depot in filling containers, packing occurred at a number of other locations in the South East Asian Theatre of Operation, including a site in Calcutta.[96] In November 1944, with the prospect of the number of Special Duties Squadrons operating in the theatre increasing to three, Force 136 explored the possibility of establishing a Parachute Package Packing Unit on similar lines to the one at RAF Henlow. It was anticipated that the new unit would be based at SOE's airfield at Jessore and be capable of packing 3,000 containers per month.[97] Although work began on this facility, objections were raised at one of SOE's Council meetings over the 'elaborate and wasteful packing station [that] was being erected' at Jessore.[98]

Supply 81

In South East Asia SOE also operated a Despatch Centre in Ceylon, known as ME82 Ceylon. By October 1943 the centre not only had sufficient storage facilities to accommodate all regional operational stores but also had enough space to pack the supplies.[99] ME82 Ceylon was also responsible for all the stores handled by a packing section based in Sigiriya.[100] In May 1945, following a decision to base a Special Duties Squadron of Liberators in Ceylon, it was decided to develop and expand the packing facilities at Sigiriya and Minneriya.[101] Before the new Air Packing Section, which was to be known as ME143 Air Despatch Ceylon, could be set up, SOE needed to acquire staff who would be responsible for air liaison, administration, handling containers and supervising the despatch of aircraft.[102] On the whole, the work of SOE's packers in the South East Asian Theatre of Operation generally received positive feedback from the field. There were, however, a number of occasions when equipment packed into the containers was found to be damaged, as it had been stored unprotected from the rain.[103]

In addition to the facilities in India and Ceylon, SOE's missions in South East Asia established supply bases in China. To handle all the stores that were transported over the Himalayan 'Hump', a depot was established at Kunming.[104] This facility, known as No. 1 Advanced Base, was responsible for the storage, despatch and handling of personnel and stores on behalf of SOE and the Ministry for Economic Warfare (MEW) (China) in the region.[105]

Over the course of the Second World War SOE established a number of small dumps of equipment around the world. These were formed in anticipation of new fronts opening up. Despite this, there were concerns within SOE that their ability to conduct operations in North and South America was hampered by their lack of equipment. In an attempt to address this, supplies were starting to be stockpiled at STS103 in Canada by June 1942. SOE had also just delivered a considerable stock of equipment to Trinidad. At this point in the war SOE was also establishing dumps of stores throughout South America, including sites in Belize, Peru, Chile and Uruguay.[106] While limpets, incendiaries and plastic explosives were made available to operatives in Recife, SOE's Chief Agents in Peru and Uruguay could access only commercial explosives. SOE also supplied comprehensive instructions for the manufacturing of homemade incendiaries and other devices from readily available items to all chief agents in South America.[107]

Notes

1 SOE and the armed forces also agreed that the costs of these supplies would be written off by the latter (TNA HS 7/46 Appendix A, p. 1).
2 TNA HS 7/46 Appendix A, p. 1.
3 Fredric Boyce and Douglas Everett, *SOE: The Scientific Secrets* (Stroud, 2009), pp. 215, 233.
4 TNA HS 7/46 Appendix C Army Store, p. 5.
5 TNA HS 7/46 Appendix C Army Store, pp. 5, 6.
6 TNA HS 7/46 Appendix C Army Store, p. 5.

82 *Supply*

7 TNA HS 7/46 Appendix A, p. 1.

8 TNA HS 7/46 Appendix A, p. 1. Equipment bearing the trade names of British or allied companies could have serious security implications for SOE's agents in the field. The difficulties SOE faced with external companies were gradually overcome as the organisation developed working relationships with the businesses.

9 TNA HS 7/46 Handbook SOE False Document Section, p. 3. When contracting private companies to manufacture sensitive equipment, SOE had to consider the potential security implications (TNA HS 7/46 Appendix A, p. 1). On 28 August 1942 the Pressed Steel Company, based in Cowley, Oxfordshire, was contracted to manufacture 153 Welman hulls. The company was informed, however, that they were producing 'floats, sweeps, Mk III'. In addition, the manufacturing of the Welmans was compartmentalised, with different components being produced by a number of companies. No one business was given access to the full designs (Boyce and Everett, *SOE*, pp. 131, 133, 215, 233).

10 TNA HS 7/46 History SOE False Document Section, p. 3.

11 TNA HS 7/27 History of the Research and Development Section of SOE, p. 5. It was within the miniature filling factory that SOE's staff could assemble and pack high explosive demolition charges in accordance with contemporary magazine regulations. Despite the facilities at The Frythe and Aston House, neither site had the capacity to produce equipment on a significant scale (TNA HS 7/27 History of the Research and Development Section of SOE, p. 5).

12 Boyce and Everett, *SOE*, p. 215.

13 TNA HS 7/46 E section 1940–45.

14 STS38 was established to prepare Polish agents to operate in hostile territory (Boyce and Everett, *SOE*, pp. 97–8).

15 Boyce and Everett, *SOE*, pp. 97–8.

16 IWM Oral History Niven, Pamela M Catherole 27078 REEL 1 08.00.

17 Boyce and Everett, *SOE*, pp. 97–8.

18 TNA HS 7/49 History and Development of the Camouflage Section 1941–45, pp. 1, 3. Jack Knock, a NCO in SOE, recalled arriving at Station XV and finding the

> gates were unlocked with a huge wire fence. VPs [Vulnerable Police with dogs] all over the place ... transferred up to a nice room, single bed, sheets, pillowcases ... blankets, not army blankets, wardrobes, tables, dressing table, mirror. Went to bed ... woken at 6 o'clock next morning by an ATS [Auxiliary Territorial Service] girl with a mug of tea ... this place had its own private lavatory, bathroom ... I had to you know help myself to breakfast. It was all there ... knife, fork everything provided. No mess tin ...Absolute luxury ... Finished my breakfast ... it was all cleared away for us by hordes of ATS girls.
> (IWM Oral History Knock, Jack Robert Edward 11471 REEL 8 13.45)

19 TNA HS 7/49 History and Development of the Camouflage Section 1941–45, p. 3. Within the grounds of Station XV SOE constructed a prop shop, a textile shop, a carpenters' shop, a printing room, an art department, a compositors' section, a plasterers' shop, a paint shop, a paint spraying shop and a metal workers' shop (TNA HS 7/49 History and Development of the Camouflage Section 1941–45 Photographs). Historic aerial photographs of Station XV indicate that a magazine compound was also constructed in the grounds of the facility. The capacity of the unit at the Thatched Barn expanded to a position whereby they could camouflage over 30 tons of arms and ammunition per month for a single Country Section (TNA HS 7/49 History and Development of the Camouflage Section 1941–45, p. 4). Staff at the Thatched Barn also had the capabilities to test equipment. The pre-war swimming pool located in the grounds was 'practically out of action for swimming because at the bottom of it was three or four

Supply   83

submersible canoes going through testing' (IWM Oral History Knock, Jack Robert Edward 11471 REEL 8 25.15).

20 TNA HS 7/49 History and Development of the Camouflage Section 1941–45, p. 3.

21 The staff at the Thatched Barn manufactured a wide variety of camouflaged material intended destined for SOE's agents in the field, including incendiary cigarettes and briefcases, and explosive logs, bicycle pumps, oil cans, rats, torches, clogs, food tins, coal and animal dung (TNA HS 7/49 History and Development of the Camouflage Section 1941–45 Part I – Devices).

22 IWM Oral History Couper, Joyce Ellen Frances 15482 REEL 1 07.30–14.45.

23 IWM Oral History Couper, Joyce Ellen Frances 15482 REEL 1 14.45.

24 TNA HS 7/27 SOE History Experimental Station 6 (War Dept.) otherwise known as Station XII, pp. 1, 2. The Auxiliary Units were formed in July 1940 by General Ironside and led by Colonel Gubbins. These units would operate behind the enemy lines in the event of an Axis invasion of the UK. See John Warwicker, *With Britain in Mortal Danger: Britain's Most Secret Army of WWII* (Bristol, 2002); David Lampe, *The Last Ditch: Britain's Secret Resistance and the Nazi Invasion Plan* (London, 2007); and Bernard Lowry and Mick Wilks, *The Mercian Maquis: The Secret Resistance Organisation in Herefordshire and Worcestershire during World War II* (Logaston, 2007).

25 TNA HS 7/27 SOE History Experimental Station 6 (War Dept.) otherwise known as Station XII, pp. 1, 2.

26 TNA HS 7/27 History of the Research and Development Section of SOE, p. 5.

27 TNA HS 7/27 History of the Research and Development Section of SOE, p. 7. Following this internal reshuffle Aston House was organised into five new departments: Design, Production, Testing, Laboratory, and Stores and Administration (TNA HS 7/27 SOE History Experimental Station 6 (War Dept.) otherwise known as Station XII, pp. 1, 2). SOE established another depot at the Knoll School, Camberley, Surrey (TNA HS 6/960 Provision of Personnel for Special Training Schools HOR/A/117 11/02/1943). Known as the Camberley Reception Depot (CRD), this unit was responsible for distributing supplies to SOE's UK facilities (TNA HS 7/51 Chapter II: The Headquarters of the Training Section, p. 8 and HS 7/46 Appendix C Army Store, p. 5).

28 TNA HS 7/27 SOE History Experimental Station 6 (War Dept.) otherwise known as Station XII, p. 2.

29 Des Turner, *Aston House Station 12: SOE's Secret Centre* (Stroud, 2006), p. 106. Much to the dismay of the commander of the local fighter squadron, no German aircraft were drawn to the glare of the fire, which was visible for miles.

30 TNA HS 7/27 SOE History Experimental Station 6 (War Dept.) otherwise known as Station XII, p. 2.

31 TNA HS 7/27 SOE History Experimental Station 6 (War Dept.) otherwise known as Station XII, p. 2.

32 Turner, *Aston House Station 12*, p. 204.

33 TNA HS 7/27 SOE History Experimental Station 6 (War Dept.) otherwise known as Station XII, p. 2.

34 TNA HS 7/27 SOE History Experimental Station 6 (War Dept.) otherwise known as Station XII, pp. 1, 3. Until July 1942 all supplies dispatched from Aston House were sent in plain or commercial cover packages. After this date, SOE obtained official classifications from the Explosives Storage and Transport Committee for all of their devices.

35 TNA HS 7/27 SOE History Experimental Station 6 (War Dept.) otherwise known as Station XII, pp. 1, 3. Aerial photographs of Aston House indicate that the magazines were not constructed to contemporary design standards. Despite the non-standard nature of these facilities, the structures were regarded as 'high-class' (TNA HS 7/46 SOE Handbook Supplies Organisation, p. 5).

84 *Supply*

36 TNA HS 7/27 War Diary History of the Arms Section, p. 2.
37 SOE requisitioned the North Road Garage as a temporary solution to house small arms while the armoury was being built at The Frythe (Boyce and Everett, *SOE*, pp. 19, 20).
38 Boyce and Everett, *SOE*, pp. 19, 20.
39 TNA HS 7/27 War Diary History of the Arms Section, p. 2.
40 TNA HS 7/27 Bride Hall.
41 TNA HS 7/27 Bride Hall.
42 TNA HS 7/27 Station VI, pp. 1, 3. SOE acquired a wide range of small arms from a variety of organisations, including the armed services and manufacturers, as well as weapons that had been confiscated by the police (TNA HS 7/27 Station VI, pp. 1, 3).
43 TNA HS 7/27 Station VI, pp. 1, 3. This figure does not include all the other weapons, including rifles and submachine guns, that Bride Hall also handled. Each month between 3,000 and 5,000 pistols and revolvers, together with ammunition, were supplied by the Small Arm Section at Station VI to SOE's Country Sections by (TNA HS 7/27 War Diary History of the Arms Section, p. 6).
44 TNA HS 7/50 History of the Packing Stations within SOE, p. 3.
45 TNA HS 7/50 Services, Supplies and Research 12/11/43; and TNA HS 7/50 History of the Packing Stations within SOE, p. 3. Locating their packing section in close proximity to the RAF's Special Parachute Section allowed SOE's staff to liaise with and learn from their RAF counterparts.
46 The office measured only 9 ft × 8 ft (2.74 m × 2.43 m) (TNA HS 7/50 History of the Packing Stations within SOE, p. 2).
47 TNA HS 7/50 History of the Packing Stations within SOE, p. 2. Between May 1942 and January 1945, SOE's unit at RAF Henlow filled 19,863 packages, manufactured 10,900 harnesses, and modified and packed 27,980 parachutes (TNA HS 7/50 History of the Packing Stations within SOE, p. 2).
48 TNA AIR 2/5203 Storing and maintenance of parachutes 05/06/41.
49 SOE maintained a presence at RAF Henlow for the remainder of the war.
50 TNA HS 7/50 History of the Packing Stations within SOE, p. 1.
51 TNA HS 7/50 Standard packages July 1944. The standard contents for the 'A350', arms and ammunition package, which was packed into a 'C' container, included five Sten guns complete with accessories and magazines, 1,500 9 mm rounds for a Parabellum and ten field dressings (TNA HS 7/50 Standard packages July 1944). On the walls of the buildings in which the containers were packed were content lists for each package. This gave the packers a crib sheet to follow when working. Each package took approximately 10 minutes to fill (IWM Oral History Hughes, Albert 28495 REEL 9 00.30).
52 TNA HS 7/50 Packing, p. 1. At the time the packing section moved to Gaynes Hall the number of staff was ten; this increased to 30 in September 1942, 80 in April 1943, 130 in September 1943 and 150 in March 1944. Over the operational life of Station 61, the staff at this facility handled over 10,000 tons of equipment (TNA HS 7/50 Packing, pp. 1, 2).
53 IWM Oral History Hughes, Albert 28495 REEL 9 03.00.
54 TNA HS 7/50 Packing, p. 1. The quality of the accommodation at Gaynes Hall was questionable. On arriving at Station 61 in July 1944 Albert Hughes and his colleagues

> were all put into one Nissan hut which was like the black hole of Calcutta. So we immediately complained and they put up a huge marque and six of us … went into the marque the rest stayed in the slums. It was so warm they didn't bother to put a ground sheet down … it was beautiful living in there.
>
> (IWM Oral History Hughes, Albert 28495 REEL 8 29.00)

Supply 85

55 IWM Oral History Hughes, Albert 28495 REEL 9 03.30.
56 IWM Oral History Hughes, Albert 28495 REEL 9 03.30.
57 TNA HS 4/349 DCDO/523 09/02/43.
58 TNA HS 4/349 DP/RU/1401 19/02/43, p. 2.
59 To ensure that the containers had the correct centre of gravity, the contents had to be carefully and skilfully packed.
60 TNA HS 7/50 History of the Packing Stations within SOE, p. 3.
61 TNA HS 7/50 Packing, p. 3. Aerial photographs taken of this facility show that the design of the buildings at Area H was similar to that of those at Station 61. It is possible that the construction of this facility was either supervised or undertaken by the MCU or other personnel from SOE (Derwin Gregory, 'Built to Resist: An Assessment of the Special Operations Executive's Infrastructure in the United Kingdom during the Second World War, 1940–1946' (unpublished PhD thesis, University of East Anglia, 2015), p. 151).
62 TNA HS 7/50 Packing, p. 3.
63 TNA HS 7/50 History of the Packing Stations within SOE, p. 4.
64 TNA HS 7/50 History of the Packing Stations within SOE, p. 4.
65 TNA HS 7/46 Appendix C Army Stores, p. 6. Following the invasion, these supplies would have been vital to the Resistance.
66 TNA HS 7/46 Appendix C Army Stores, p. 6. The location of Medical Supplies Packing Station (ME10) is unknown.
67 TNA HS 7/46 Appendix C Army Stores, p. 6.
68 TNA HS 7/169 Visit to Massingham, Cairo, Maryland, Jungle and Naples by L/IT 23rd February/31st March, 1944, p. 5. Throughout 1943 SOE's Force 133 operated a number of packing stations in Libya at airfields in Derna and Torca (TNA HS 7/61 HQ SOM History and Problems, p. 3). In November of that year plans were developed to establish an operational base at San Pancrazio for missions to the Balkans, northern Italy and central Europe. The packing station for this facility would be a joint enterprise between Massingham and Cairo (TNA HS 8/240 *Massingham Monthly Review* for the period ended 2nd November 1943, pp. 1–2). In January 1944 Force 133 moved their packing station to the airfield at Brindisi (TNA HS 7/61 HQ SOM History and Problems, p. 3). The South, East and West African Missions also established substantial dumps of arms, ammunition, explosives and special devices throughout Africa. These were located in Britain's four colonies in West Africa, as well as in Mombasa, in the east. In February 1943 SOE was considering setting up stores inside the Ordinance Store at Simonstown. These dumps would be supplied from SOE in the UK as well as from items obtained locally from army sources (TNA HS 3/11 East African mission: terms of reference and general organisation East African Mission Terms of Reference 02/08/1941, p. 2; TNA HS 3/74 SOE Missions in West and East Africa 26/09/1942, p. 2; and TNA HS 3/83 Report on visit to South Africa 04/02/1943, p. 20).
69 TNA HS 7/169 Visit to Massingham, Cairo, Maryland, Jungle and Naples by L/IT 23rd February/31st March, 1944, p. 5.
70 TNA HS 7/169 Visit to Massingham, Cairo, Maryland, Jungle and Naples by L/IT 23rd February/31st March, 1944, p. 14.
71 Force 133 was the cover name for SOE's operations in the Balkans.
72 TNA HS 7/169 Visit to Massingham, Cairo, Maryland, Jungle and Naples by L/IT 23rd February/31st March, 1944, p. 18.
73 TNA HS 7/119 Force 136 – Jubbulpore Depot – Brief History, p. 1. SOE's facilities at the arsenal were basic. Office furniture had to be assembled from a number of old packing cases (TNA HS 7/119 Force 136 – Jubbulpore Depot – Brief History, p. 1). On 27 May 1942 the magazine (No. 8) that had been allocated to SOE at Jubbulpore burnt down. This contained all SOE's stores, except high

86 *Supply*

explosives and items containing explosives (TNA HS 7/119 GB Stewart Esq c/o Capt AC Brown, ACOO, Jubbulpore Arsenal 28/05/1942, p. 1 and TNA HS 7/119 Important Telegram 457 28/05/1942).

74 TNA HS 7/119 Force 136 – Jubbulpore Depot – Brief History, p. 1.

75 A 'godown' is another name for a warehouse.

76 TNA HS 7/119 Force 136 – Jubbulpore Depot – Brief History, p. 1. The Jubbulpore Depot had close and cordial relations with both civil and military authorities: the Jubbulpore Ammunition and Ordnance Depot, as well as the Gun Carriage Factory and Ordnance Factory, Khamaria, assisted the depot. Staff at the Jubbulpore Depot were encouraged to take part in sport and healthy recreations in their spare time. Within the facility a miniature firing range was constructed that proved very popular with everyone, including members of the Arsenal and Ordnance Depot (TNA HS 7/119 Force 136 – Jubbulpore Depot – Brief History, pp. 3, 4).

77 TNA HS 7/119 Appendix A. Notes on Container Packing (at Jubbulpore), p. 1. Four supervisors oversaw the packers' work (TNA HS 7/119 Appendix A. Notes on Container Packing (at Jubbulpore), p. 1).

78 TNA HS 7/119 Appendix A. Notes on Container Packing (at Jubbulpore), p. 1.

79 TNA HS 1/229 Letter from AD to CD AD/748 21/09/1943, p. 1.

80 TNA HS 7/117 SFDC History, p. 1. The site was approximately 9 miles (14.5 km) from Poona and 2 miles (3.2 km) from Kirkee. Owing to the Special Forces Development Centre's (SFDC) proximity to Mumbai, it was decided that this facility should be the Transit Depot for all the FANYs seconded to SOE arriving in India. This resulted in the expansion of accommodation, so that 100 FANYs could be processed at the SFDC. After the war this facility was used to accommodate personnel awaiting repatriation (TNA HS 7/117 SFDC History, p. 8).

81 TNA HS 7/117 SFDC History, p. 1.

82 TNA HS 7/117 SFDC History, p. 2.

83 The small packing shed had a capacity of 10 tons (TNA HS 7/117 Stores Department, p. 1).

84 TNA HS 7/117 Stores Department, p. 1.

85 TNA HS 7/117 Functions and organisation of Development Section, SFDC, p. 3.

86 TNA HS 7/117 Stores Department, p. 1. As the SFDC was designed to hold only a working stock of supplies, arrangements were made with the S Ordnance Depot, formerly K Sub-Depot, Dehu Ammunition Depot, to allow SOE access to 52,000 ft^2 (4,831 m^2) of storage space at their facility. The S Ordnance Depot also acted as a railhead for the receipt and bulk storage of non-explosive stores for the SFDC. SOE also arranged that the S Ordnance Depot's Group V Depot would take rail receipts and store bulk explosives and ammunition. S Ordnance Depot was approximately 20 miles (32.2 km) from the SFDC, while the Group V Depot was about 8 miles (12.9 km) distant (TNA HS 7/117 Stores Department, p. 2).

87 TNA HS 7/117 History of Development and Production Sections SFDC, January 1944–September 1945, p. 1. The Development Section was designed to be a scaled-down version of SOE's Station XII (TNA HS 7/117 History of Development and Production Sections SFDC, January 1944–September 1945, p. 1).

88 TNA HS 7/117 Stores Department, p. 1.

89 TNA HS 7/117 SFDC History, pp. 5, 8.

90 TNA HS 7/117 Stores Department, p. 1.

91 TNA HS 7/117 Stores Department, p. 1. It was intended that when Jubbulpore Depot was closed the magazines could be handed back to GHQ (TNA HS 7/117 Stores Department, p. 1). In July 1945 Force 136 were also in the process of developing a depot on Lake Victoria in Rangoon (TNA HS 1/325 Letter from HQ(GC) Force 136 to Force 136 Depot, Jubbulpore Z/S.13354 14/07/1945, p. 1).

Supply 87

92 TNA HS 7/117 SFDC History, p. 3. One of the small depots established by SOE in India was located at Fort St George, Madras. In August 1945, for example, an inspection of this depot recorded 200 Sten Guns Mk II, 30,000 rounds of 9 mm ammo, 5,000 explosive clams and 11,991 lbs (5,439 kg) of explosives (TNA HS 7/118 Inspection of Stores held at Madras Insp/B/54 06/08/1945, p. 1).

93 TNA HS 7/117 SFDC History, p. 3.

94 TNA HS 7/117 SFDC History, p. 8. The Metal Box Company, Bombay, also manufactured aluminium containers into which SOE packed medical stores. Until January 1943, medical stores were packed in a building at the EWS(I). With increasing demands for supplies, this facility could no longer cope. Messrs Kemp and Co., Manufacturing Chemists, Bombay, were then contracted to make the containers and pack the supplies (TNA HS 7/116 Medical History Force 136, p. 1).

95 TNA HS 7/117 SFDC History, p. 8.

96 TNA HS 1/281 Force 136 Establishments Summary of Functions 06/05/1945, p. 2. Stores at Calcutta were held in two locations: in Force 136's city compound and in Bally. The former contained an effective stock of equipment that could meet operational demands, while Bally was a legacy facility about which very little was known by the organisation in May 1944 (TNA HS 1/279 Letter from BGS HQ Force 136 to Deputy Commander, HQ Group 'A' Force 136 06/11/1944, p. 1; and TNA HS 7/118 Report on inspection of stores at Calcutta Insp/10 02/05/1944, p. 1).

97 TNA HS 1/279 Letter from Calcutta to London 08/11/1944, p. 1. During an inspection of Jessore in January 1945 containers that were awaiting despatch to the field were stored loose in standard bomb dump bays measuring 30 ft × 33 ft (9.1 m × 10.1 m), which were enclosed on three sides by concrete walls 7 ft (2.1 m) high and roofed with thatching (TNA HS 7/118 Inspection of Stores held in Calcutta/Jessore Insp/31 08/01/1945, p. 6).

98 TNA HS 8/202 SOE Council Minutes of Meeting held on Friday, June 15th, 1945.

99 TNA HS 7/116 Despatch Centre – Ceylon 30/10/1943, p. 2.

100 TNA HS 1/277 QO/GFN/3/902, p. 2. The QMG Branch of ME82 was also responsible for all training stores in Ceylon (TNA HS 1/277 Establishment – ME82 SC/A/WE/20 23/11/1944).

101 TNA HS 1/281 Summary of functions Appendix B to SD/43/115 11/05/1945, p. 1. Supplies were also packed in Ceylon into containers destined for transportation to the field by submarine (TNA HS 7/116 Submarine Despatch Centre Ceylon, p. 6).

102 TNA HS 1/281 Summary of functions Appendix B to SD/43/115 11/05/1945, p. 1.

103 TNA HS 7/105 Operational Report – Wolf (Kengtung SSS) by Maj GE Pennell, RA Appendix IX Stores – General, TNA HS 7/105 Final Report on Operation Tiger and Rabbit Part III – Q; and TNA HS 7/105 Report on Operation Tiger Part III – 'Q'. Concerns were sometimes expressed that the packers were not taking sufficient care when assembling the containers.

104 TNA HS 1/168 SOE China. Arrangements were also made with the Governor of Burma to set up a supply base in Burma to support SOE's operations in China (TNA HS 1/207 History of SOE Oriental Mission, p. 46).

105 TNA HS 1/281 Force 136 Establishments Summary of Functions 06/05/1945, p. 2. Overall charge of No. 1 Advanced Base was given to the Officer Commanding SOE's ME93, which was also located in Kunming (TNA HS 1/131 Directive to OC, ME 93 (Kunming) 10/07/1945, p. 1).

106 TNA HS 7/73 SO in Latin America – its past history, present resources and future possibilities 02/06/1942, p. 4. Despite the construction of dumps by SOE throughout South America, a number of them were not supplied with equipment.

107 TNA HS 7/73 SO in Latin America – its past history, present resources and future possibilities 02/06/1942, p. 4.

88 *Supply*

References

Archives

The National Archives (TNA), London

AIR 2/5203: ROYAL AIR FORCE: Squadrons and Units (Code B, 67/34): Formation of special duty flight: No.138 Squadron.

HS 1/131: M.E.93; Hong Kong volunteers; European personnel.

HS 1/168: Organisation and coordination.

HS 1/207: History of SOE Oriental Mission; Killery Mission.

HS 1/229: Organisation and co-ordination; SEAC stores.

HS 1/277: War establishment: No 82 Ceylon sub-mission.

HS 1/279: Military establishments: 92 (Gurkha Force Nucleus) to 94 (Jedburgh operations).

HS 1/281: Military establishments: 143 (Air Liaison Section) to 145 (Radar, India).

HS 1/325: SCS policy and forward bases.

HS 3/11: East African mission: terms of reference and general organisation.

HS 3/74: West African missions; SIS and SOE; Prof Cassin's report; Franck mission (NEUCOLS and FRAWEST); US cooperation.

HS 3/83: South Africa Mission: reorganisation of SOE; draft directive for mission; prohibited areas adjoining Portuguese East Africa.

HS 4/349: Ministerial correspondence: SOE/FO/NKVD/OSS liaison.

HS 6/960: SKIDAW training; PENNINE – preparations outside Spain to meet possibility of invasion.

HS 7/27: SOE Research and Development section 1938–45.

HS 7/46: E section 1940–45; radio communications division; false document section; supplies organisation.

HS 7/49: History and development of camouflage section 1941–45.

HS 7/50: Planning and supply of air dropping equipment 1941–45.

HS 7/51: Training section 1940–45; industrial sabotage training 1941–44.

HS 7/73: Review of SO activities in Latin America.

HS 7/105: Burma country section: reports on individual operations by staff and operational officers.

HS 7/116: Force 136: Ceylon Despatch Centre; medical section; security section; political warfare section.

HS 7/117: Force 136: Special Forces Development Centre 1943–45.

HS 7/118: Force 136: Inspection Department history and reports; technical stores.

HS 7/119: Force 136: Jubblepore arms depot.

HS 7/169: MASSINGHAM: Special Projects Operational centre (SPOC); operation in Corsica; BALACLAVA naval section; para-naval work.

HS 8/202: Committees: SOE Council minutes.

Imperial War Museum (IWM), London

Couper, Joyce Ellen Frances (Sound Archive interview number 15482).

Hughes, Albert (Sound Archive interview number 28495).

Knock, Jack Robert Edward (Sound Archive interview number 11471).

Niven, Pamela M Catherole (Sound Archive interview number 27078).

Secondary sources

Boyce, Fredric and Everett, Douglas. *SOE: The Scientific Secrets* (Stroud, 2009).

Gregory, Derwin. 'Built to Resist: An Assessment of the Special Operations Executive's Infrastructure in the United Kingdom during the Second World War, 1940–1946' (unpublished PhD thesis, University of East Anglia, 2015).

Lampe, David. *The Last Ditch: Britain's Secret Resistance and the Nazi Invasion Plan* (London, 2007).

Lowry, Bernard and Wilks, Mick. *The Mercian Maquis: The Secret Resistance Organisation in Herefordshire and Worcestershire during World War II* (Logaston, 2007).

Turner, Des. *Aston House Station 12: SOE's Secret Centre* (Stroud, 2006).

Warwicker, John. *With Britain in Mortal Danger: Britain's Most Secret Army of WWII* (Bristol, 2002).

5 Transportation

Once SOE had packed their supplies into containers, they were ready for delivery to the field. The weapons that were sent to the resistance 'were most gratefully received ... [and when the supplies included food,] that was just too wonderful for words'.[1] Not only was transportation vital for getting equipment abroad, it was also essential for getting agents to their area of operation.

Following the Fall of France in June 1940, the Secret Intelligence Service (SIS) came under increasing pressure from the directors of Naval, Military and Air Intelligence to provide a minimum of 72 hours warning of a German invasion. To meet this requirement, it was essential that the organisation had access to intelligence from occupied Europe. The task of smuggling information out of France and transporting agents to the field was assigned to Commander Frank Slocum of SIS's Operations Section. As the RAF had little capacity at the time to support Slocum, he focused his efforts on establishing a maritime link with the French coast. Initially, operations were conducted using any fast surface craft Slocum could borrow. Between 20 June and 12 October 1940, he managed to organise 16 attempts to the north coast of France, five to the Channel Islands, six to Belgium and six to the Netherlands.[2]

Independent of Slocum, another section within SIS was also examining ways to transport agents to the continent. Following his escape from France on 20 June 1940,[3] Section D's Leslie Humphreys was tasked with creating a link back to occupied France, and within a month he was ready to attempt to land three agents by sea. To enable this operation, Humphreys approached Slocum for assistance. At this time SIS's Operations Section was beset by demands on their transport, and as he classed Section D's activities as low priority, Slocum was not willing to support Humphreys. Humphreys, therefore, had to seek out transportation that would be under Section D's exclusive control.[4]

Section D commissioned Captain John Dolphin to locate a small vessel that would be suitable for establishing a line of communication with occupied Europe. The results of this search led to the requisitioning of a Belgium motor yacht moored at Newlyn, Cornwall. Following a refit, the yacht was renamed No. 77. Despite now having the ability to infiltrate agents into

DOI: 10.4324/9781315180106-5

France by sea, the first operation was not undertaken until after the formation of SOE. On 1 August 1940 the crew of No. 77 set sail for France with Captain Gerry Holdsworth of the Intelligence Corps and three agents aboard. Following contact with a German patrol boat, the mission was forced to turn back. For the next ten operations, SOE relied on the services of Slocum's unit; however, all the attempts were abandoned before reaching the French coast. The failure of SIS's Operations Section further strengthened SOE's resolve to run independent transportation networks.[5]

In the autumn of 1940 SOE reassigned Holdsworth, now a commander, to Newlyn. From there he was tasked with finding a suitable location from which a maritime link to France could be established. Eventually, Holdsworth decided to establish his new base on the Helford Estuary, Cornwall.[6] On 5 November 1940, he approached the naval officer-in-charge at Falmouth, Cornwall, to obtain permission to establish this new facility. Authorisation was duly received and the Helford Estuary became a clandestine maritime hub.[7]

Initially, Holdsworth's new base was located at Helston. This site proved to be too far upstream, as vessels found they could access the facility only at high tide. The Helford was then scoured for another suitable location, which was found at Ridifarne, situated on the north bank above the Helford Passage. Because of a natural pool in the estuary at this site, boats could remain afloat at the facility on all tides.[8]

In early 1942 Slocum was attached to Rear-Admiral John Godfrey's Naval Intelligence Division (NID) and was allocated the position of NID (Clandestine). This coincided with the Admiralty issuing a directive placing all SOE vessels at Helford under the operational control of NID. The aim of this was to bring the mission schedules of different organisations under a centralised control. Not only was this intended to restrict the possibility of operations clashing, but the Admiralty could also limit the activities of these units. The Royal Navy felt that too many missions in the English Channels could have led to an increase in enemy patrols. This would compromise the safety of all missions, clandestine or otherwise. With the issuing of this directive, SOE lost its independent maritime link to France.[9]

SOE, however, managed to maintain a sea link to occupied Europe through a connection between Norway and the Shetland Islands. The close proximity of the Scottish islands to Scandinavia, combined with their sparse population, made them ideal for harbouring a clandestine fleet.[10] Plans to establish a land-based facility from which Norwegian fishing boats could operate were first discussed in 1940. Initially conceived as a joint base with SIS, it eventually became a purely SOE operation.[11]

The first shore facility established by SOE on the Shetland Islands was at Lunna House on the Lunna Voe. This overlooked a small bay that provided the Norwegian fishing boats with a natural harbour, sheltered from the waves of the Atlantic Ocean and the North Sea. The physical isolation of Lunna House also hid the activities of the crews from prying eyes.[12] As the war

92   *Transportation*

progressed the existence of a clandestine fleet on the Shetland Islands became common knowledge both locally and in Norway, and eventually the operations were christened the 'Shetland Bus'.[13] By the end of 1941, to help meet increasing operational demands, SOE decided to open a supplementary base on the Scottish mainland. The location for this new facility was Burghead, on the Moray Firth. By the close of the season, the base was operational and under the command of Captain H Marks.[14]

As the war progressed, the remoteness of Lunna House proved counterproductive and it eventually began to affect the flotilla's operational efficiency. The site was accessible via only one road that had been constructed over peat. During the winter months the route was prone to subsidence under the weight of the trucks resupplying the facility. Whenever the road was damaged, the base would be left isolated until it could be repaired. This limited the crews' opportunities for rest and relaxation as well as cutting SOE's shipwrights' access to the islands' pre-existing engineering facilities. In order not to be reliant on Shetland's workshops to maintain ships, SOE would have to have invested in infrastructure at Lunna Voe. The engineers and shipwrights would also have needed access to stockpiles of equipment and materials with which to make the repairs. If these had been provided the base would have been too conspicuous to aerial reconnaissance.[15]

Following a visit to Lunna Voe in 1942 by Colonel John Wilson, head of SOE's Norwegian Section, it was agreed that the 'advanced operational Base had proved [too] remote'.[16] While planning the relocation of the main activities of the clandestine fleet, a decision was taken to retain accommodation at Lunna Voe for the most secret operations.[17] The shortlist of potential sites on the Shetland Islands drawn up by SOE included Lerwick on the east coast and Scalloway on the west. Scalloway was eventually selected for the new base, as Lerwick was deemed too cosmopolitan and the capacity of the harbour was being fully utilised by the Royal Navy. In addition, a maritime engineering firm in Lerwick had offered SOE use of their workshops.[18]

During the process of relocating to Scalloway, SOE requisitioned a number of buildings throughout the town. The facilities – shipwrights' workshops, storage facilities, sergeants' mess and a radio workshop – were based in two condemned houses, a disused coal store, an old weaving shed and a herring-curing station, while staff were housed in four new Nissen huts and an old net factory that had been converted into barracks. Various wooden huts on the edge of Scalloway were also used as accommodation and as an officers' mess. As the number of Norwegian officers employed by the base grew, an empty hotel in the town was acquired for their billets. Behind the main street, a rented property housed the cipher staff and intelligence records. Properties were also taken over to house the motor transport workshop, an armourer, and for storing equipment.[19]

At the time that SOE relocated their activities to Scalloway only one slipway existed on the main island. As this was regularly being used by the Royal Navy, SOE had only limited access to this facility. In order to address this issue, SOE decided to construct their own slipway. It was originally planned that the Admiralty would undertake the building work on their behalf, but when it became clear that work would not start before the winter SOE sought permission to complete the work themselves. Permission was duly received and funding was allocated to the task.[20]

The main challenge faced by SOE's engineers during the construction was that they had no experience of building slipways. To keep costs to a minimum, as SOE was reluctant to ask for further resources in the construction of the slipway, the team scavenged materials from across the islands.[21] Once the necessary equipment had been sourced and assembled, SOE arranged for Royal Navy divers to lay the slipway's concrete ramp.[22] Work on the structure, christened the 'Prince Olav Slipway', was finished in just two months,[23] after which SOE started work on a new pier. As available resources were limited, a pile driver was manufactured from a disused army water tower and used to sink the foundations. The pier was also welded together in an attempt to speed up the construction process.[24]

Although SOE's UK-based operations developed maritime links with both France and Norway, the transportation of agents and supplies by sea was far from ideal. As it was not always possible to beach the ship to unload, stores would have to be transferred to specially designed surf-boats so they could be brought ashore. This procedure could take in excess of one and a half hours to complete, which increased the ships' risk of discovery.[25] Once the agents and supplies had been landed, they then faced a dangerous journey through enemy-occupied territory to their final destination. Patrols, curfews and checkpoints exacerbated the risk faced by agents moving across country.[26] Further challenges to clandestine maritime activities in the European Theatre of Operation occurred on 23 March 1942, when Hitler issued Führer Directive No. 40. This directive gave rise to the Atlantic Wall and the increasing militarisation of the European coastline.[27] It was essential, therefore, that SOE acquired a different means of transportation to deliver supplies and agents to pinpoint locations deep within occupied Europe, and the solution appeared to be aircraft.

It was the opinion of Air Marshal Arthur 'Bomber' Harris, of Bomber Command, that strategic bombing would win the war.[28] This command not only regarded clandestine warfare as 'unethical'[29] but also felt that it was 'an unworthy and inexcusable travesty of our conduct of the war to suggest that our policy is determined [by SOE]'.[30] Harris also viewed the Ministry for Economic Warfare (MEW), as 'amateurish, ignorant, irresponsible and mendacious'.[31] It was not until 21 August 1940 that the RAF eventually released aircraft to form No. 419 (Special Duties) Flight at North Weald airfield, Essex. On 1 March 1941 the flight was disbanded and reformed as No. 1419 (Special Duties) Flight at RAF Stradishall, Suffolk.[32] Two months later, on 16 May, Harris complained that 'only a short while ago strenuous political manoeuvres took place which resulted in our being bullied, quite unnecessarily, into raising the establishment of this flight in aircraft and crews'.[33]

94 *Transportation*

Although political pressure was applied on the RAF to increase the number of aircraft available to the secret services, SOE was not the original recipient of the increased operational capacity. At the 287th War Cabinet meeting held on 14 August 1941, the committee decided that 'sabotage should be generally directed in accordance with the bombing aim policy'.[34] It was also agreed that, in view of the 'paramount importance of good intelligence, the provision of sorties for *SO2 should not be allowed to interfere with the requirements of SIS*'.[35]

Despite the increase in political support for the secret services, the RAF was still reluctant to release aircraft to support the transportation of agents and supplies. On 23 March 1942 Air Chief Marshall Sir Wilfred Freeman KCB DSO MC, vice chief of the Air Staff, berated Harris that his 'command still does not seem to realise ... [the] great importance [of subversive warfare]'.[36] The following month, Freeman reiterated this message when he informed Harris that

> H.M. Government attach the greatest importance to political and *subversive warfare*, for the successful conduct of which the co-operation of your Command is essential. The importance both of propaganda and subversive activities has recently been re-emphasised by the Defence Committee and the Chiefs of Staff Committee.[37]

On 25 August 1941 the RAF disbanded No. 1419 (Special Duties) Flight and reformed it as No. 138 Squadron.[38] The number of aircraft allocated to the secret services operating from the UK increased on 15 February 1942 following the formation of another squadron assigned to special duties, No. 161 Squadron.[39] Initially, Bomber Command equipped these units with inter-war aircraft that were being withdrawn from front line service.[40] By 24 March 1943 the two squadrons had 18 aircraft and No. 138 Squadron had sufficient crews to operate 15 four-engine aircraft, while No. 161 Squadron could only equip five. Combined, these two units were operating at the strength of a normal squadron.[41]

Despite increasing the number of special duty aircraft that were available to the secret services, Harris remained vocal in his objections.[42] Believing that the

> present system of specialising squadrons is extraordinarily wasteful and diametrically opposed to our theory of versatility and economy ... I [Harris] will, accordingly, if these squadrons are returned to me or traded off in lieu of other of my squadrons to Coastal Command, undertake all reasonable requirements now undertaken or foreshadowed by 138, provided they are reasonable.[43]

Although Harris objected to supporting clandestine activities, the number of sorties conducted by No. 138 and No. 161 Squadrons increased significantly after January 1941.[44]

As the number of aircraft based in the UK that were allocated to the secret services increased from 1942, it was felt that a dedicated airfield was required to accommodate them.[45] After much discussion, RAF Tempsford, Bedfordshire, was allocated to No. 138 and No. 161 Squadron. Located on heavy soils and at the bottom of a valley, the airfield was prone to flooding and fog.[46] High ground to the south-east and north-east also restricted the approaches to the airfield. Concerns were, therefore, raised at the time that some of the runways were unserviceable to fully laden bombers during take-off.[47] SOE questioned whether No. 138 Squadron should move to the airfield after the RAF had 'condemned Tempsford as far as their own Squadrons are concerned'.[48] Overall, the base was regarded as a 'poor airfield'.[49] Despite lodging objections with the RAF, No. 138 Squadron was relocated to Tempsford on 11 March 1942, followed by No. 161 Squadron in April.[50]

In an attempt to disguise the activities of RAF Tempsford, an extensive and superfluous camouflage scheme was devised. Developed by Major Jasper Maskeyne and the Royal Engineers' Camouflage Experimental Station, roof slates were removed, windows were deliberately broken, curtains were replaced with sacks and buildings were clad in wood to make them resemble stables.[51] The overall camouflage scheme was intended to make RAF Tempsford appear as if it was a disused airfield.[52] On first arriving at the base in 1942, one anonymous pilot officer thought that

> this must be some elaborate leg-pull for, at a glance, the whole place looked derelict. There was a huddle of buildings roughly the shape and size of Nissen huts but they looked like cowsheds, but I didn't know that until much later. They were grouped round a farm. Its name was Gibraltar Farm. ... There were some hangars, so superbly camouflaged that it took me quite a time to realise that they were hangars ... There were runways, strangely narrow ones channelled out of fields of vegetables. You hardly noticed them. The whole place was odd. Not exactly up to standard ... Gibraltar was a real farm. No doubt about that. But instead of land-girls ... there were more guards hanging around the muckyards and there was a duck-pond.[53]

Running alongside the western edge of RAF Tempsford was the Great Northern Railway. This served as the main rail link between London and Edinburgh. In 1942 the officer commanding 'A' Flight of No. 161 Squadron was on the train and overheard a

> small boy [say] to [his] mother: 'Oh, look Mummy. There's a torpedo on that black Lysander.' Young man: 'That's not a torpedo. That is a long range petrol tank. I wonder what they use them for.' In view of this conversation, and the possibility of an enemy agent being a passenger in one of the 300 trains which pass each day, I thought it advisable to bring this to your attention.[54]

96　*Transportation*

It is possible, therefore, that RAF Tempsford's elaborate camouflage scheme was developed as an attempt to hide the activities of the squadrons from the ground.

The main complex of buildings utilised by SOE at RAF Tempsford was known as Gibraltar Farm and, by 1944, these had been allocated to 'special duties'.[55] It was in these structures that the organisation stored its maps, plans and operational records. Within this group of buildings was Gibraltar Barn, in which agents, who had been transported to the airfield in the back of a blacked-out car, would collect their equipment and undertake final checks before boarding their plane.[56] As the work that was conducted in the barn was top secret, the building was off-limits to most of the airfield's personnel.[57]

By 1942 SOE and the RAF were coordinating their missions through the latter's Intelligence Directorate, AI2(c).[58] All plans made by SOE had to be submitted at the monthly conference with the deputy director of intelligence responsible for Europe (DDI2) and the officer commanding No. 138 Squadron. In practice, it was the squadron that had final say on whether a specific operation could be flown. The decision as to which sorties were to be flown each day was determined by the squadron based on the 12:00 metrological reports.[59] As operational approval was normally given late in the day, there was often little time available for SOE to prepare agents and equipment for despatch.[60]

In addition to transporting agents and supplies, the two special duty squadrons based at RAF Tempsford were tasked with conducting bombing raids.[61] Both DDI2 and the officer commanding RAF Tempsford agreed that No. 138 and No. 161 Squadrons should be employed on bombing operations outside of the moon period.[62] Although SOE's air liaison officer agreed to this in principal, they felt that the aircraft should specialise in low-level, pinpoint hit-and-run missions. Operations of this nature would suit the aircrews' experience of navigating by dead reckoning. As time and resources had been invested in training the aircrews, SOE also expressed concerns over the dangers faced by the aircraft during a bombing mission.[63]

Before a bombing raid was launched, the squadrons required authorisation from higher up in the RAF. On several occasions prior to July 1942, operations had to be cancelled with fully loaded aircraft sitting on the runway ready to take off, as the officer commanding Tempsford could not obtain approval from the Group. The largest obstruction to Bomber Command authorising a mission was that they required details of the intended target by 09:30 on the morning of the operation. Generally, the officer commanding Tempsford would not know what aircraft he had available for raids until later in the day after the meteorological reports came in.[64] Owing to these constraints, aircrews operating out of RAF Tempsford between March 1942 and July 1942 dropped only 82,000 lbs of bombs.[65] The number of bombing operations undertaken by No. 138 and No. 161 Squadrons could have been increased if the agreement procedure 'for these two units were less cumbersome'.[66]

Throughout the Second World War only 'two methods of transporting personnel and equipment to the field are open [to SOE around the world], by air or by sea'.[67] Although air transportation was to prove the more important method for UK-based operations, both means were employed in the other theatres of war. In December 1941 Slocum visited Gibraltar to explore the possibility of establishing a new naval base for clandestine operations in the region. This trip was motivated by the increasingly fortified nature of coastal regions of northern France and the Low Countries. Slocum, therefore, was scoping out less defended beaches on which he could land supplies and agents.[68]

While in Gibraltar Slocum learnt that Poles, Czechs and SOE were already mounting missions from the Rock into the western Mediterranean and along Morocco's Atlantic coast. It was his opinion that the operational sphere's naval and air authorities had insufficient control over these groups. The craft employed on these missions were also inadequate for the task and were often hindered by friendly patrols. Without the various units coordinating their operations, there was the slim possibility that two boats would arrive at the same beach at the same time. By the time of Slocum's visit, these independently operating groups were beginning to annoy the Royal Navy. The small craft would often set out from Gibraltar with no regard to the military situation at sea and without notifying the port authorities. As the Battle of the Atlantic was in full swing, the Royal Navy welcomed Slocum's proposal to take charge and reorganise the clandestine maritime operations based in Gibraltar. Following a series of consultations, Slocum established a Special Flotilla with all existing clandestine craft placed under the control of the captain commanding the Eighth Submarine Flotilla.[69]

The clandestine fleet, which comprised the two small feluccas *Dogfish* and *Seawolf*, was operated by a Polish unit and was known as the Coast Watching Flotilla; it was soon joined by HMS *Tarana*, a modern 347-ton 150-foot (45.7 m) trawler that had been refitted at Portsmouth as a Q-ship. At night this ship, decked out in the appearance of a royal naval vessel, would slip out of Gibraltar flying the White Ensign. By dawn she had undergone a transformation and looked like a typical Portuguese trawler. When the *Tarana* reached her destination, she would be moored offshore while her rowing boat delivered the supplies to the beach.[70]

Within the Mediterranean SOE also conducted maritime operations from Massingham. The first mission conducted by this facility, in December 1942, was to Corsica and used a submarine of the Royal Navy's Eighth Flotilla. Following the island's liberation in September 1943, SOE established a base on Corsica.[71] Known as Balaclava, the facility was set up as a base from which clandestine operations could be launched to the coasts of Italy and southern France by Coastal Forces and high speed craft. Balaclava would also operate as a hub for the transportation of stores and personnel by sea between Corsica, Sardinia, North Africa and southern Italy. In addition, the staff were directed to reconnoitre an unfrequented part of the coast from which they could deliver small boat training as required.[72]

98   *Transportation*

On 28 September 1943 Balaclava's advance party left Algiers for Corsica. On board FPV2017 were enough supplies and equipment to ensure that the new base was self-sufficient for at least three months. Initially based at Calvi, the headquarters moved to Basti three days after the Germans evacuated the city.[73] As the first officer of Balaclava was an American, the base had excellent relations with the nearby units of the United States Army Air Force (USAAF) and the Office of Strategic Services (OSS).[74] From this base, Balaclava would conduct maritime operations each month during the 14 days of the 'non-moon' period. Between missions, the unit repaired boats, conducted trials of equipment and made improvements to their craft. The crews that operated the boats were also kept busy with training exercises and manoeuvres.[75]

In November 1943 SOE's Force 133 began work on an advance base in south-east Italy to support guerrillas operating in the Balkans. This facility was tasked with supplying troops and agents with arms, explosives, warlike stores, food, clothing and medical equipment in addition to providing transportation to the field. It was the responsibility of Brigadier Miles to identify the most suitable location for the base in the Bari-Monopoli-Brindisi area.[76] Eventually a maritime link to the Balkans was established by a sub-unit based at Noci Bari, while air transportation was provided by the RAF's No. 334 Wing at Brindisi airfield. In November 1943 the advance base aimed to deliver 3,000 tons of equipment per month to the Balkans. To achieve this, the unit began building up a working stock of two months' worth of supplies. In addition, a reserve of two months' equipment was stockpiled, totalling 12,000 tons.[77]

To efficiently transport agents and supplies across the Mediterranean and Middle East Theatre of Operations SOE required access to aircraft. During Massingham's early days, the lack of available planes held back operations into Corsica, Italy and the South of France.[78] During 1942 a flight of four Liberators from No. 108 Squadron RAF conducted special operations in the Mediterranean. In May 1943 an additional 14 Halifaxes were added to the flight and the unit was reformed as No. 148 Squadron. The squadron was then mainly involved in delivering supplies for Force 133 to Yugoslavia, although the aircraft made the occasional trip to other Balkan countries. No. 1575 Flight, which was later reformed into No. 624 Squadron, joined No. 148 Squadron in special operations in June 1943. Later in 1943 a further flight, No. 1586 (Polish) Flight, was tasked with special duties in the Mediterranean.[79]

Until the liberation of Corsica towards the end of 1943, there was only, on average, a maximum of four aircraft available each night to conduct operations. As the aircrews and planes would require periods of rest, uninterrupted operations could not be conducted for any great length of time. During the planning of an operation, Massingham's Air Operations Section would liaise with the RAF. The aircraft that were allocated to special duties were mainly based at Blida, Algeria, which was located at the base of the Chrea Mountains, 13 miles (20.9 km) from Massingham.[80] Previously used by the French

Air Force, the facility had the capacity to handle the wide range of different aircraft used for special duties.[81]

In September 1943 a decision was taken to relocate all special duty aircraft involved in supplying the South of France to Brindisi, Italy.[82] These units were formed into No. 334 Wing in November, and the formation assumed control of all special duties aircraft in the theatre. In February 1944 the wing expanded when it was joined by 50 C-47s of the USAAF 62 Troop Carrier Group. At the same time, 18 Savoia-Marchetti SM.82s and 18 Cants of the Italian Air Force, operating from Lecce, were also placed under the control of No. 334 Wing. The following month, No. 267 Squadron joined the wing and, in July, a Russian Air Group consisting of 12 C-47s and 12 Yak fighters was also attached.[83]

In January 1944 Force 133 decided to increase the amount of supplies being delivered to France. This was in anticipation of the imminent invasion of the country.[84] To meet these new demands, No. 624 Squadron was relocated to Blida in February 1944.[85] This move left just one Halifax squadron at Brindisi, reducing Force 133's capacity to deliver supplies to Italy and the Balkans. To replace this loss of aircraft, attempts were made to access a number of C-47s.[86]

The transportation of supplies and agents was also an important component of SOE's work in the South East Asian Theatre of Operations. Although it was possible to travel overland to Burma from India and China and to French Indo-China from China, these long journeys were far from ideal.[87] The preferred means of transportation, as with the other theatres of war, were by sea and air.[88]

The first two agents dropped into Siam in May 1942 departed from the India Air Landing School at Dinjan, Assam. Over the following six months, this base carried out another ten sorties, six successful. In June 1943 No. 1576 (Special Duties) Flight, which was equipped with Hudsons, was formed at Chaklala and tasked with supporting the clandestine services operating in the South East Asian Theatre.[89] On 1 February 1944 the flight was reformed as No. 357 (Special Duties) Squadron.[90] The squadron's A Flight, which comprised Dakotas, Hudsons and Liberators, was initially based at Digri, Bengal, but moved to Jessore in September 1944, while B Flight's Catalinas operated out of Redhills Lake in Madras.[91] After April 1945 the Lysanders of No. 357 Squadron's C Flight flew out of Meiktila, Burma.[92] In May, following the liberation of Rangoon, the flight moved further south, to Mingaladon.[93]

In April 1944 the number of planes available for special duties increased further with the creation of No. 628 (Special Duties) Squadron. This squadron flew Catalinas out of Redhills Lake until it was disbanded in October 1944. In the following month No. 358 (Special Duties) Squadron was formed to support clandestine organisations operating in Asia. In January 1945 the number of aircraft available increased further when No. 160 Squadron was transferred to special duties.[94] The squadron's Liberators, which operated from Kankesanturai and Minneriya, Ceylon, dropped agents and supplies

100 *Transportation*

into Malaya and Sumatra from April 1945.[95] Aircraft flying special duties missions on behalf of Force 136 to Malaya also utilised the airfield on the Cocos Islands from July 1945.[96]

When the aircraft undertaking missions on behalf of SOE reached the drop zone, agents would have to be dropped blind if no reception committee was available.[97] In addition to the normal dangers associated with a blind drop, there was the threat of punji sticks erected in the drop zone. One group of Kachins had a particularly narrow escape when, after overshooting their drop zone in the Burma's Shan States, they discovered that the whole area was covered with these booby traps. Although these were unlikely to kill, wounds could easily turn septic, seriously compromising the mission.[98]

SOE's agents and supplies were also transported by sea in the South East Asian Theatre. Before having access to aircraft, SOE had to rely on the submarines of the Royal Navy. The Admiralty would normally approve these missions only if they fitted in with their routine patrols.[99] Undertaking these operations was dangerous for the submarines, as they had to navigate shallow water to get the agents to their destination.[100] As the submarine could not deliver the agents and supplies directly to shore, collapsible canoes known as 'folboats' would be carried on board. During some of the earlier missions junks would meet the submarines at predefined rendezvous points. Once transferred aboard, these craft would drop the agents and supplies ashore when it was safe[101] – while surfaced and unloading agents and supplies, the submarine was exposed to enemy attack. Journeys in the submarines were hot, cramped and lengthy for SOE's agents; one team spent three weeks at sea before their mission was aborted.[102] Despite the dangers and discomfort associated with this form of transportation, in July 1943 SOE requested permission to establish their own submarine force; however, this came to nothing.[103] The operational need for this fleet disappeared as more aircraft became available for special duties.[104]

To allow agents and supplies to be transported by sea throughout the South East Asian Theatre of Operation without suspicion, SOE managed to acquire a number of locally made vessels.[105] Initially, the London headquarters were adverse to the use of country craft. Owing to the vast distances the boats were expected to cover, their poor quality and the need to get agents and supplies ashore quickly, they regarded these craft as unsuitable. Eventually London withdrew their objections and SOE continued to transport agents and supplies using country craft in South East Asia.[106] Agents and supplies that were to be transported by sea were generally despatched from ME95 Marine Training and Despatch Centre, Trincomalee.[107] Besides training agents in para-naval activities, the base accommodated SOE's operational craft, which included Welmans and Sleeping Beauties.[108]

Although maritime links played a role in SOE's global operations, almost

> every phase of SOE activity is governed by the amount of air transport available. This applies not merely to the forward provisioning of stores,

parachutes and containers, but also to the number of personnel required to be trained, the number of signals links to be served and the size or establishment of all country sections and other installations such as packing stations.[109]

The uncertainty that surrounded SOE's access to aircraft around the globe was a major handicap to forward planning.[110]

Notes

1 Roderick Bailey, *Forgotten Voices of the Secret War: An Inside History of Special Operations during the Second World War* (London, 2008), p. 257.
2 Brook Richards, *Secret Flotillas: Clandestine Sea Operations to Brittany 1940–44 Volume 1* (Barnsley, 2012), pp. 25, 26, 30.
3 Michael Foot, *SOE in France* (London, 1966), p. 21.
4 Richards, *Secret Flotillas Volume 1*, pp. 85–6.
5 Richards, *Secret Flotillas Volume 1*, pp. 86–7.
6 As there were few strategic targets near the Helford Estuary, it was hoped that the development of the base would go relatively unnoticed (Richards, *Secret Flotillas Volume 1*, p. 99).
7 Richards, *Secret Flotillas Volume 1*, pp. 97, 99. Holdsworth's intended area of operation was the Brittany coast (Richards, *Secret Flotillas Volume 1*, p. 97). This rugged coastline, dotted with coves, inlets and uninhabited islands, provided numerous locations where vessels could unload and stockpile stores out of sight (T Le Goff and D Sutherland, 'The Revolution and the Rural Community in Eighteenth-Century Brittany', *Past and Present* 62 (1974), p. 100). The rocky nature of the area meant also that it was unsuitable for a seaborne invasion; German coastal defences were, therefore, less developed (J Kaufmann and Robert Jurga, *Fortress Europe: European Fortifications of World War II* (Conshohocken, 1999), pp. 383, 388).
8 Richards, *Secret Flotillas Volume 1*, p. 99.
9 Richards, *Secret Flotillas Volume 1*, pp. 140–1. Despite losing operational control of the Helford Flotilla, the number of missions undertaken by the NID on behalf of SOE remained relatively constant throughout the war (see Richards, *Secret Flotillas Volume 1*, pp. 304–30).
10 Kaare Iversen, *Shetland Bus Man* (Lerwick, 2004), p. xiii.
11 TNA HS 7/174 History of the Norwegian Section 1940–45, p. 11.
12 David Howarth, *The Shetland Bus: A Classic Story of Secret Wartime Missions across the North Sea* (Lerwick, 2010), p. 88.
13 Howarth, *The Shetland Bus*, pp. 88–9.
14 TNA HS 7/174 History of the Norwegian Section 1940–45, p. 43.
15 Howarth, *The Shetland Bus*, pp. 88–9.
16 TNA HS 7/174 Chapter 1942, p. 40.
17 TNA HS 7/174 Chapter 1942, p. 40.
18 Howarth, *The Shetland Bus*, pp. 88–9.
19 Howarth, *The Shetland Bus*, pp. 95–6.
20 Howarth, *The Shetland Bus*, pp. 95–6.
21 The winch was found discarded on Fair Isle, an engine was removed from a wrecked fishing boat and the tracks came from Aberdeen (Howarth, *The Shetland Bus*, pp. 95–6).
22 The slipway's concrete ramp descended 170 ft (51.8 m) (Howarth, *The Shetland Bus*, pp. 95–6).

102   Transportation

23 The slipway had the capacity to winch vessels up to 110 ft (33.53 m) in length and with a dead weight of 120 tons (Howarth, *The Shetland Bus*, pp. 95–6).

24 Howarth, *The Shetland Bus*, pp. 95–6.

25 Richards, *Secret Flotillas Volume 1*, pp. 197, 250, 263.

26 TNA AIR 20/8242 SOE Air Operations 23/02/1943, p. 1.

27 George Forty, *Fortress Europe: Hitler's Atlantic Wall* (Hersham, 2002), p. 12.

28 Richard Muller, 'The Origins of MAD: A Short History of City-Busting', in *Getting MAD: Nuclear Mutual Assured Destruction, Its Origins and Practice*, ed. Henry Sokolski (Carlisle, 2004), p. 36.

29 Boye Lillerud, '"Flipping the COIN": Unity of Effort and Special Operations Forces', *Security in Practice* 16.752 (2008), p. 20.

30 Charles Webster and Noble Frankland, *The Strategic Air Offensive against Germany 1939–1945*, Vol. 3 (London, 1961), p. 88.

31 Webster and Frankland, *Strategic Air Offensive*, p. 88.

32 Alan Lake, *Flying Units of the RAF: The Ancestry, Formation and Disbandment of all Flying Units from 1912* (Shrewsbury, 1999), p. 84.

33 TNA AIR 2/5203 Minute Sheet 16/05/41.

34 TNA CAB 79/13 287th Meeting War Cabinet 14/08/41.

35 TNA CAB 79/13 287th Meeting War Cabinet 14/08/41. Author's emphasis.

36 TNA AIR 20/2901 Letter from Freeman to Harris 23/03/1942. Author's emphasis.

37 TNA AIR 20/2901 S.46368/III/VCAS 16/04/1942. Author's emphasis.

38 Jeff Jefford, *RAF Squadrons: A Comprehensive Record of the Movement of all RAF Squadrons and Their Antecedents since 1912* (Shrewsbury, 2001), p. 63.

39 Lake, *Flying Units of the RAF*, p. 233.

40 Jefford, *RAF Squadrons*, pp. 63, 66.

41 TNA AIR 14/1121 3G/S.8009/59/SOA 24/03/43.

42 TNA AIR 20/2901 ATH/DO/6 28/03/1942, p. 1.

43 TNA AIR 20/2901 ATH/DO/6 28/03/1942, p. 1.

44 TNA AIR 20/8255, TNA AIR 20/8334, TNA AIR 20/8343 and TNA AIR 20/8252.

45 TNA AIR 14/1121 RAF Station Tempsford 3G/S8730/29/Org 24/03/1942.

46 TNA AIR 14/1120 JEAB/DO/90 20/01/1942, p. 2. When deciding where to build an airfield, soil type, drainage, obstructions to flying and access to local hardcore and brick supplies were all taken into account (David Smith, *Britain's Military Airfields 1939–45* (Wellingborough, 1989), p. 46).

47 TNA AIR 14/1120 JEAB/DO/90 20/01/1942, p. 2.

48 TNA AIR 20/8343 GC Ops 06/09/1941.

49 TNA AIR 14/1120 ACASI/38A/42, p. 1.

50 Jefford, *RAF Squadrons*, pp. 63, 66. The main satellite airfield for No. 138 and No. 161 Squadrons was RAF Tangmere, West Sussex. This was also home to 11 Group Fighter Command and 84 Group 2 Tactical Air Force (TAF) (Jonathon Falconer, *RAF Airfields of World War 2* (Hersham, 2012), pp. 187–9). Aerial photography of RAF Tempsford indicates that it was constructed as a standard Class A bomber airfield. Initially, four T2 type hangars were erected, but by the end of 1942 a further B1 type hangar had been built to the south of the site. In 1943 two further T2 hangars were constructed to the north of the airfield. Tempsford also had 47 pan hardstandings and four Blister hangars.

51 Aerial photographs show that the airfield's runways were painted to resemble field patterns in an attempt to break up their outlines (English Heritage FNO/141 8OTU 08/09/1942 3).

52 Bernard O'Connor, *RAF Tempsford: Churchill's Most Secret Airfield* (Stroud, 2010), p. 19. The attention to detail of RAF Tempsford's camouflage scheme

was potentially excessive. At the height at which the Luftwaffe reconnaissance pilots were flying, Maskeyne's minor architectural features would have been invisible. It would also not have been possible to hide the obvious signs of human occupation, including pathways, tyre marks and aircraft.

53 Quoted in O'Connor, *RAF Tempsford*, pp. 196–7.

54 TNA AIR 40/2579 Security 22/07/1942.

55 During the construction of RAF Tempsford, a number of pre-existing buildings located within the perimeter track were retained and utilised by the RAF and branches of the secret service. Another complex of buildings classified as 'special duties' appear on the 1944 site plan, on the airfield's southern perimeter track (RAF Museum Tempsford Record Site Plan DGW 4330/44). It is likely that these structures accommodated SIS personnel.

56 It was in Gibraltar Barn that agents would be checked to ensure they did not have any compromising material about their person. All bus tickets and postage stamps, for example, would have to be confiscated before they boarded their plane.

57 O'Connor, *RAF Tempsford*, pp. 19, 49, 60.

58 TNA HS 4/143 Air Policy 06/04/1942, p. 1.

59 The Squadron would occasionally make a decision about whether a sortie could be flown later in the day using the 14:00 Metrological Reports (TNA HS 4/143 Air Policy 06/04/1942, p. 1).

60 TNA HS 4/143 Air Policy 06/04/1942, pp. 1, 2.

61 At around the time No. 161 Squadron relocated to RAF Tempsford, in April 1942, construction of the airfield's bomb dump was completed (TNA AIR 28/820 Operations Record Book April 1942, p. 2).

62 TNA AIR 20/8170 OB Ops 6598 22/07/42.

63 TNA AIR 20/8170 Special Targets for 138 and 161 Squadrons: Notes of meeting at Tempsford on the 12th July, 1942.

64 TNA AIR 20/8170 OB Ops 6598 22/07/42.

65 Eighty-two thousand pounds of explosives was equivalent to six fully loaded Halifaxes. Each Halifax could carry a maximum of 13,000 lbs of explosives (Kenneth Merrick, *Halifax: An Illustrated History of a Classic World War II Bomber* (London, 1980), p. 223).

66 TNA AIR 20/8170 OB Ops 6598 22/07/42.

67 TNA AIR 20/8242 SOE Air Transport Requirements 01/01/1942, p. 1.

68 Brook Richards, *Secret Flotillas: Clandestine Sea Operations in the Western Mediterranean, North African and the Adriatic 1940–1944 Volume 2* (Barnsley, 2013), p. 88.

69 Richards, *Secret Flotillas Volume 2*, pp. 89–90.

70 Nicholas Rankin, *Defending the Rock: How Gibraltar Defeated Hitler* (London, 2017), pp. 434–5.

71 TNA HS 7/169 Part VII Operations from Massingham, p. 3.

72 TNA HS 7/169 Balaclava – Naval Section September 1943 to August 1944, p. 1.

73 SOE's Balaclava was the first Special Service unit to arrive in Corsica with the intention of using the island as a base of operations (TNA HS 7/169 Balaclava – Naval Section September 1943 to August 1944, p. 1).

74 In addition to Balaclava, Basti was home to the headquarters of the USAAF 63rd Fighter Wing, Coastal Forces, Inter-Service Liaison Department (ISLD, a cover name for the SIS) and OSS (TNA HS 7/169 Balaclava – Naval Section September 1943 to August 1944, pp. 1–2).

75 TNA HS 7/169 Balaclava – Naval Section September 1943 to August 1944, pp. 1–2.

76 Force 133 also operated a small craft facility at Haifa for operations to Greece and in the Aegean Sea (TNA HS 7/170 Section XVIII Special Seaborne Operations, p. 2).

104   *Transportation*

77 TNA HS 7/170 GHQ Middle East Forces Directive NO187 26/11/1943, pp. 1, 2–3.
78 TNA HS 7/169 Part VII Operations from Massingham, p. 1.
79 TNA HS 7/170 Section XVI Results of Air Operations, pp. 1–2.
80 From the middle of 1944, when American aircraft became available for work into the south of France, another airfield in Algeria, Maison Blanche, was also used for special operations (TNA HS 7/169 Part VII Operations from Massingham, p. 1).
81 TNA HS 7/169 Part VII Operations from Massingham, p. 1. Studies were conducted on the viability of using Catalinas for special operations in the Adriatic, but it was determined that these aircraft would be vulnerable to enemy fighters while on the water off enemy-occupied territory (TNA HS 7/169 Para-naval work in the Western Mediterranean, p. 2).
82 In November 1943 it was proposed to establish an operational base at San Pancrazio for missions into the Balkans, northern Italy and Central Europe. The packing station would be a joint enterprise between Massingham and Cairo (TNA HS 8/240 Massingham Monthly Review for the period ended 2nd November 1943, pp. 1–2). In November 1944, owing to the oncoming winter weather and poor flying conditions, plans were also developed to establish a joint SOE OSS airfield in France. It was intended that this base would infiltrate supplies and personnel into Piedmont, Italy. As a result of the obstructionist attitude of the local French command only a limited amount of stores and personnel was infiltrated into Italy. During the Franco-Italian border dispute of May 1945, the base proved to be a highly profitable source of intelligence (TNA HS 7/170 Section IV Resisting in Italy, p. 4).
83 TNA HS 7/170 Section XVI Results of Air Operations, pp. 1–2.
84 In July 1944 the Mediterranean Allied Airforce was considering providing an airfield in the Livorno area as a forward base for the air supply of southern France. It was anticipated that the base might also be used to supply partisan forces in north-west Italy. If the base was established two squadrons of Dakotas would be based at the airfield. This facility would also require the support of a packing station (TNA HS 3/163 Directive G/805 26/07/1944, p. 1).
85 TNA HS 7/170 Section XVI Results of Air Operations, pp. 1–2.
86 TNA HS 7/61 HQ SOM History and Problems, p. 4.
87 The ideal location for a base from which SOE could penetrate Japan and Manchuria was Siberia. Before the USSR entered the war, SOE was adverse to the idea. When Germany invaded the USSR there was an opportunity to establish a mission in Siberia. The outbreak of war with Japan intervened before London submitted plans for an exchange of missions. With the collapse of British forces in the East hopes for a Siberian base ended (TNA HS 1/207 History of SOE Oriental Mission, pp. 8–9).
88 Charles Cruickshank, *SOE in the Far East* (Oxford, 1983), p. 32.
89 Cruickshank, *SOE in the Far East*, p. 32.
90 Alan Ogden, *Tigers Burning Bright: SOE Heroes in the Far East* (London, 2013), pp. 28–9.
91 Cruickshank, *SOE in the Far East*, p. 32. The Catalina flying boat enabled SOE to insert and extract parties offshore or in wide rivers (Ogden, *Tigers Burning Bright*, p. 30).
92 The Lysanders would land on makeshift jungle airstrips to deliver supplies and agents. At Mewaing, Burma, a 600-yard (548.6 m) all-weather strip was constructed from split bamboo (Cruickshank, *SOE in the Far East*, pp. 33–4).
93 Cruickshank, *SOE in the Far East*, p. 32. In June 1945 it was hoped that a single airfield close to Rangoon could provide accommodation for all special duty aircraft. Ideally, this facility would support Liberators and Dakotas and take the place of RAF Jessore. Owing to the difficulties in building an airstrip capable

of handling heavy bombers that was reliable during the monsoon, this facility was never constructed (TNA HS 1/325 SD Operations – Bases in Burma 13/06/1945, p. 1).

94 On 31 July/1 August 1945 a Liberator of No. 160 Squadron, flown by Flight Lieutenant JA Muir, was airborne for 24 hours 10 minutes. This mission was from Minneriya to Kota Tinggi and the crew spent 85 minutes over the target area (Cruickshank, *SOE in the Far East*, p. 33).

95 Cruickshank, *SOE in the Far East*, pp. 32–3.

96 TNA HS 7/111 Extracts from Despatch on Air Operations, SEA, by ACM Sir Keith Park 3rd May – 12th September, 1945, p. 4.

97 The dropping of agents could be 'camouflaged' by synchronising missions with bombing raids. Leaflets would also be dropped along the flight path to try and convince the enemy that the aircraft was on a routine propaganda sortie (Cruickshank, *SOE in the Far East*, p. 36).

98 Cruickshank, *SOE in the Far East*, p. 34.

99 Cruickshank, *SOE in the Far East*, p. 36.

100 Ogden, *Tigers Burning Bright*, p. 27.

101 Cruickshank, *SOE in the Far East*, pp. 36–7.

102 Ogden, *Tigers Burning Bright*, p. 27.

103 In September 1943 submarines were SOE's preferred means of transport to delivery agents and supplies to Burma, Malaya and Sumatra. At the time, SOE had occasional access to two Dutch submarines based at Colombo. Operations had to fit around patrols and resulted in fewer than one sortie per month (TNA HS 1/229 SOE – Far East Group Transport Facilities and Requirements September 1943, p. 1). Submarines of the Royal Navy were also the only means of reaching the Andaman Islands and Malaya from 1942 to December 1944. These craft were based at Colombo and Trincomalee (TNA HS 7/116 Submarine Despatch Centre Ceylon, p. 7).

104 Cruickshank, *SOE in the Far East*, p. 36.

105 In September 1943 SOE's Marine Section was temporarily located in Calcutta (TNA HS 1/229 SOE – Far East Group Transport Facilities and Requirements September 1943 Chart No. II).

106 The Royal Navy also operated a fleet of motor launches on behalf of SOE's India Mission (Cruickshank, *SOE in the Far East*, p. 101).

107 Cruickshank, *SOE in the Far East*, pp. 17, 100–1.

108 TNA HS 1/280 WE for ME No. 95 SD/23/99 18/12/1944, p. 1. ME95 also held operational stores that were issued to those agents despatched to the field from this facility.

109 TNA HS 7/61 HQ SOM History and Problems, p. 4.

110 TNA HS 7/61 HQ SOM History and Problems, p. 4.

References

Archives

The National Archives (TNA), London

AIR 2/5203: ROYAL AIR FORCE: Squadrons and Units (Code B, 67/34): Formation of special duty flight: No.138 Squadron.

AIR 14/1120: Specialist units at Tempsford Beds and satellites location and administration.

AIR 14/1121: Specialist units at Tempsford Beds and satellites location and administration.

AIR 20/2901: Special Operation Executive operations: aircraft.

106   *Transportation*

AIR 20/8170: OPERATIONS: France and Low Countries CODE 55/2/3: Special targets to be bombed by 138 and 161 Squadrons.

AIR 20/8242: ROYAL AIR FORCE: Squadrons and Units (Code 67/34): 138 Squadron (1419 Flight): policy.

AIR 20/8252: OPERATIONS: General (Code 55/1): RAF Tempsford: daily summaries of special operations.

AIR 20/8255: OPERATIONS: General (Code 55/1): RAF Tempsford: monthly operation statistics.

AIR 20/8334: OPERATIONS: General (Code 55/1): 1419 Flight (later 138 Squadron): operational reports.

AIR 20/8343: OPERATIONS: General (Code 55/1): 138 and 161 Squadrons: general.

AIR 28/820: TEMPSFORD.

AIR 40/2579: 419 (SD) Flight [later, 138 (SD) Squadron]: operations.

CAB 79/13: Minutes of meetings nos. 251–300.

HS 1/207: History of SOE Oriental Mission; Killery Mission.

HS 1/229: Organisation and co-ordination; SEAC stores.

HS 1/280: Military establishments: 95 (Marine Research Training Centre) to 100 (HQ Australia), 121, 122 and 141.

HS 1/325: SCS policy and forward bases.

HS 3/163: Mediterranean Group: Moli di Bari HQ; operational directives to country sections and stations.

HS 4/143: Poles and Czechs: combined policy; air policy; Poles in South America; SOE relations with OSS; sabotage; secret armies; third front.

HS 7/61: History of HQ SOM (Special Operations Mediterranean) by Lt Col Beevor and Lt Col Pleydell Bouverie; 15th army group liaison mission to German C-in-C, south west by Colonel H M Threlfall.

HS 7/111: SOE oriental mission May 1941–Mar 1942; historical narrative South East Asia Command (SEAC) Theatre SOE India , May 1942–Aug 1945; air operations in support May-Sept 1945.

HS 7/116: Force 136: Ceylon Despatch Centre; medical section; security section; political warfare section.

HS 7/169: MASSINGHAM: Special Projects Operational centre (SPOC); operation in Corsica; BALACLAVA naval section; para-naval work.

HS 7/170: Allied Forces Headquarters (AFHQ) special operations Mediterranean theatre 1942–45.

HS 7/174: Norwegian section 1940–45.

HS 8/240: Directors and heads of sections: Massingham (the Algiers base operating into France).

RAF Museum, London

DGW 4330/44 Tempsford Record Site Plan.

Secondary sources

Bailey, Roderick. *Forgotten Voices of the Secret War: An Inside History of Special Operations during the Second World War* (London, 2008).

Cruickshank, Charles. *SOE in the Far East* (Oxford, 1983).

Falconer, Jonathon. *RAF Airfields of World War 2* (Hersham, 2012).

Foot, Michael. *SOE in France* (London, 1966).

Forty, George. *Fortress Europe: Hitler's Atlantic Wall* (Hersham, 2002).

Howarth, David. *The Shetland Bus: A Classic Story of Secret Wartime Missions across the North Sea* (Lerwick, 2010).

Iversen, Kaare. *Shetland Bus Man* (Lerwick, 2004).

Jefford, Jeff. *RAF Squadrons: A Comprehensive Record of the Movement of all RAF Squadrons and Their Antecedents since 1912* (Shrewsbury, 2001).

Kaufmann, J and Jurga, Robert. *Fortress Europe: European Fortifications of World War II* (Conshohocken, 1999).

Lake, Alan. *Flying Units of the RAF: The Ancestry, Formation and Disbandment of all Flying Units from 1912* (Shrewsbury, 1999).

Le Goff, T and Sutherland, D. 'The Revolution and the Rural Community in Eighteenth-Century Brittany', *Past and Present* 62 (1974), pp. 96–119.

Lillerud, Boye. '"Flipping the COIN": Unity of Effort and Special Operations Forces', *Security in Practice* 16.752 (2008).

Merrick, Kenneth. *Halifax: An Illustrated History of a Classic World War II Bomber* (London, 1980).

Muller, Richard. 'The Origins of MAD: A Short History of City-Busting', in *Getting MAD: Nuclear Mutual Assured Destruction, Its Origins and Practice*, ed. Henry Sokolski (Carlisle, 2004).

O'Connor, Bernard. *RAF Tempsford: Churchill's Most Secret Airfield* (Stroud, 2010).

Ogden, Alan. *Tigers Burning Bright: SOE Heroes in the Far East* (London, 2013), pp. 28–9.

Rankin, Nicholas. *Defending the Rock: How Gibraltar Defeated Hitler* (London, 2017).

Richards, Brook. *Secret Flotillas: Clandestine Sea Operations to Brittany 1940–44 Volume 1* (Barnsley, 2012).

Richards, Brook. *Secret Flotillas: Clandestine Sea Operations in the Western Mediterranean, North African and the Adriatic 1940–1944 Volume 2* (Barnsley, 2013).

Smith, David. *Britain's Military Airfields 1939–45* (Wellingborough, 1989).

Webster, Charles and Frankland, Noble. *The Strategic Air Offensive against Germany 1939–1945*, Vol. 3 (London, 1961).

6 Communications

It was essential that a reliable and efficient communication system existed between the areas of operation and SOE's headquarters; without this link, agents and the global resistance would have been isolated. Wireless communications were vital for reporting enemy activities, arranging for the extraction of personnel, coordinating operations and organising missions.[1] In the field, wireless operators were highly prized by the resistance.[2] SOE was quick to appreciate the value of two-way wireless traffic and invested in the development of a global communication network.

Despite the importance of communications to clandestine operations, SOE was not always responsible for their own networks. On the formation of the organisation the Secret Intelligence Service's (SIS) Colonel Claude Dansey argued that they should retain control of SOE's wireless networks.[3] The head of SIS Sir Stewart Menzies, 'C', was also

> absolutely opposed to any other Secret W/T [wireless telegraphy] Service being set up in the U.K. I fought long enough to try and maintain one Secret Service, and this would be another step in the wrong direction, apart from the unlikelihood of S.O.2 being able to set up anything for many months which would give efficient results.[4]

In September 1940 SOE finally agreed that all traffic originating from within the organisation was to be handled by SIS. Under this arrangement Menzies maintained the right to reject any message he deemed compromising to SIS's security.[5] SOE was under no illusion that 'C. telegrams take complete preference over [ours]'.[6]

At the outbreak of the Second World War, it was the responsibility of SIS's Section VIII to communicate with agents operating abroad.[7] Initially, the organisation based their home station facilities in the main house at Bletchley Park. By the end of 1939 the limited capacity of this site meant that plans were drawn up to relocate the unit to Whaddon Hall, Buckinghamshire. SIS's new base, which became known as the 'Main Line' station, was responsible for handling the organisation's traffic from embassies and overseas

DOI: 10.4324/9781315180106-6

missions, and covert stations on the continent, and occasionally for communicating directly with agents.[8]

In May 1940 SIS began work constructing their first wireless facility dedicated to handling agents' traffic alone. By the autumn of that year work on the new receiver station at Nash, Buckinghamshire, was complete. The finished complex comprised a shed, in which the receiving equipment was installed, and a brick-built generator building with attached battery store. SIS opened a second receiver station along similar lines at Upper Weald, Buckinghamshire later in the war.[9] The transmitters for both of these facilities were located at Manor Farm, Calverton, Buckinghamshire.[10]

SIS's receiver at Nash was staffed by a complement of nine men on a three-watch system using non-standardised equipment. One member of this team, Jack White, recalled that the station operated eight receivers: seven HROs, manufactured by the National Radio Company, and his personal battery operated AR88. At Manor Farm SIS assembled a collection of various American 750W and British 100W and 30W transmitters. To ensure that the American equipment was maintained effectively, four engineers from the US Civilian Technical Corps were based at this facility.[11] Among Section VIII's staff responsible for handling wireless traffic, there was a feeling that SIS viewed communicating with their agents as a lower priority than intercepting enemy transmissions.[12] Even within SOE there was an awareness 'that the information which "C" gets from his own direct agents in foreign countries represents what I would call an almost negligible proportion of the total information which he receives from wireless intercepts (Order of Battle)'.[13]

It was inevitable that because another organisation, which would inevitably prioritise their own communications, controlled SOE's wireless networks, there would be delays in the processing and handling of SOE messages. As SOE grew, and the organisation generated more traffic, these holdups would be exacerbated.[14] By March 1942 SOE had noticed that despite their messages being marked as highest priority, they were not being handled in an appropriate manner. On further investigation the organisation determined that it took SIS four days to deliver a telegram from SOE's Balkans or Middle East Missions back to the UK.[15] Of even greater concern to SOE was the ability of C to impose a form of 'inquisitive censorship over the whole of our [SOE's] activities'.[16]

By controlling SOE's wireless networks, SIS was also able to limit the former's capacity to send agents abroad. It was the opinion of some within SIS that they had the authority to restrict the number of agents SOE handled to 'the capacity of the receiving scheme ... [and] by the fact that to increase the number to any extent will constitute a menace to security'.[17] During April 1941 between 300 and 400 SOE recruits were undergoing training in the UK.[18] This number of prospective agents, however, was too many for the 'necessary arrangements made by S.I.S. for the reception of their messages as and when they arrive in the countries where it is proposed that they should operate'.[19]

110   *Communications*

As SIS's handling of SOE's communications was having a negative impact on the latter, SOE realised that they needed to control their own networks. While discussions were ongoing between SOE and SIS, SOE began construction on their new wireless stations. By December 1941 work was underway on the facility at Grendon Underwood, Buckinghamshire. On the 17th of that month, however, SOE's Captain Chalk reported that with the 'present section [of personal at Grendon Underwood] and the possible opening of the [wireless] station in March, I feel that I shall almost be forced to attempt to operate almost every channel myself during the first month or two'.[20] In Chalk's opinion, the operators' work was 'bad even for army standards. It will be quite impossible for any of them to be good enough for their proposed job for some months after their arrival at the station'.[21]

In February 1942 SIS finally agreed to transfer operational control of SOE's wireless traffic to the organisation. One of the conditions of this agreement was that SOE had to ensure that all necessary 'security requirements were met'.[22] C also retained the right to reduce the number of channels operated by SOE if it was

> found that interference or embarrassment to S.I.S. communications resulted ... One more condition ... is that it must be clearly understood that S.O.E. will not, under any circumstances, undertake any communications for the representatives of any Allied Power without reference to me.[23]

On 27 March 1942 SOE agreed to SIS's conditions.[24] SOE began preparing for the transfer of control and were ready to handle some of their own traffic by 22 May 1942.[25] A partial handover of the wireless networks then occurred on 1 June.[26] Nine days later, SOE felt that they were only just 'now *starting* to run our own wireless communications'.[27]

SOE's first Home Station was known as Station 53a. The receiver was located at Grendon Underwood, Buckinghamshire, while the transmitter was based in Charndon, Buckinghamshire.[28] The establishment of the receiver did not, however, occur without incident. Despite the discussion of this facility by SOE and SIS for a number of months, Captain Richard Gambier-Parry, head of SIS's Section VIII, began protesting in April 1942 that he had only just been informed of the wireless station's location.[29] It had, however, been Gambier-Parry who suggested that SOE should establish their new receiver at Grendon Underwood.[30] His concerns were over the proximity of SOE's site to his most important receiving stations and the possibility of interference, as both organisations worked within the same frequency band.[31] On 13 April 1942 Gambier-Parry was of the opinion that:

> it would be much better if we went into the matter now between our two selves and settled any possible causes of future disagreement before they arise, rather than wait until we have to take them formally to the W/T

Board, should your detailed proposals be of a nature likely to cause embarrassment to existing services. As you will remember, there is a clause in 'C's letter to C.D. [the head of SOE] covering this particular point, and reserving to him the right to ask you to curtail your activities should they result in interference with existing services. It therefore makes it obviously desirable that we should start right and not get into a position where friction might result.

I imagine that with the establishments your organisation possesses up and down the country, there should be no difficulty in finding a place for your W/T centre which could not possible involve 'C' in having to fall back on his rights in the matter.[32]

Eventually SOE convinced SIS to drop their objections to Grendon Underwood. Initially, SOE established the Signal Office of the Home Station in a downstairs room of the main house. The transmitter for this station was located in a small purpose-built structure in the hamlet of Charndon.[33] This facility was connected to Grendon Underwood by a 20-pair cable that enabled the 18 250W transmitters to be operated by remote control. As the activities of SOE abroad expanded, however, the capacity of Grendon Underwood and Charndon proved insufficient to handle the increasing traffic volume, resulting in a considerable loss of efficiency and flexibility in SOE's wireless networks.[34] In addition, by June 1942 the organisation was facing equipment shortages. On the 28th of that month SOE expressed concerns that the 'manufacturers have not yet been able to supply the R.A.F., and in turn us, with the quantity [of receivers] that we require for working'.[35]

In order to address the overcrowding caused by attempts to increase Grendon Underwood's capacity, SOE began constructing a new signal office within the estate in October 1942. This structure proved a considerable improvement over the existing facilities in the main house. Within the new Signal Office 18 operating positions were installed, four of which were equipped for automatic sending. The superintendent who oversaw the wireless operators had the ability to connect any position to any transmitter from their desk. In addition, the superintendent was provided with the necessary equipment to monitor all the receivers. While SOE was upgrading Grendon Underwood's Signal Office, work also began on expanding the transmitter complex at Charndon.[36]

Although this programme of work increased SOE's capacity in the UK to handle wireless traffic, demand continued to outstrip capacity. At a SOE Communications Committee meeting held on 19 August 1942, the possibility of establishing an additional Home Station was raised.[37] Eventually, a decision was taken to construct a purpose-built structure instead of adding to the pre-existing facilities.[38] The proposed function of the new station was to lighten Grendon Underwood's workload.[39] On 14 December 1942 SOE began construction on their second Home Station, which was to be known as Station 53b.[40]

112   *Communications*

When completed in March 1943 the receiver complex, at Poundon, Oxfordshire, was substantially larger than SOE's first facility at Grendon Underwood.[41] Installed in the main building were 40 operating positions, of which over half were adapted for automatic sending. In an attempt to economise on antennae, SOE installed new Wide Band Receiving Amplifiers at Poundon. This arrangement meant that as many as 50 receivers could be operated simultaneously from each amplifier.[42] The transmitter site for Station 53b was located nearby, at Godington. Into the purpose-built structure SOE installed 34 250W transmitters, together with their remote control apparatus.[43] Connecting all this equipment required over 6,000 ft (1,828.8 m) of lead-covered wire. To ensure that malfunctioning equipment could be quickly replaced, SOE mounted the transmitters at Godington on a series of platforms.[44] The structure that housed the transmitters was designed to be large and airy, with banks of equipment arranged along the two main walls.[45] SOE's layout of Station 53b's transmitter and receiver site were in keeping with contemporary design standards.

To reduce the likelihood of radio detection units pinpointing the transmitter's location, it was highly desirable that agents operated in the same frequency for short periods. It was, therefore, essential that the wireless staff based in SOE's Home Stations could change the frequency of every transmitter with great speed.[46] The 250W transmitters that SOE had access to took 4–5 minutes on average to achieve this transition. In an attempt to reduce this time, SOE began developing new wireless equipment for their Home Stations. The result of this research was a Wide Band Transmitting Amplifier that worked with a three-wire rhombic antennae. The new equipment not only provided a good radio signal over a wide area but also allowed the Home Station to transmit on 12 channels simultaneously.[47] More importantly, the set-up enabled SOE's Home Station wireless operators to change frequency in as little as 30 seconds.[48]

Despite the installation of the Wide Band Transmitting Amplifiers at Godington, SOE still lacked the capacity to handle all wireless traffic being sent from and received in the UK. In an attempt to address this, it was decided to upgrade Station 53a's transmitter at Charndon. Instead of installing the Wide Band Transmitting Amplifiers into the existing structure, a new building was constructed based on Godington's design. This new space not only allowed SOE to increase the number of transmitters it operated but also allowed them to install a new 'trouble-free' remote control system.[49]

On 14 December 1942 Colonel William 'Wild Bill' Donovan, CD's opposite number in the Office of Strategic Services (OSS), was informed by SOE that they were developing plans for a third UK Home Station.[50] By January 1943 SOE proposed that this new facility, which would be named Station 53c, should be built, equipped, staffed and operated by the OSS.[51] Under these plans, the new Home Station, despite being staffed by Americans, would operate under the control of the officer commanding Station 53. In addition, a British chief signal master would be permanently based at the facility to ensure that it co-operated with Stations 53a and 53b. It was anticipated that once the new facility had been constructed it would be at least six months before it would be fully staffed by Americans. As a stopgap, it was proposed that SOE personnel would run the new Home Station. Following the transfer of Station 53c to the OSS, SOE planned on retaining control over the enciphering and deciphering of messages originating from this Home Station.[52] The transmitter for Station 53c was eventually located at Twyford, Buckinghamshire, while the receiver was based in a new complex at Poundon. When all three Home Stations were operational, wireless traffic to south-western Europe was allocated to Station 53a, Central Europe to Station 53b and Scandinavia to Station 53c.[53]

While plans were being developed for the construction of Station 53c, it was reported that SOE Home Stations were an 'administrative and technical mess ... [whose staff were] ill trained and many were psychologically unsuited to the emotional stress imposed by clandestine Signals'.[54] These issues appear to have been overcome by the run-up to Operation OVERLORD and the invasion of mainland Europe. During the planning phases, SOE was allocated 200 frequencies for clandestine activities and a further 66 for joint military operations.[55] Although this was significantly fewer than the field army's allotment of 1,000 frequencies and the field air force's 400, it was ahead of the naval forces' 75.[56] The allocation of a large number of frequencies to SOE demonstrated a recognition of the important role that the organisation and the resistance would play in the invasion. At the request of the War Office, SOE also supplied all the special forces units involved in Operation OVERLORD with 'one time pads'.[57]

In addition to communicating with agents operating in enemy-controlled territory, SOE's UK-based Home Stations were in contact with a network of wireless facilities established across the globe. Early attempts by SOE to communicate with their overseas missions were often chaotic, as 'there was a gross lack of Signals knowledge, and no co-ordination with the London H.Q.'.[58] By the middle of 1943 new wireless equipment had started to arrive at the missions, helping to improve the situation. Some of the missions, however, reacted unfavourably to the innovations sent out from London. In an attempt to convince their overseas staff of the value of the new wireless equipment SOE dispatched signal officers to educate the missions. Once they had been persuaded of the benefits of the technology, the missions began making demands for the latest equipment that far exceeded the available supply.[59]

The possibility of establishing a transatlantic clandestine wireless network with America was first discussed in the summer of 1941. SIS hoped to establish a line of communication that would not only aid American-British co-operation but also assist in the joint interception of enemy traffic. In October 1941 William Stephenson, head of the British Security Coordination (BSC), arranged for representatives of SIS's Section VIII, Gambier-Parry, to visit Washington to discuss with him the establishment of a worldwide clandestine communication network.[60] At the time of this meeting, communications

114 *Communications*

between BSC in the USA and SIS in the UK were handled by the Federal Bureau of Investigation's (FBI) transmitter at Maryland. As SIS refused to disclose their ciphers or the message in clear text, Gambier-Parry realised that he could not always rely on the American transatlantic wireless link. On 19 November 1941 he informed Stephenson that he intended to establish an independent communication network with Toronto, Canada. It was intended that this new facility would handle all SIS traffic between North America and the UK, as well as top-grade cryptographic material.[61]

Soon after Gambier-Parry's visit to Washington, Benjamin deForest Bayly, who had been appointed by Stephenson to run BSC's communications section, began exploring the possibility of establishing a transatlantic clandestine wireless network. In order to appraise himself of SIS's requirements, Bayly flew to Britain for three weeks of fact finding. Planning of the new wireless network coincided with ongoing discussions between SOE and the BSC over the possibility of establishing a training school in Canada. Eventually it was decided that, instead of constructing two bases, the training school and wireless station could co-exist at the same facility. When SOE's instructors arrived at the newly constructed Special Training School (STS) 103 in December 1941, they were joined by three members of the Royal Signals Corps. It was the responsibility of these wireless operators to train students in the use of radios and to establish a wireless station that was to eventually become known as HYDRA.[62]

To equip this new radio station, Bayly sourced wireless equipment that had been confiscated from North American amateur radio operations as a security precaution. In May 1942 the first 2,500W transmitter was delivered to the facility.[63] Shortly afterwards it was joined by a 10kW high-frequency water-cooled transmitter that had previously been operated by the WCAU radio station in Philadelphia. When messages were received by this station, staff would then forward them to BSC office in New York over commercial telex lines.[64]

SOE's use of commercial cables and wireless routes in North America was not unique to this continent. By 7 June 1942 all communications between SOE's overseas missions and London were being carried over a commercial system of cables and wireless networks. These messages would often arrive in Britain via convoluted routes. Communications from Durban were sent either by landline to Cape Town and then to the UK by wireless or cable or to Salisbury, Nairobi, Aden or Colombo before being transmitted the rest of the way by wireless.[65] Messages that originated in Cairo could either be transmitted directly by radio or were sent by cable to Alexandria, then to the Port of Sudan and finally to Aden, at which point they sent by wireless to the UK.[66] By June 1942 SOE's mission in India had to rely mainly on a communications link between Britain and Kirkee.[67] All communication between the organisation's facilities in India was conducted using landlines.[68] SOE's reliance on commercial means of communication did, however, raise concerns in 1942, as some in the organisation felt that because they were not prepared for the 'possibility of breakdown in existing communications' they were 'taking an unwarrantable risk'.[69]

Communications 115

In January 1942, despite being able to contact the UK via cables, SOE raised the possibility of establishing a wireless station in Gibraltar.[70] Concerns were, however, raised at the end of April as to whether this proposed facility would be allowed, under the arrangements with C, to communicate with SOE's new UK Home Stations.[71] SOE's Council finally agreed that a direct line of communication should be established immediately between Grendon and Gibraltar in June 1942.[72] On 28 January 1943, following an inspection of SOE's wireless arrangements in Gibraltar, it was reported back to London that at both facilities 'the personnel and the general set up gives one a good view – one or two of the N.C.Os [non-commissioned officers] are certainly worth commissions, judged by the average army standard of to-day ... The equipment is good and adequate'.[73] Although by the spring of 1943 most of Gibraltar's wireless responsibilities had passed to Massingham, the facilities in the Rock came under increasing pressure in July as a result of Operation HUSKY and the Italian surrender. During this period the traffic handled by Gibraltar increased to approximately 160,000 groups per week. This pressure was relieved only when other stations in the region started to assist the work of this facility.[74]

Throughout the Mediterranean and Middle East Theatre, SOE operated a number of wireless stations. Operations run by the organisation in the Balkans were initially served by emergency wireless stations hastily established in offices in Cairo, Haifa, Istanbul and Smyrna. Owing to the strategic situation in Egypt during the summer of 1942, SOE's wireless facility in Cairo suffered a series of setbacks as efforts were turned to developing a signals system in case the Middle Eastern front collapsed. Later in the year the Cairo War Station was also caught unprepared following a series of Allied victories and the expansion of the British Liaison Missions in the Balkans. While it was still trying to establish itself and train its staff, traffic at the Cairo facility increased to approximately 100,000 groups per week. By the spring of 1943 this number had risen to 150,000–200,000. Owing to the volume of messages handled by the Cairo War Station, there were times when normal traffic was delayed by 3.5 days, meaning that stations in the field might have to wait seven days for a response to any communication. These issues were not resolved until the autumn of 1943, by which time traffic was being diverted to other wireless stations in the region.[75]

When SOE's main base in the Mediterranean, known as Massingham, was issued its Operational Instructions, the facility was instructed that it had to establish and maintain wireless communications with England, Cairo, Malta and Gibraltar, and any future stations in the region. Massingham was also tasked with the responsibility of maintaining radio contact with some of SOE's field agents.[76] At the beginning of 1943 plans were developed to install a more powerful plant at the base, which would allow Massingham to increase their capacity to handle wireless traffic.[77] The power for the wireless equipment was supplied by a small RAF 9kVA generator set housed in a shed adjoining the main radio building.[78] Overseeing the operation of the wireless station was Major Corbatt, 'a keen worker and strict disciplinarian [who] exercises close control over the work of each member of his staff'.[79]

Following Italy's surrender in 1943, a wireless section from Massingham joined the Maryland Mission at Brindisi. The station later relocated to Monopoli near Bari, before eventually settling in the Siena area. In the autumn of 1943 SOE's Force 133, which were keen to improve communications with the Balkans, decided to establish another wireless station in Italy. This resulted in the creation of an elaborate facility at Torre a Mare, near Bari, which opened in August 1944. At the time, Bari was also home to SOE's Force 399's wireless station.[80] When Special Operations (Mediterranean) (SOM) formed in April 1944, SOE's wireless stations at Monopoli, Bari and Torre a Mare were all placed under the control of this new headquarters.[81] Although this encouraged more coordinated planning, it was too late in the war to replace the three bases with a new main wireless station in Italy. Monopoli, Bari and Torre a Mare, therefore, continued operating independently.[82]

Wireless communications were particularly important in the Far East, where agents worked far from base with no other means of passing messages. Two of the Indian Mission's radio stations were located in Calcutta: one worked with agents in Burma, Siam and Indo-China; and the other was a Psychological Warfare Branch facility. The Mission also had a station in Colombo that communicated with agents in Malaya and Sumatra.[83] At both Calcutta and Colombo SOE established 'Guard' Stations. As these remained open 24 hours a day, they provided agents who had failed to get in touch via standard channels a means to reach their base.[84] SOE also ran a small wireless facility at Kunming that communicated with agents operating in French Indo-China.[85] Following a review of the Indian Mission's wireless facilities in early 1944, SOE's Council were informed that the inspectors were 'very pleased with the arrangements India had already made and the excellent way in which they had carried out certain difficult and important operations'.[86]

Following the agreement reached between SIS and SOE in March 1942, SOE established a global network of wireless facilities. This enabled the organisation to communicate with their missions abroad as well as agents in the field. In 1942 the number of staff running SOE's global communications network was 96; by 1944 this had increased to 2,962.[87] SOE's work in the field of wireless communications demonstrated to some in the organisation that they were 'on the whole more hardworking and enthusiastic [than SIS], and that we are not afraid of challenging them when they try to double-cross us'.[88] It was felt, however, that this contributed to SIS viewing SOE as 'very dangerous rivals'.[89]

Notes

1 Roderick Bailey, *Forgotten Voices of the Secret War: An Inside History of Special Operations during the Second World War* (London, 2008), p. 186; Roderick Bailey, *The Wildest Province: SOE in the Land of the Eagle* (London, 2008), p. 57; Jorgen Haestrup, *Secret Alliance: A Study of the Danish Resistance Movement 1940–45*, Vol.

Communications 117

1 (Odense, 1976), p. 189; and Harry Kedwood, *In Search of the Maquis: Rural Resistance in Southern France 1942–1944* (Oxford, 1994), p. 182.

2 Pierre Lorain, *Secret Warfare: The Arms and Techniques of the Resistance* (London, 1983), p. 34.

3 Anthony Read and David Fisher, *Colonel Z: The Secret Life of a Master of Spies* (London, 1984), p. 270.

4 TNA HS 8/358 C/6050 21/03/1941, p. 2.

5 David Stafford, *Britain and European Resistance 1940–1945: A Survey of the Special Operations Executive with Documents* (London, 1980), p. 38. At the time this agreement was signed, SIS had only limited experience in the field of wireless communications. Sir Mansfield Smith-Cumming, the first C, began contemplating using the technology only in the spring of 1912. He saw wireless communications as a means to obtain intelligence quickly during periods of political tension that might signal a threat to British interests. It took another 26 years for SIS to establish a communications group, Section VIII, under Captain Richard Gambier-Parry. One of Gambier-Parry's most difficult and urgent challenges was to provide SIS's agents with wireless sets, as commercial technology had proved unsuitable (Keith Jeffrey, *MI6: The History of the Secret Intelligence Service 1909–1949* (London, 2010), pp. 10, 30, 262, 318).

6 TNA HS 8/358 SO2 Communications through C 09/03/1941, p. 1.

7 Jeffrey, *MI6*, pp. 262, 318.

8 Geoffrey Pidgeon, *The Secret Wireless War: The Story of MI6 Communications 1939–1945* (Richmond, 2008), pp. 27, 80, 81, 82–3, 114, 262.

9 SIS's receiver station at Upper Weald was slightly larger than the one at Nash. This facility comprised of two sheds for the receiver equipment alongside the brick-built generator and battery store. Messages were received at this station by aerials formed of semi-vertical wires suspended from relatively low cantilever wires. It took SIS until 1944 to arrange for a crew of aerial erectors to improve this *ad hoc* receiving system. Over the course of the war, SIS also established wireless facilities at Dower House, Buckinghamshire; Windy Ridge, Buckinghamshire; Tattenhoe Barn, Buckinghamshire; and Creslow Manor, Buckinghamshire (Pidgeon, *The Secret Wireless War*, pp. 82, 287, 295).

10 Pidgeon, *The Secret Wireless War*, pp. 80, 81, 82–3, 114, 262, 287, 295.

11 The US Civilian Technical Corps was a quasi-military organisation established in 1941 to assist the UK in the war effort within the UK.

12 Pidgeon, *The Secret Wireless War*, pp. 114, 285–6, 295.

13 TNA HS 8/321 M/OR/170 19/01/1942.

14 TNA HS 8/358 SO2 Communications 05/04/1941, p. 1.

15 TNA HS 8/358 SO2 Communications through C 09/03/1941, p. 2.

16 TNA HS 8/358 SO2 Communications through C 09/03/1941, p. 2.

17 TNA HS 8/358 To CD from E 16/03/1941, p. 1.

18 TNA HS 8/358 S.O.2 Communications 05/04/1941, p. 1.

19 TNA HS 8/358 S.O.2 Communications 05/04/1941, p. 1.

20 TNA HS 8/357 Personnel and Establishment of Military Station No. 8 17/12/1941, p. 3.

21 TNA HS 8/357 Personnel and Establishment of Military Station No. 8 17/12/1941, p. 1.

22 TNA HS 8/321 C/8686 05/02/1942. Following the transfer of the wireless networks, SOE was concerned that SIS was finding alternative ways to read their traffic. On 7 August 1942 they ordered an investigation into the possibility of SIS tapping the teleprinters between London and Station 53 (TNA PRO HS 8/357 DCDO/1173 07/08/1942). Although they determined that the 'line does not actually run through the Broadway Building, it is technically possible for "C" to

118 *Communications*

tap our traffic at some point along the route without our being aware of the fact' (TNA HS 8/357 MS/KV/804 09/08/1942).

23 TNA HS 8/321 Communications 26/03/1942.

24 TNA HS 8/360 Communications 27/03/1942.

25 TNA HS 8/360 ADP/TC/1195 22/05/1942.

26 Michael Foot, *SOE: The Special Operations Executive 1940–46* (London, 1993), p. 157.

27 TNA HS 8/360 ARB/SGB/1306 10/06/1942. Author's emphasis.

28 TNA HS 7/34 Station Construction Section, p. 1. Grendon Underwood had previously been STS53 and a school for training agents in the use of wireless communications.

29 TNA HS 8/321 CD/OR/1565 17/04/1942, p. 1.

30 TNA HS 8/321 CD/OR/1565 17/04/1942, p. 1.

31 TNA HS 8/321 Gambier-Parry to Ozanne 13/04/1942, p. 1. Because of his reservations about Grendon Underwood, Gambier-Parry wrote to SOE expressing his concerns that they might have completed 'a lot of constructional work until the possibilities of interference have been thoroughly explored' (TNA HS 8/321 Gambier-Parry to Ozanne 13/04/1942, p. 1). The site had already been vetted for potential signal interference by the General Post Office (GPO) (TNA HS 8/321 CD/OR/1565 17/04/1942, pp. 1–2).

32 TNA HS 8/321 Gambier-Parry to Ozanne 13/04/1942, pp. 1–2.

33 This new structure measured 20 ft × 12 ft (6.1 m × 3.66 m) (TNA HS 7/34 Station Construction Section, p. 1).

34 TNA HS 7/34 Station Construction Section, p. 1. Between 17 July and 28 August 1942, 423 messages were received at Station 53 from SOE's agents in the field. Over this 43-day period, 149 messages arrived from the Fighting French, 128 from other French agents, 74 from Belgium, 38 from the Netherlands and 34 from other countries in which SOE operated (TNA HS 8/363 Mutilated Messages 04/09/1942). In this period SOE was receiving, on average, six messages per day from the resistance in France. By July 1943 this figure had increased significantly to 120 messages per day (Jean-Louis Perquin, *The Clandestine Radio Operators: SOE, BCRA, OSS* (Paris, 2011), pp. 8, 26, 28, 29).

35 TNA HS 8/357 MS/G/720 28/06/1942. Station 53 handled one message per day from agents in the Netherlands between 17 July and 28 August 1942. Following the arrival of agent 'RLS' into the field on 28 February 1942, Major Hermann Giskes, the Abwehr officer in charge of Operation NORDPOL, reported that the number of messages his operation transmitted to the UK increased to several per day (Hermann Giskes, *London Calling North Pole* (London, 1953), p. 62). If Giskes' recollections are correct, then these figures indicate that Station 53 did not have the capacity to handle all the wireless traffic originating in the field.

36 TNA HS 7/34 Station Construction Section, p. 1. The new extension, into which SOE installed six 250w transmitters, measured 35 ft × 18 ft (10. 7 m × 5.5 m) (TNA HS 7/34 Station Construction Section, p. 1).

37 TNA HS 8/357 Minutes of Ad Hoc Communications Committee Meeting in MS' Office on Wednesday, 19th August, 1942, p. 3.

38 TNA HS 7/34 Station Construction Section, p. 9.

39 TNA HS 8/357 Minutes of Ad Hoc Communications Committee Meeting in MS' Office on Wednesday, 19th August, 1942, p. 3.

40 TNA HS 7/34 Station Construction Section, p. 9. SOE's capacity to handle agents' wireless traffic was initially hampered by limitations on equipment and the lack of qualified staff. Before the construction of Station 53b, it was likely that SIS continued communicating on behalf of SOE.

41 TNA HS 7/34 Station Construction Section, p. 10; and Leo Marks, *Between Silk and Cyanide: The Story of SOE's Code War* (London, 1998), p. 142. The main

receiver building at Poundon measured 40 ft × 40 ft × 12 ft (12.19 m × 12.19 m × 3.66 m) (TNA HS 7/34 Station Construction Section, p. 10).

42 TNA HS 7/34 Station Construction Section, p. 10.

43 The main building at Godington was 100 ft × 24 ft (30.48 m × 7.32 m) and incorporated features allowing open wire feeder routes. This equipment transmitted messages over 32 di-pole and two rhombic antennae that were erected in the field surrounding the complex. These were made from six 20 ft (6.1 m), one 80 ft (24.38 m) and 15 100 ft (30.48 m) masts and required over 10,000 ft (3,048 m) of wire and 3,000 spreaders in the down leads (TNA HS 7/34 Station Construction Section, pp. 10, 11).

44 TNA HS 7/34 Station Construction Section, pp. 10, 11.

45 Derwin Gregory, 'Communicating with the European Resistance: An Assessment of the Special Operations Executive's Wireless Facilities in the UK during the Second World War', *Post-Medieval Archaeology* 50.2 (2016), pp. 293, 299. Arranging the transmitters along the walls with space in the middle of the room allowed technicians maximum accessibility to inspect and maintain the equipment. This layout was in keeping with the design of other contemporary wireless facilities (see H Thomas and R Williamson, 'A Commercial 50-Kilowatt Frequency-Modulation Broadcast Transmitting Station', *Proceedings of the Institute of Radio Engineers* 29.10 (1941), p. 539; and Peter Eckersley and Noel Ashbridge, 'A Wireless Broadcasting Transmitting Station for Dual Programme Service', *Journal of Institute of Electrical Engineers* 68.405 (1930), p. 195). In order to limit the impact the generator might have on the delicate wireless equipment at Poundon and Godington, the power plant was installed in a separate building. The generator at Godington was also bolted to a concrete pad inset into the floor of the building (Gregory, 'Communicating with the European Resistance', p. 294). If the engineers did not carefully consider the positioning of the generator, the noise and vibrations from these machines could affect the delicate wireless sets. It was essential that silence prevailed in the transmitter room for the comfort of the technicians operating the equipment. This also made it easier to locate faults caused by arcing and sparking (Eckersley and Ashbridge, 'A Wireless Broadcasting Transmitting Station', p. 204).

46 This also restricted the German interceptors' ability to transcribe messages in their entirety (TNA HS 7/34 Station Construction Section, pp. 10, 11).

47 Each channel gave a field strength equal to that from a 250w transmitter connected to a resonant half-wave dipole (TNA HS 7/34 Station Construction Section, pp. 10, 11).

48 TNA HS 7/34 Station Construction Section, pp. 10, 11.

49 TNA HS 7/34 Station Construction Section, pp. 11, 12. The new 'trouble-free' remote control system required over 3,000 m of twin lead-covered wire to operate. Transmission occurred over 35 dipoles and two rhombic antennae formed from 16,000 ft (4,876.8 m) of wire and five 120 ft (36.6 m), 12 100 ft (30.5 m), four 80 ft (24.4 m) and two 60 ft (18.3 m) masts. The feeder route also required 100,000 ft (30,480 m) of copper wiring (TNA HS 7/34 Station Construction Section, pp. 11, 12).

50 TNA HS 8/37 Confidential Memorandum for Colonel Donovan 14/12/1942, p. 1.

51 TNA HS 7/283 OSS/SOE, p. 61. The transmitter for Station 53c was located at Twyford, Buckinghamshire, while the receiver was at Poundon.

52 TNA HS 7/283 OSS/SOE, p. 61.

53 TNA HS 8/37 Confidential Memorandum for Colonel Donovan 14/12/1942, p. 1.

54 TNA HS 7/33 Progress at the Base Station, p. 4.

55 Pidgeon, *The Secret Wireless War*, p. 2.

56 TNA HS 7/34 Signal Planning Section, p. 2.

120   *Communications*

57 Marks, *Between Silk and Cyanide*, p. 459. One time pads are a form of encryption that cannot be cracked.
58 TNA HS 7/33 SOE Signals, p. 7.
59 TNA HS 7/33 SOE Signals, p. 7.
60 The BSC was originally established by the British as a counter-espionage and intelligence agency in North America. As the war progressed, the organisation increasingly became a conduit for intelligence that was passed between the USA and the UK (David Stafford, *Camp X: SOE and the American Connection* (Viking, 1987), p. 165).
61 Stafford, *Camp X*, pp. 165, 168, 170.
62 Stafford, *Camp X*, pp. 168, 170, 171.
63 This transmitter, known as 'the little rig', was originally operated from a private residence in Toronto (Stafford, *Camp X*, p. 171).
64 Stafford, *Camp X*, pp. 170–1, 172–4. Between New York and Buffalo, messages were transmitted over Western Union commercial cables, and then a Canadian National cable took them from Fort Erie to HYDRA. The BSC also utilised cables between New York, Ottawa and Washington. In order to protect the contents of the messages, they were sent via a Telekrypton cipher machine adapted by Bayly and renamed 'Rockex'. Initially the 'Rockex' could transmit 100 words per minute. This was later increased to 300 words when a photo-electric keyer was introduced. Eventually, this machine, which was capable of handling the volume of traffic generated by the BSC, was used to encipher all communications between the BSC and the UK (Stafford, *Camp X*, pp. 172–4).
65 Messages originating from Freetown, Sierra Leone, could be sent directly to the UK via cables, or had to be sent to Bathurst, South Africa, before being transmitted wirelessly (TNA HS 8/361 Communications Main Line 7 June 1942, p. 1). SOE operated a number of small wireless facilities throughout Africa. In 1942 the organisation felt that their Frawest Mission, operating in West Africa, would need War Stations at Freetown, Accra and Lagos (TNA HS 3/74 Report on Frawest Mission 11/11/1942, p. 14). SOE also controlled a number of wireless stations in Africa that were used for broadcasting propaganda material: the 'Madagascar Line' was run from the government radio station in Mauritius, while 'Radio Gambia' was operated by SOE on behalf of PWE (TNA HS 8/198 SOE Notes on a Meeting of Directors, held on 26.1.42, p. 2; and TNA HS 3/11 General; mission to Portuguese East Africa; account of operations in Africa An Account of SOE Operations in Africa, p. 5).
66 In January 1942 SOE established a small wireless facility on Malta (William Mackenzie, *The Secret History of SOE: Special Operations Executive 1940–1945* (London, 2002), p. 737). Messages originating from this facility were sent to Alexandria before being forwarded to their intended destination (TNA HS 8/361 Communications Main Line 7 June 1942, p. 1).
67 Communications were also possible via a low-powered transmitter located in Colombo (TNA HS 8/361 Communications Main Line 7 June 1942, p. 1).
68 TNA HS 8/361 Communications Main Line 7 June 1942, p. 2. By September 1943 internal signals in India were coordinated from a main station at Meerut. This provided a link to Calcutta, Madras, Colombo, Trinco, Bombay, Poona, Quetta, Cairo, Chaklala, Chingking, Delhi, Kunming, Imphal, Falam, Fort Hertz, Tamu and Nazira (TNA HS 1/229 SOE – Far East Group Plans/130/1322 September 1943, pp. 1–2).
69 TNA HS 8/361 Communications Main Line 7 June 1942, p. 2.
70 TNA HS 8/198 SOE Notes on a Meeting of Directors, held on 5.1.42, p. 2; and TNA HS 8/361 Communications Main Line 7 June 1942, p. 2. One of the main reasons SOE established the wireless facility at Gibraltar was to communicate

Communications 121

with stations they thought they might need to set up Spain. The link between Grendon and Gibraltar was part of a global network of wireless stations planned by SOE. It was intended that this network would comprise the UK Home Stations, main stations in Algeria and Cairo, subsidiary links in Gibraltar and Malta for the Mediterranean theatre, small stations at Freetown, Lagos and Durban for Africa, and bases in India, Ceylon and Australia for the Far East (Mackenzie, *The Secret History of SOE*, pp. 736–8).

71 TNA HS 8/198 Notes on a Meeting of the SO Council, held on 30.4.42, p. 2.

72 TNA HS 8/361 MS/CML/165 1 June 1942. At the beginning of Operation TORCH and the invasion of North Africa, SOE's radio station in Gibraltar was the sole channel to North Africa. SOE's signal detachment, known as Angel, based in Casablanca and communicating with Gibraltar, was also responsible for handling the US Army's traffic, as they were having trouble with their radio to Gibraltar. Angel also handled the priority traffic of the US Admiral John Hall, as he had lost all his radio equipment (TNA HS 7/68 Torch and the SOE Signals Stations at Gibraltar, pp. 1, 6). Hall thanked Angel and 'all concerned in passing his important traffic, saying that their efficiency and speed had proved invaluable in his operations during a difficult period' (TNA HS 7/68 Torch and the SOE Signals Stations at Gibraltar, p. 7).

73 TNA HS 8/19 Letter from M to CD 28 January 1943.

74 Mackenzie, *The Secret History of SOE*, p. 738. Between May and August 1944 Gibraltar was working with about 60 outstations in the south of France (Mackenzie, *The Secret History of SOE*, p. 738).

75 Mackenzie, *The Secret History of SOE*, pp. 737–8.

76 HS 8/19 MASSINGHAM Operational Instruction No. 1, p. 2; and TNA HS 7/169 Part II Conception of Massingham and its Formation, p. 6.

77 TNA HS 8/240 Review of SOE Activities for the period 15th December 1942 to 15th January 1943, p. 10.

78 TNA HS 3/182 Visit to Massingham, Cairo, Maryland, Jungle and Naples by L/IT 23rd February/31st March, 1944, p. 4. Massingham also had another 9kVA generator set which was kept as a stand-by in case of equipment failure.

79 TNA HS 3/182 Visit to Massingham, Cairo, Maryland, Jungle and Naples by L/IT 23rd February/31st March, 1944, p. 4. During an inspection of Massingham in February 1944, it was reported that the Signal Receiving and Despatching Station was 'well arranged and equipped except for the automatic tape machine transmitter which is of obsolete type, in poor condition and frequently gives trouble. This should be replaced by a more modern instrument'.

80 Force 399 was a cover name for SOE's operations in Yugoslavia.

81 SOM was an Anglo-American special forces command (Bailey, *The Wildest Province*, p. 268).

82 Mackenzie, *The Secret History of SOE*, pp. 738–9. Some of SOM HQ facilities were centralised at Siena (Mackenzie, *The Secret History of SOE*, p. 739).

83 Charles Cruickshank, *SOE in the Far East* (Oxford, 1983), p. 39, TNA HS 1/229 SOE – Far East Group Plans/130/1322 September 1943, pp. 1–2; and TNA HS 1/229 SOE – Far East Group Plans/130/1322 September 1943, pp. 1–2. As a temporary measure in November 1944, pending the opening of a Colombo-Paris wireless link, French traffic that originated in Kandy was sent via the Colombo-London link (TNA HS 7/35 Special Signal Instruction No. 60).

84 Cruickshank, *SOE in the Far East*, p. 39. Plans were developed in the summer of 1944 to double the number of wireless channels at the War Stations at Calcutta and Colombo. Although this would require additional diesel generators and four new mechanics at each site, it would be possible operate a 24-hour watch (TNA HS 1/275 War Establishments – Military Establishment No. 9 SE/8 18/09/1944, p. 4).

122 *Communications*

85 TNA HS 1/229 SOE – Far East Group Plans/130/1322 September 1943, pp. 1–2; and Cruickshank, *SOE in the Far East*, p. 39. On 30 September 1945 the licence for SOE's wireless stations in Chungking and Kunming expired. At the same time, the Chinese raised objections about the continuation of SOE's Chungking Station, which was located in the Embassy grounds. As a result of these pressures the facility was relocated to another compound in the city (TNA HS 1/159 Report by Lt Col RN Seddon on visit to China 31/10/1945, pp. 1, 2).

86 TNA HS 8/200 SOE Council Minutes of meeting held on Tuesday, April 4th, 1944. At a SOE Council meeting held on 10 November 1944 concerns were expressed that the mainline stations at Delhi, Calcutta and Colombo were all being considerably increased to an unnecessary degree. It was suggested that an investigation should be conducted to make sure that there was no overlap in the work of the various organisations operating in the South East Asian Theatre of Operation (TNA HS 8/201 SOE Council Minutes of Meeting held on Friday, November 10th, 1944).

87 HS 7/33 SOE Signals, p. 2. In 1942 six officers and 30 other ranks (ORs) staffed SOE's wireless stations in the UK, three officers and six ORs staffed Gibraltar, six officers and 25 ORs staffed the Middle East stations and five officers and 15 ORs staffed the Far East. By 1944 this had increased to 92 officers, 1,020 ORs and 720 non-military personnel in the UK; 26 officers, 250 ORs and 29 non-military in Gibraltar; 30 officers, 409 ORs and 135 non-military in the Middle East; and 20 officers, 164 ORs and 68 non-military in the Far East (HS 7/33 SOE Signals, p. 2).

88 TNA HS 8/321 M/OR/170 19/01/1942.

89 TNA HS 8/321 M/OR/170 19/01/1942.

References

Archives

The National Archives (TNA), London

HS 1/159: Research and Investment Institute (R.I.I.).

HS 1/207: History of SOE Oriental Mission; Killery Mission.

HS 1/229: Organisation and co-ordination; SEAC stores.

HS 1/275: War establishment: No 9 Signals.

HS 3/11: East African mission: terms of reference and general organisation.

HS 3/74: West African missions; SIS and SOE; Prof Cassin's report; Franck mission (NEUCOLS and FRAWEST); US cooperation.

HS 3/182: Visit to Massingham, Cairo, Maryland, Jungle and Naples; destruction of heavy machine shop at Pozzuoli.

HS 7/33: Section I: signals; appendices A and B.

HS 7/34: Section I: signals; appendices C and D.

HS 7/35: Section I: signals; appendix E.

HS 7/68: TORCH: north African landings; SOE signals stations at Gibraltar.

HS 7/283: Office of Strategic Studies (OSS) /SOE Oct 1942–Jun 1943 (page 1–185).

HS 8/19: Massingham (codename for SOE's Algiers base operating into France): OSS and SOE in North Africa (country name recorded as North America on cover page).

HS 8/37: OSS.

HS 8/198: Committees: SOE Council minutes.

HS 8/199: Committees: SOE Council minutes.

Communications 123

HS 8/200: Committees: SOE Council minutes.
HS 8/201: Committees: SOE Council minutes.
HS 8/202: Committees: SOE Council minutes.
HS 8/240: Directors and heads of sections: Massingham (the Algiers base operating into France).
HS 8/321: Liaison: SIS.
HS 8/357: Communications: Equipment supplies and requirements.
HS 8/358: Communications: Relations with SIS.
HS 8/360: Communications: Organisation of communications.
HS 8/361: Communications: SOE signals station.
HS 8/363: Communications: Appreciations and exercises.

Secondary sources

Bailey, Roderick. *Forgotten Voices of the Secret War: An Inside History of Special Operations during the Second World War* (London, 2008).
Bailey, Roderick. *The Wildest Province: SOE in the Land of the Eagle* (London, 2008).
Cruickshank, Charles. *SOE in the Far East* (Oxford, 1983).
Eckersley, Peter and Ashbridge, Noel. 'A Wireless Broadcasting Transmitting Station for Dual Programme Service', *Journal of Institute of Electrical Engineers* 68.405 (1930), pp. 1149–70.
Foot, Michael. *SOE: The Special Operations Executive 1940–46* (London, 1993).
Gregory, Derwin. 'Communicating with the European Resistance: An Assessment of the Special Operations Executive's Wireless Facilities in the UK during the Second World War', *Post-Medieval Archaeology* 50.2 (2016), pp. 289–304.
Haestrup, Jorgen. *Secret Alliance: A Study of the Danish Resistance Movement 1940–45*, Vol. 1 (Odense, 1976).
Jeffrey, Keith. *MI6: The History of the Secret Intelligence Service 1909–1949* (London, 2010).
Kedwood, Harry. *In Search of the Maquis: Rural Resistance in Southern France 1942–1944* (Oxford, 1994).
Lorain, Pierre. *Secret Warfare: The Arms and Techniques of the Resistance* (London, 1983).
Mackenzie, William. *The Secret History of SOE: Special Operations Executive 1940–1945* (London, 2002).
Marks, Leo. *Between Silk and Cyanide: The Story of SOE's Code War* (London, 1998).
Pidgeon, Geoffrey. *The Secret Wireless War: The Story of MI6 Communications 1939–1945* (Richmond, 2008).
Read, Anthony and Fisher, David. *Colonel Z: The Secret Life of a Master of Spies* (London, 1984).
Stafford, David. *Britain and European Resistance 1940–1945: A Survey of the Special Operations Executive with Documents* (London, 1980).
Stafford, David. *Camp X: SOE and the American Connection* (Viking, 1987).
Thomas, H and Williamson, R. 'A Commercial 50-Kilowatt Frequency-Modulation Broadcast Transmitting Station', *Proceedings of the Institute of Radio Engineers* 29.10 (1941), pp. 537–45.

7 Conclusion

One of the most persistent criticisms of SOE was that the organisation was 'amateurish'. These accusations tend to focus on SOE's early history. It was, however, never true that those individuals employed by SOE were complete novices to secret service work. A number of people responsible for running SOE had actually previously worked for the Secret Intelligence Service (SIS).[1]

One of the most vocal opponents of SOE was actually SIS. Following the Venlo incident in 1939, SIS's reputation was tarnished.[2] When Section D was removed from the organisation in 1940, SIS started to feel threatened. Within SOE there were concerns that SIS felt that if SOE was 'not squashed quickly ... we [SOE] will squash them'.[3] By focusing on SOE's supposedly 'amateurish' nature, attempts were made during the war to undermine the organisation's legitimacy to operate independently. Following the end of hostilities, there were some who continued wartime inter-bureaucratic rivalries. The image of SOE as an irresponsible, amateurish organisation, consorting with foreign radicals and revolutionaries, became firmly entrenched in post-war assessments.[4]

This examination of SOE's agent-facing infrastructure challenges the accusations of 'amateurism'. The organisation's support facilities were generally of a high standard and innovative. SOE's UK-based wireless stations are the best illustration of the organisation's willingness to incorporate state-of-the-art equipment into their facilities. These Home Stations combined advanced technology with contemporary design standards. SOE also invested in the development of innovative wireless sets. By combining high-tech radio sets and Home Stations, it was hoped that agents could be provided with a reliable and efficient means of communication.

The professionalism of SOE's agent-facing infrastructure was also reflected in their global network of training bases. Almost immediately following the organisation's formation, a programme for instructing students in aspects of clandestine warfare was devised. As this system was ideally suited to SOE's needs, only minor alterations were made to it throughout the remainder of the war. To ensure that the training was of a high standard, instructors embedded a heightened level of realism into their syllabuses. Central to these courses were models, military equipment, industrial machinery and innovative

DOI: 10.4324/9781315180106-7

Conclusion 125

training facilities. Through the combination of state-of-the-art techniques and a focus on realism, SOE tried to ensure that their students were thoroughly prepared for their missions. In addressing the charge of 'amateurism', it is significant that, following the dissolution of SOE in 1946, SIS took over not only the organisation's Research and Development Section but also their Training Section. Contemporaries of SOE acknowledged that in the 'training of underground workers ... S.O.E. has done pioneer work of value'.[5]

Despite early failures, which gave SOE a bad name, by the summer of 1941, one year after it was established, the organisation was beginning to show its worth.[6] On the night of 7 June 1941, a group of SOE-trained agents managed to destroy eight transformers at the Pessac Transformer Station, France, during Operation JOSEPHINE B.[7] Following the success of this operation, Hugh Dalton informed Churchill that his organisation had proved that 'industrial targets, especially if cover [*sic*] only a very small area, are more effectively attacked by SOE methods than by air bombardment'.[8] Post-strike photographic analysis estimated that at that time only 25 per cent of the RAF's payload landed within 5 miles (8 km) of the designated target.[9] SOE was starting to demonstrate the strategic value of small groups of highly trained and determined agents.

Only 15 days after the success of JOSEPHINE B, Operation BARBAROSSA, the Axis invasion of the Soviet Union, commenced. Immediately the Chiefs of Staff subcommittee of the War Cabinet commissioned a study on what actions Britain could take. On 23 June the Joint Planning Staff reported that raids on the French and Norwegian coast might have an impact on German operations on the Eastern Front. They also advocated an increase in the RAF's bombing campaign against German industry, infiltrating agents into the Caucasus, Central Asia and Persia and attacking the Baku oilfields.[10]

For the first 13 weeks following the invasion, Britain could do little except offer the Soviets moral support.[11] At this stage of the war Churchill lacked the operational capacity necessary to open a second front.[12] The Chiefs of Staff were also unwilling to change strategy, as they felt the Soviets would soon capitulate. Owing to the lack of support, by 4 September 1941 Stalin's patience was at breaking point. His representatives began suggesting that they would be willing to consider a separate peace treaty with Hitler. Within a month, Britain had dispatched the first convoy loaded with fighter aircraft to Russia.[13]

Despite Britain's heavy investment of resources in the bombing offensive, Stalin still insisted that troops were landed in mainland Europe.[14] For a country suffering from equipment shortages, SOE offered a cost-effective method of tying down large numbers of Axis troops.[15] Agents could also have a negative impact on the combat effectiveness of the enemy.[16] By establishing facilities that could design, develop and camouflage booby traps, it was SOE's intention to undermine the morale of Axis soldiers. Devices included exploding rusty bolts, coal, wooden logs, food tins, engineer's oilcans, torches, Chinese stone lanterns, Balinese carvings and Japanese sauce tins.[17] By December 1944 Station XV had manufactured 138 explosive bicycle pumps, 100

126   *Conclusion*

exploding rats, 19 incendiary tobacco tins and 36 pairs of exploding clogs.[18] Although they were produced in relatively small numbers, the fear of booby traps could lead to heightened levels of anxiety among troops and reluctance to follow orders.[19] SOE's agents could, therefore, tie down large numbers of troops while decreasing their fighting capability.

By the end of 1941 operations conducted by SOE had demonstrated their strategic value and attitudes within Whitehall towards the organisation were beginning to change. Political pressure now starting to be applied to those organisations that had initially been reluctant to support SOE.[20] The unfriendly feelings towards SOE within departments the organisation had to work with resulted in inefficiency, however.[21] By July 1942 Sir John Hanbury-Williams and Edward Playfair deemed that these relationships were now generally satisfactory on both sides, but they could not 'give nearly such a favourable account of SOE's relations with SIS'.[22] This relationship had got so bad by 1942 that observers believed that

> if things do not improve on the S.I.S. side, they are bound to get worse on the S.O.E. side:-
>
> > 'Cet animal est tres mechant:
> > Quand on l'attaque il se defend.'
>
> These bad relations ... lead to inefficiency, wasted effort, some duplication and it may be at times danger of life and liberty to devoted men [and women], is not open to doubt.[23]

By August 1942 the levels of distrust had reached a point where SOE was concerned that SIS was tapping their phone lines. Although SOE could not prove these allegations, they still recommended installing Typex machines at their facilities.[24]

SOE's relationships with the RAF and the Royal Navy, however, were not as clear-cut. Initially, these branches of the armed services were reluctant to support clandestine warfare in situations where it directly affected their operations. Mounting political pressure on the RAF, however, led to their decision to release aircraft to Special Duties squadrons operating out of the UK. As the war progressed, aircraft and airfields were also made available in both the Mediterranean and Middle East Theatre and in the South East Asian Theatre.

Although the transportation of agents and supplies by air was SOE's preferred means, the organisation also utilised maritime vessels operating from bases around the world. Until 1942 SOE ran a 'private' navy in the English Channel. As the Royal Navy were concerned about the strategic implications of these independent operations in home waters, they arranged for the Helford Flotilla to be transferred to the Naval Intelligence Division (Clandestine) (NID(C)). The facilities of the Shetland Bus, however, remained important to SOE throughout the war. In the other theatres of war, SOE's maritime infrastructure, which coordinated and operated ships, boats and submarines, remained vital for the movement of agents and supplies to the field.

It was also essential to SOE's operations to develop relationships with foreign organisations and one of their closest collaborations was with the Office of Strategic Services (OSS). SOE was to play an important role in teaching their American counterparts the art of clandestine warfare. In the UK this mentoring partly took the form of SOE's involvement in the establishment and operation of OSS facilities. At both Area H and Station 53c, SOE maintained a presence to oversee the work of the Americans. In the Mediterranean and Middle East Theatre, OSS personnel would often be based at, and assist in running, SOE's facilities.

SOE was also often criticised for their 'alleged wastefulness and extravagance'.[25] In an effort to undermine SOE, Lieutenant Colonel Claude Dansey of SIS christened the organisation the 'Stately 'Omes of England'.[26] Although it is true that SOE's global network of agent-facing facilities was extensive, each site played a role. Owing to the nature of clandestine operations, SOE required facilities in the different theatres to train large numbers of agents, supply them with purpose-designed equipment and communicate with them while they were in the field.

It was the preference of the minister for economic warfare, Hugh Dalton, that SOE should use only 'houses [that had] already [been] requisitioned'.[27] If the organisation needed a new property in the UK, they first had to approach the War Office's Land Branch. If they had nothing suitable, SOE then contacted the Ministry of Works to find a site on their behalf.[28] Occasionally, SOE would search the local advertisements for suitable accommodation that they might be able to requisition.[29] In January 1941 SOE established a Properties Section that was responsible for vetting all the organisation's demands for new premises and land within the UK. This section also had to check that all requests had obtained the necessary internal approval, as well as being financially sanctioned. Once the Properties Section were happy that the demands had been authorised and were justified, they set about acquiring, preparing, furnishing and maintaining the premises.[30] SOE was, however, happy to allocate multiple roles to the properties they already operated. Massingham, for example, was a training facility, a maritime hub and a communications centre. Back in the UK, Grendon Underwood, which had previously been used as a training centre, was converted into SOE's first Home Station.[31] When facilities became surplus to requirements, it was also the responsibility of the Properties Section to dispose of them.[32]

It was SOE's policy to restrict new construction work at their facilities to the essentials, as far as possible. Staff were made aware that the 'reduction of building work to a minimum is a matter of greatest National importance, Commandants [of Country Establishments] will therefore ensure that requests for maintenance and alterations to premises are made only when absolutely essential'.[33]

128   *Conclusion*

Over the course of the war, the War Office gained a bad name in the UK as a result of the damage done to houses by military units. SOE, however, demonstrated to owners that they treated houses with respect.[34] To ensure that private property was protected, SOE arranged for everything within a requisitioned house to be removed before taking over a site.[35] If items could not be removed from the site, they were to be sealed off and regularly inspected by the commanding officer of the facility. In order to limit the physical impact of their activities on requisitioned structures, officers from SOE's Properties Section would inspect the sites periodically.[36] Although they aimed to visit each facility every six months, more pressing matters prevented this target being reached until the summer of 1944, when SOE employed a Properties Section officer specifically to inspect their facilities.[37] These activities not only ensured that SOE maintained a good reputation among property owners but limited potential compensation claims following the end of hostilities.[38]

At the outbreak of the Second World War, there were few facilities operated by the British government around the globe dedicated to clandestine warfare. Following SOE's formation in 1940, the organisation had to expand while developing their operational procedure and organising missions. These 'amateurish' early operations had a lasting impact on how other organisations viewed SOE. After demonstrating the strategic value of clandestine warfare, political support for the organisation was more forthcoming, enabling SOE to expand their network of agent-facing facilities and to increase their activities. By the end of the war, SOE had an extensive network of facilities around the world, vital in the planning, preparing and supporting of clandestine missions against the Axis powers.

Notes

1 TNA FO 1093/155 Minute 27/03/1942, p. 4.
2 On 9 November 1939 Captain Best and Major Stevens, key figures in SIS's Dutch network, were captured by German intelligence following fundamental failings in SIS's operational procedures. This mistake compromised SIS's European network (Nigel Jones, 'Introduction', in *The Venlo Incident: A True Story of Double-Dealing, Captivity, and a Murderous Nazi Plot*, ed. Sigismund Best (London, 2009), p. xiv).
3 TNA HS 8/321 M/XX/441 10/03/1942.
4 David Stafford, *Britain and European Resistance 1940–1945: A Survey of the Special Operations Executive with Documents* (London, 1980), p. 5.
5 TNA HS 8/281 Suggested Note for Cabinet or Prime Minister, p. 2.
6 TNA CAB 301/51 Report on SOE, p. 3. Churchill was of the opinion, however, that it takes a minimum of five to ten years to establish successfully a new secret service (Keith Jeffery, *MI6: The History of the Secret Intelligence Service 1909–1949* (London, 2010), p. 157).
7 William Mackenzie, *The Secret History of SOE: Special Operations Executive 1940–1945* (London, 2002), p. 246.
8 Mackenzie, *The Secret History of SOE*, p. 246.

Conclusion   129

9 Roger Beaumont, 'The Bomber Offensive as a Second Front', *Journal of Contemporary History* 22.1 (1987), p. 7.

10 Abraham Roof, 'A Separate Peace? The Soviet Union and the Making of British Strategy in the Wake of 'Barbarossa', June–September 1941', *Journal of Slavic Military Studies* 22.2 (2009), p. 247.

11 Roof, 'A Separate Peace?', pp. 239, 249.

12 Beaumont, 'The Bomber Offensive', p. 4.

13 Roof, 'A Separate Peace', pp. 241, 250.

14 Jonathan Fenby, *Alliance: The Inside Story of How Roosevelt, Stalin and Churchill Won One War and Began Another* (London, 2008), p. 66.

15 See Lester Grau, *The Bear Went Over the Mountain: Soviet Combat Tactics in Afghanistan* (London, 2001); Ahmed Hashin, *Insurgency and Counter-Insurgency in Iraq* (London, 2006); Daniel Marston and Carter Malkasian, eds, *Counterinsurgency in Modern Warfare* (Oxford, 2008); and E. Smith, *Counter-Insurgency Operations 1: Malaya and Borneo* (Shepperton, 1985).

16 When operating in a combat zone soldiers not only face the imminent danger of loss of life but also witness the death and mutilation of their comrades (Charles Moskos, *The American Enlisted Man: The Rank and File in Today's Military* (New York, 1970), p. 141). Among troops there is often a greater fear of mines and booby traps that strike without warning and that are designed to maim. The threat of roadside bombs and booby traps leads to heightened anxiety among soldiers on the frontline and in the rear (Richard Holmes, *Acts of War: The Behaviour of Men in Battle* (London, 2004), pp. 209, 211).

17 Roderick Bailey, *Secret Agent's Handbook: The Top Secret Manual of Wartime Weapons, Gadgets, Disguises and Devices* (London, 2008).

18 TNA HS 7/49 History and Development of the Camouflage Section 1941–45 Part I – Devices. Station XV had also manufactured 185,813 tyre bursters, 43,700 incendiary cigarettes, 700 exploding wooden logs, 50 exploding torches, 24 exploding food tins and 3.5 tons of exploding coal by December 1944 (TNA HS 7/49 History and Development of the Camouflage Section 1941–45 Part I – Devices).

19 Holmes, *Acts of War*, p. 214; Theodore Nadelson, *Trained to Kill: Soldiers at War* (Baltimore, 2005), p. 91.

20 TNA AIR 20/2901 Freeman to Harris 23/03/1942.

21 TNA CAB 301/51 Report on SOE, p. 3.

22 TNA CAB 301/51 Report on SOE, p. 9, 11.

23 TNA CAB 301/51 Report to the Minister of Economic Warfare on the Organisation of SOE, p. 11.

24 TNA HS 8/357 MS/KV/804 09/08/1942.

25 TNA CAB 301/51 Report on SOE, p. 4.

26 Robert Marshall, *All the King's Men: The Truth Behind SOE's Greatest Wartime Disaster* (Glasgow, 1989), p. 58.

27 TNA HS 8/337 Letter to Jebb from Hicks 08/09/1941.

28 TNA HS 8/337 Draft of Suggested Reply to Mr George Hicks' Letter to the Minister dated 28th August, 1941, p. 1.

29 TNA HS 8/337 Letter to Gaitskell from Venner 03/09/1941.

30 TNA HS 7/15 Properties Section History 06/03/1946, p. 1. During the process of SOE requisitioning Gaynes Hall in 1942 for their new packing facility, the unhappy owner wrote to Buckingham Palace expressing their concerns. The palace responded that Queen Elizabeth had been 'satisfied that the desire of the Government Department concerned is neither thoughtless nor frivolous, but is founded upon considerations which have a serious national justification' (TNA HS 8/337 Buckingham Palace 13/10/1941).

130 *Conclusion*

31 TNA HS 8/321 CD/OR/1565 17/04/1942, p. 1.
32 TNA HS 7/15 Properties Section History 06/03/1946, p. 1.
33 TNA HS 7/15 Property Arrangements at Country Establishments, p. 1.
34 TNA HS 8/337 Draft of Suggested Reply to Mr George Hicks' Letter to the Minister dated 28th August, 1941, p. 1.
35 TNA HS 7/15 Property Arrangements at Country Establishments, p. 1; and TNA HS 7/15 Properties Section History, p. 7.
36 In order to protect the walls at a number of country houses they requisitioned in the UK SOE installed wooden panelling (TNA HS 7/15 Properties Section History, p. 7).
37 TNA HS 7/15 Properties Section History, p. 7.
38 TNA HS 7/15 Property Arrangements at Country Establishments, p. 1.

References

Archives

The National Archives (TNA), London

AIR 20/2901: Special Operation Executive operations: aircraft.
CAB 301/51: Hanbury Williams report on the Special Operations Executive (SOE).
FO 1093/155: Special Operations Executive (SOE) organisation: relations between SOE and the Secret Intelligence Service (SIS).
HS 7/15: D FIN/2 section: FANY pay and allowances; properties section.
HS 7/49: History and development of camouflage section 1941–45.
HS 8/281: Policy and Planning: Future of SOE.
HS 8/321: Liaison: SIS.
HS 8/337: Organisation and administration: Property.
HS 8/357: Communications: Equipment supplies and requirements.

Secondary sources

Bailey, Roderick. *Secret Agent's Handbook: The Top Secret Manual of Wartime Weapons, Gadgets, Disguises and Devices* (London, 2008).
Beaumont, Roger. 'The Bomber Offensive as a Second Front', *Journal of Contemporary History* 22.1 (1987), pp. 3–19.
Fenby, Jonathan. *Alliance: The Inside Story of How Roosevelt, Stalin and Churchill Won One War and Began Another* (London, 2008).
Grau, Lester. *The Bear Went Over the Mountain: Soviet Combat Tactics in Afghanistan* (London, 2001).
Hashin, Ahmed. *Insurgency and Counter-Insurgency in Iraq* (London, 2006).
Holmes, Richard. *Acts of War: The Behaviour of Men in Battle* (London, 2004), pp. 209, 211.
Jeffery, Keith. *MI6: The History of the Secret Intelligence Service 1909–1949* (London, 2010).
Jones, Nigel. 'Introduction', in *The Venlo Incident: A True Story of Double-Dealing, Captivity, and a Murderous Nazi Plot*, ed. Sigismund Best (London, 2009).
Mackenzie, William. *The Secret History of SOE: Special Operations Executive 1940–1945* (London, 2002).

Marshall, Robert. *All the King's Men: The Truth Behind SOE's Greatest Wartime Disaster* (Glasgow, 1989).

Marston, Daniel and Malkasian, Carter, eds. *Counterinsurgency in Modern Warfare* (Oxford, 2008).

Moskos, Charles. *The American Enlisted Man: The Rank and File in Today's Military* (New York, 1970).

Nadelson, Theodore. *Trained to Kill: Soldiers at War* (Baltimore, 2005).

Roof, Abraham. 'A Separate Peace? The Soviet Union and the Making of British Strategy in the Wake of 'Barbarossa', June–September 1941', *Journal of Slavic Military Studies* 22.2 (2009), pp. 236–52.

Smith, E. *Counter-Insurgency Operations 1: Malaya and Borneo* (Shepperton, 1985).

Stafford, David. *Britain and European Resistance 1940–1945: A Survey of the Special Operations Executive with Documents* (London, 1980).

Index

accommodation 5, 33, 36, 38, 41, 43, 45, 47, 49, 53, 61, 64, 66, 76, 78, 84, 92, 127

Africa, SOE in 17, 44; Accra 17, 120; Algiers 18, 19, 26, 78 (*see also* Massingham); Algeria 44, 98, 104, 121; ammunition dumps 85; Bathurst 17, 120; Cairo 17, 18, 25, 26, 78, 85, 104, 114, 115, 120, 121; Cape Town 17, 44, 114; Durban 17, 114, 121; Freetown 17, 120, 121; Kenya 44; Lagos 17, 120, 121; Madagascar 26; Missions 85; Nigeria 44; Sierra Leone 44; South Africa 44; training in 44; wireless communications 114, 120

Albania, SOE's mission to 27

Aston House, Hertfordshire (Station XII): fire at 74, 83; magazine at 74; production of supplies at 72, 73, 82; research and development at 6, 61, 83; storage at 73–4

Audley End, Essex (STS43) 40, 75

Australia, SOE in 17

Auxiliary Units, the 9, 83

Balaclava, maritime base 97–8, 103

Balkans, SOE in 26, 42, 85, 98, 99, 104, 109, 115, 116

Balloon Development Establishment, Cardington 65

Bayly, Benjamin deForest 114

Beaulieu, Hampshire, training at 11, 15, 36

Bletchley Park 6, 108

bomb dumps 87, 103

booby traps 42, 100, 125–6, 129

Bride Hall, Hertfordshire (Station VI) 74–5, 84

Briggins, Essex, Station XIV 72

British Security Coordination (BSC) 113–14, 120

Burma, SOE in 17

Camouflage and Technical Unit, Cairo 78

Camouflage School, Monopoli 77–8

Camouflage Section 73, 82

camouflaging: of airfields 95–6, 102–3; of equipment 72–3, 83, 125–6

Canada, SOE in 49–50; STS103 (Camp X) 36, 49–50, 81, 114

Caribbean, SOE in 81

carrier pigeon service 13

CELINI Line 12

Ceylon Country Section 47–8

Chamberlain, Neville 8

CHERUB Circuit 12, 24

Chichley Hall, Buckinghamshire (STS46) 38

China, SOE in *see* Far East, SOE in

Churchill, Winston 8

clandestine warfare 9–10, 93, 94, 126, 127; communications 41; equipment 61; propaganda 5, 8, 16; raids on enemy installations 5

Coast Watching Flotilla for clandestine craft 97

communications 108–9, 113, 116, 117; SIS control of 108–10; SOE control of 110; *see also* wireless equipment; wireless facilities

Corsica *see* Balaclava, maritime base

Crete, SOE in 17

Cruickshank, Charles 3

Czechoslovakian agents 38

Dalton, Dr Hugh 7–9, 22, 125, 127

Danish Country Section 38

134 *Index*

Dansey, Lieutenant Colonel Claude
108, 127
debriefing of agents 31, 34, 46
Department EH 5, 22

Eastern Warfare Schools (EWSs) 45–6,
47, 48, 87

Far East, SOE in 17, 26; 81, 116, 122
Fawley Court, Buckinghamshire (STS41)
38, 74
firing ranges 42, 52
Fishguard, Pembrokeshire (Station IXc)
66, 69
Foot, Michael 3, 21
Force 133 78, 85, 98, 99, 103, 116
Force 136 26, 56, 79, 80, 86
Force 399 27, 121
Forgery Section 72
France, SOE in 2, 12–14, 17, 19, 26, 42,
50, 90–1, 93, 97, 99, 104, 118, 121, 125
Freeman, Air Chief Marshall Sir
Wilfred 94
French Section 43
The Frythe Residential and Private
Hotel, Welwyn, Hertfordshire (Station
IX): Engineering Section 62–3;
magazines 68; production of supplies at
72, 82; research and development 73;
testing facilities 64; Thermostat Hut
63, 68; wireless research at 6, 61, 62

Gambier-Parry, Captain Richard 110,
113–14, 117, 118
Gibraltar 97, 115, 120–1, 122
Government Code and Cypher
School(GCCS) 1, 6
Gubbins, Colin 9, 33, 42

Hambro, Sir Charles 9
Harris, Air Marshal Arthur 'Bomber'
93, 94
Hatherop Castle, Gloucestershire
(STS45) 38
Helford estuary, Cornwall, maritime base
at 69, 91, 101
Helford Flotilla 101, 126
holding camps 48, 55, 56
Holdsworth, Captain Gerry 91, 101
Holland, Major Jo 6, 7
The House on the Shore, Hampshire
(STS33) 15
Howbury Hall, Bedfordshire (STS40) 12

India, SOE in 17, 26; GSI(K) Depot
78, 80, 85, 86; Indian Forward
Broadcasting Unit (IFBU) Training
Camp 48; Indian Mission 45, 47, 48,
66, 78; Marine Research and Training
Centre 66, 69; SOE's headquarters
(ME80) 17, 18; Special Forces
Development Centre (SFDC) 79–80,
86–7; storage facilities 78, 85, 86, 87;
training in 45–7, 48, 49, 56; wireless
communications 114, 116, 120, 121,
122; *see also* Eastern Warfare Schools
industrial sabotage 6, 16, 39–40
intelligence 2, 90
Istanbul, SOE in 17
Italy, SOE in 18, 27, 55, 98, 99, 116;
training in 44

Java, SOE in 17
Jebb, Gladwyn 7, 23
Jedburghs 11, 19, 23, 48
JESCHKE Circuit 13

liaison between organisations 19, 27, 48,
84, 96, 98
Liddell Hart, Basil 2
Lord Hankey 7
Lord Selborne 9

MacKenzie, William 2, 20
Malay Country Section 47, 48
Manus, Max 14–16, 25
Marine Section 105
Massingham, Advanced Operational
Base in North Africa: Air Operations
Section 98; Camp 14 43; Camp 25
44; formation of 18, 26–7; location
of 18; maritime operations from 97,
127; 'museum' at 42; Naval Training
Establishment 43, 54; responsibilities
of 26; staffing of 19; storage at 77;
training at 40, 42–4, 54, 127; wireless
communications 115–16, 121, 127
Medical Units 77
Mediterranean Allied Airforce 104
Mediterranean Theatre 18, 77, 98, 115,
126, 127
Mediterranean: Special Operations
(Mediterranean) (SOM) 18, 116, 121
Menzies, Sir Stewart ('C') 7, 9, 108
Middle East Theatre 98, 115, 126, 127
Military Intelligence (Research) (MI(R))
4, 6–7, 8, 9, 31, 51

Index   135

Ministry for Economic Warfare (MEW)
8, 81, 93
Ministry of Information (MoI) 8
Ministry of Supply 72
Ministry of Works 64, 66, 127
Mobile Construction Unit (MCU) 66
Morton, Sir Desmond 7, 8
Moscow, SOE in 17

Naval Intelligence Division (NID) 91,
101, 126
Nelson, Sir Frank 8, 9, 23
New York Mission 50
New Zealand, SOE in 17
Newitt, Professor Dudley 61, 73
Norsk Hydro Plant, Telemark 10
North Weald airfield, Essex 93
Norwegian agents 38
Norwegian Campaign, the 9
Norwegian Section 92

Office of Strategic Services (OSS) 11, 18,
27, 43, 76–7, 98, 112–13, 127
Operation BARBAROSSA 125
Operation BUNDLE 15, 16
Operation FOXLEY 10
Operation GUNNERSIDE 10, 40
Operation HUSKY 115
Operation JOSEPHINE B 125
Operation MARDONIUS 15
Operation MOST III 10
Operation OVERLORD 63, 71,
77, 113
Operation TORCH 42, 121
Operational Research Section 65
Operations Section 41; of SIS 90–1
Oriental Mission 17, 44–5

'passing', agents' ability to 31, 36
physical fitness 34
Polish agents 82
Polish military: Military Wireless
Research Unit (PMWR) 64–5, 68, 69;
wireless operators 7
Polish Section 40
Political Warfare Executive (PWE)
1, 5, 8
private sector, use of 60, 71, 72, 76, 79,
87, 92
Properties Section 26, 63, 127, 128
Protected Areas 51
prototypes, testing of 63, 64, 65–6, 69
psychological warfare 46, 47, 129

Queen Mary's Reservoir, Staines, Surrey
(Station VIII) 65–6

Radio Communication Division
(RCD) 63
RAF Henlow 75, 84; Special Parachute
Section 65, 84
RAF Jessore 49, 104
RAF Ringway (STS51) 11, 15, 41, 53, 65
RAF Stradishall 93
RAF Tangmere 102
RAF Tempsford 65, 95–6, 102, 103;
Gibraltar Barn 96, 103; Gibraltar
Farm 96
railways 69, 71, 79, 95
recruitment 32, 33
requisitioned buildings 127; treatment of
128, 130
Research and Development Section 60;
expansion of 60; external research 60,
64; private sector 60, 71, 72, 76, 79, 82,
87; reorganisation of 61; universities
60; wireless 64–5, 68, 69, 124
resistance groups 1, 8, 10, 39, 40, 46, 90,
108, 113; in China 26; in France 77,
118; European 2, 10, 75, 76–7
Robichaud, Albert 11–14, 24
Royal Air Force (RAF): Bomber
Command 96; Intelligence Directorate,
AI2(c) 96; Parachute Training
Squadron 41
Royal Army Ordnance Corps 74
Royal Navy 47
Royal Ordnance Factory Elstow,
Bedfordshire 71
Royal Signals Corp 65, 114

sabotage: of aircraft 16; of ships 16; *see also*
industrial sabotage
safe houses 17, 25
Scotland: Arisaig House, Inverness-shire
7; Burghead, Moray, maritime base
at 92; Inverie House, Inverness-shire
(STS24) 7, 15; Inverlochy Castle,
Inverness-shire (STS26) 15, 51;
Lochailort, Inverness-shire, STC at
7; Scalloway, Shetland Islands, base at
92–3; Shetland Islands, maritime base
at 91–2, 101–2
Seaman, Mark 3
Secret Intelligence Service (SIS; MI6) 1,
90; headquarters 17; Section VIII 108,
109, 110, 117; *see also* Department

136   *Index*

EH; Military Intelligence (Research) (MI(R)); Section D
Secret Service (MI5) 1
Section D 4, 5–7, 60, 61, 124; Station XVII, Brickendonbury 6, 39
Sections: E 71–2; F (French) 11; RF (Free French) 11; X 10
Shetland Bus 92, 126
Signal Stations 27
Singapore, SOE in 17
Slocum, Commander Frank 90, 91, 97
Small Arms Section 74
South America, SOE in 17, 81, 87
South East Asian Theatre 48, 56, 81, 99, 126; depots in 78, 81, 87; GHQ New Delhi 17; training in 44, 49
special duties flights 93, 94, 96, 98, 99
Special Operations Executive (SOE): archive 2, 3, 4, 21; command and control infrastructure 17; Country Sections 3, 22, 25, 32, 38, 46; creation of 1, 4, 8; criticism of 2–3, 8, 49, 76, 124, 127; funding of 1, 26; histories of 1–4; manner of operation 1; organisation of 8, 22, 73; relations with branches of the military 47, 71, 75, 94, 97, 98, 105, 126; relations with SIS 8–9, 10, 108, 109, 116, 117, 124; satellite offices 17; signals detachment 121; staffing of 1, 31, 72, 113, 118, 122; *see also* Sections; Stations
Special Projects Operational Centre in the Mediterranean (SPOC) 18–19, 27; SPOC (Forward) 19
Special Training Centre (STC), Lochailort 7
Special Training Schools (STSs) 31; STS3, Stodham Park 15; STS4/STS7, Winterfold 33; STS5, Wanborough Manor 32; STS17, Brickendonbury 39–40; STS24, Inverie House 15; STS26, Inverlochy Castle 15; STS33, The House on the Shore 15; STS38 82; STS39, Wall Hall 12; STS40, Howbury Hall 12; STS41, Fawley Court 38, 74; STS43, Audley End, Essex 40, 75; STS45, Hatherop Castle 38, 39; STS46, Chichley Hall 38; STS50 11; STS51, RAF Ringway 11, 15, 41, 53, 65; STS51a, Dunham House 41; STS51b, Fulsham Hall 41; STS51c, York House 41; STS52, Thame Park 41, 43, 52; STS63,

Warnham Court 40; STS101 45; STS103 (Camp X) 36, 49–50, 81, 114; *see also* training
Stafford, David 3, 21
Stations: 53a, Grendon Underwood 110–11, 112, 113, 118, 127; 53b, Poundon 111–12, 113, 119; 61, 53c, Twyford 112–13, 119, 127; Gaynes Hall 15, 65, 75, 76–7, 84, 129; VI, Brides Hall 74–5, 84; VIII, Queen Mary's Reservoir, Staines 65–6; IX, The Frythe 6, 61–4, 72, 73, 82; IXc, Fishguard 66, 69; XIV, Briggins 72; XV, The Thatched Barn 14, 73, 82, 83, 125; XII, Aston House, Stevenage 6, 61, 72, 73–4, 82, 83
Stephenson, William 113–14
Stockholm, SOE in 17
Stodham Park (STS3) 15
storage: accounting 74; of ammunition 79; capacity 74, 78, 79, 80, 81; of equipment 73, 81; of explosives 6, 40, 74, 79; of parachutes 75; of small arms 74, 84; *see also* supplies
Stuart, Sir Campbell 5
students: ethnic origins 45; numbers of 31, 33; security risks presented by 32–3, 46–7, 51, 52
submarines: Sleeping Beauty 100; Welfreighter 68; Welman 63, 65–6, 67–8, 69, 82, 100; X-Craft 67
supplies: Area H 77, 85, 127; dropping of 68; medical 77, 85, 87; obtained from the military 71; obtained from the private sector 71, 72, 82; packing of 75–7, 78–9, 80, 81, 84–5, 97, 104; transport by road 71; transport by submarine 87; transport by train 71; *see also* storage
supply dumps 77
Switzerland, SOE in 17

Thame Park, Oxfordshire (STS52) 41, 43, 52
time delay fuzes 67
training 6, 31–2, 39, 51, 124–5; advanced 36, 38, 48, 50; container dropping 49, 53; demolition and sabotage 39–40, 42, 44, 45, 46, 54; development of 31; extended exercises 37, 39, 42; explosives 40; fieldcraft 34, 36; finishing 11, 36, 37, 43, 47, 50, 54; Finishing Schools 36–7; hand-to-hand combat 34–5; Holding Schools 37–9, 41, 43; instructors 32, 42,

44, 45, 46, 54, 56; jungle warfare 45, 46, 56; microphotography 12; Operational Holding Schools 39; overseas schools 41–2, 54, 124; parachute 34, 41, 42, 43, 44, 48–9; paramilitary 34, 44, 45, 46, 48, 54; Paramilitary Schools 33, 39; 'paranaval' 35, 43, 46; Preliminary Schools 32–3; propaganda 37, 47, 50; radar 49; signals 48; Students Assessment Board (SAB) 33–4, 39; submarine 47; syllabi 33, 34, 39, 42, 43, 47; weapons 34, 35, 46, 52; wireless 40–1, 42, 43, 44, 45; *see also* Special Training Schools (STSs)

Training Section 31, 33, 38, 41, 46

transport 90, 99; by aircraft 41, 93–7, 98–9, 101, 104–5; by boat 90–3, 97–8, 100, 103, 126; by rail 71; by road 71; by submarine 87, 100, 105; parachute drops 99, 100, 105

United States Army Air Force (USAAF) 98, 103

US Civilian Technical Corps 109, 117

Venlo incident 124, 128

Victoria and Albert Museum, Kensington 73

Wall Hall, Hertfordshire (STS39) 12

Wanborough Manor, Surrey (STS5) 32

War Cabinet 8, 94, 125

War Office 2, 6, 60, 66, 71, 72

war, nature of 3, 39

Washington DC, SOE in 17

weapons 6, 14, 34, 36, 42, 60, 74, 75, 76, 84; small arms 74–5, 79, 84

Whaddon Hall, Buckinghamshire 108–9

Winterfold, Surrey (STS4/STS7) 33

wireless equipment 41, 65, 112, 113, 119, 120, 124

wireless facilities 109–11, 118, 121, 124; global 113–15, 116, 121; Station 53a, Grendon Underwood 110–11, 112, 113, 118, 127; Station 53b, Poundon 111–12, 113, 119; Station 53c, Twyford 112–13, 119, 127; transatlantic 113–14, 120

wireless frequencies 119

Wireless Production Unit 72

wireless traffic 108–9, 111, 118

Woburn Abbey Riding School, Bedfordshire 5, 22

Wykeham House, Stanmore, PMWR facilities at 64–5, 69

Wylie, Neville 3

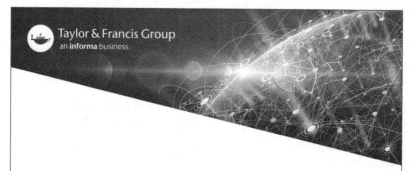